Women in Iran from the Rise of Islam to 1800

T0287900

Women in Iran from the Rise of Islam to 1800

Edited by
Guity Nashat and Lois Beck

UNIVERSITY OF ILLINOIS PRESS

URBANA AND CHICAGO

© 2003 by the Board of Trustees
of the University of Illinois
All rights reserved
Manufactured in the United States of America
1 2 3 4 5 C P 5 4 3 2 1

∞ This book is printed on acid-free paper.

Library of Congress Cataloging-in-Publication Data
Women in Iran from the rise of Islam to 1800 /
edited by Guity Nashat and Lois Beck.
p.   cm.
Includes bibliographical references and index.
ISBN 0-252-02839-2 (cl. : alk. paper)
ISBN 0-252-07121-2 (pbk. : alk. paper)
1. Women—Iran—History.
2. Women—Iran—Social conditions.
I. Nashat, Guity.
II. Beck, Lois.
HQ1735.2.W656   2003
305.42'0955—dc21   2002152213

CONTENTS

ACKNOWLEDGMENTS

THIS BOOK HAS BEEN in the making for some years, and the editors are grateful for the patience and steadfast support of the scholars whose contributions appear here. They also appreciate the efforts of those at the University of Illinois Press who aided the project.

Guity Nashat thanks Lois Beck, her colleague and friend of many years and coeditor of this volume, for coordinating revisions with the contributors and preparing the final manuscript for submission to the press. She expresses gratitude to Gary Becker, who has been a source of support and encouragement. Her late teacher, Marshall Hodgson, taught her not to judge the past but to try to understand it on its own terms. This useful lesson allowed her to appreciate the contributions of generations of Iranian women living under sometimes difficult circumstances.

Lois Beck appreciates the many people who facilitated her cultural anthropological research in Iran during the past three decades, especially because her experience living among rural, nomadic tribal, and ethnic-minority peoples has given her a wider understanding of the topic of "women in Iran" than she would have gained only by engaging in historical studies of Iran. She thanks Julia Huang for her proficiency in the use of computers and her good-humored support, and she acknowledges the assistance she received from Washington University and its Department of Anthropology. Jamsheed Choksy, Layla Diba, and Shireen Mahdavi offered her their experitse and assistance during the last months of finalizing the volume.

A NOTE ON TRANSLITERATIONS

THE SYSTEMS OF TRANSLITERATION used in this volume are modified versions of the format recommended by the *International Journal of Middle Eastern Studies.* The editors reluctantly exclude all diacritical marks from transliterated words coming from Persian, Arabic, Turkish, and related languages, with the exception of the ayn (') and hamza (') when they fall in the middle of a word. Confronted by the many different systems of transliteration and the amazing array of diacritical marks used by the contributors in their original submissions, we decided that a relatively uniform system was needed. Other than the issue of diacriticals, we have tried to respect the integrity of each contributor's system of transliteration and generally have not imposed a uniform spelling of certain words—for example, these and other variations occur: madrasa/madreseh and Mohammad/Muhammad. We follow generally accepted spellings of certain other words, such as shari'a and ulama.

Most transliterated words in Persian, Arabic, Turkish, and related languages are italicized on their first use in each chapter but not thereafter, and most such words are accompanied by short definitions in English on their first appearance. Because of their frequent use in the volume, we do not italicize the following words on first use: chador/chadur (veil-wrap), hadith (traditions of the prophet), imam (religious and/or political leader), madrasa/madreseh (school, sometimes religious), shari'a (Islamic law), and ulama (religious scholars).

CHRONOLOGY OF DEVELOPMENTS IN THE NILE-TO-OXUS REGION WITH EMPHASIS ON EVENTS IN THE IRANIAN HIGHLANDS

10,000 to 4000 B.C.E.

Beginnings of agriculture; emergence of settled life; spread of villages; invention of the plow.

4000 to 2000 B.C.E.

Emergence of urban society in Mesopotamia; invention of writing; increase in specialization affecting the division of labor along gender lines; rise of city-states and the earliest unified state in Elam; emergence of formal religious thought, science, and literature; emergence of commerce.

2000 to 550 B.C.E.

Birth of Zoroaster; arrival of earliest Indo-European tribes in the Iranian highlands; rise of Babylonian and Assyrian kingdoms; emergence of the Median state in northwestern Iran; growth of trade and expansion of cultural exchanges; development of confessional religions, Zoroastrianism in northeastern Iran and the Abrahamic tradition in the eastern Mediterranean.

550 to 330 B.C.E.

Rise of the Achaemenid empire and emergence of a politically unified region from the Aegean sea to the Indus valley; adoption of Zoroastrianism by the Achaemenid dynasty; development of an imperial tradition; expansion of urban life and rise of new towns; expansion of regional and international trade; defeat of the Achaemenids by Greeks and Macedonians.

330 B.C.E. to 224 C.E.

Rise of the Seleucid Kingdom and infusion of Greek thought and scientific tradition in the former Achaemenid areas; rise of the Parthian state and restoration of Iranian hegemony over Iran and Mesopotamia; rise and spread of Christianity; continuation of Zoroastrianism and emergence of the magi class as the religion's guardians.

224 to 651 C.E.

Rise of the centralized Sasanian empire; adoption of Zoroastrianism as the state religion by Sasanians; endemic wars between the Zoroastrian Sasanian and Christian Byzantine empires; expansion of urban life and trade in Iran and Mesopotamia; expansion of imperial and bureaucratic traditions by the Sasanians; eruption of the Mazdakite rebellion (485–531); birth of the Prophet Muhammad in Mecca (570); foundation of Islam (610); death of the Prophet Muhammad (632); rapid conquest of eastern and southern portions of the Byzantine empire and most of the Sasanian empire by Arab Muslims.

651 to 750 C.E.

Consolidation of Arab rule over conquered areas; rise of the Umayyad dynasty (661–750), with its capital in Damascus, Syria; expansion of conquest into north Africa and Spain in the west and Transoxiana in the east; conversion of some non-Arabs to Islam; adoption of the urban cultural traditions of the conquered people by Arab Muslims; emergence of opposition to the Umayyads; efforts by scholars to develop standards of behavior for Muslims.

750 to 950 C.E.

Rise of the Abbasids (750–1258), who established their capital in Baghdad, Iraq; emergence of an absolutist empire and reassertion of older Iranian cultural traditions under Islamic guise; flowering of urban life and trade; acceleration of conversion to Islam among Zoroastrians, Christians, and Jews; seclusion of women in some urban areas; emergence of Arabic as the universal language of Islam; erosion of central authority and emergence of provincial states throughout the Nile-to-Oxus region, such as the Tahirids (820–875), Sunni Khurasanians who governed in northeastern Iran; Abbasid caliphs accepted by the majority of Muslims as symbols of Islamic unity but not religious authority; emergence of an independent body of theologians and legists, devoted to the development of the shari'a (Islamic religious law) as guidelines for faith and correct behavior.

950 to 1258 C.E.

Emergence of semi-independent and independent states from Spain to the Oxus; in the Iranian highlands and Iraq they were: the Saffarids (866–1006), who ruled south-central and eastern Iran and present-day Afghanistan; the Samanids (875–1005), who claimed descent from Sasanians and chose Bukhara as their capital; the Ghaznavids (977–1186), founded by Sultan Mahmud, who chose Ghazna as their capital; the Buyids (932–1062), founded by three brothers from the Caspian region, who controlled western and central Iran and Iraq; the Seljuqs (1030–1194), founded by a leader of a Turkish tribal confederation, who controlled the central lands of Islam from the Oxus to Syria and Anatolia; and the Khwarazmshahs (1137–1225), a Turkish dynasty in Transoxiana and Khurasan. Emergence of the Persian language and literary tradition beginning with the Samanids; emergence of Persian as the official language in many Iranian provincial cities and capitals; arrival of Turkish tribal groups in the Iranian highlands, primarily from the north and northeast; use of the Turkish language in some urban and rural areas in Iran after the arrival of the Seljuqs; beginning of the Mongol invasion in 1225; fall of Baghdad and end of the Abbasid caliphate in 1258.

1258–1501 C.E.

Rise of the Mongol Ilkhanids in Iran and Iraq; gradual conversion of Mongols to Islam; adoption of some urban values and practices by the Mongol elite; fostering of Persian literary, artistic, and historical traditions; weakening of Mongol hegemony after the death of the Ilkhan Abu Saʻid in 1335; eruption of civil war; rise of Timur (1381–1405) and reconquest of central lands; increase in Turkic tribal peoples and influences in Iran, Iraq, Syria, and Anatolia; emergence of rival Timurid contenders; resumption of civil war; disruption of trade and gradual decline in population.

1501–1724 C.E.

Rise of the Safavids, who proclaimed Shiʻi Islam as the state religion, leading to hostility and war with the Sunni Ottomans (1299–1924) and with other Sunni powers in Transoxiana; restoration of stability, trade, and urban life in Iran; fostering of sciences, philosophy, art, architecture, and history by the Safavid dynasty; rise of Isfahan, the capital from the time of Abbas the Great (1588–1629), as a major center of intellectual, scientific, and artistic activity; the fall of the Safavids in 1724.

1724–94 C.E.

Eruption of civil war among various tribal confederations in the name of various Safavid pretenders; emergence of Nadir Afshar (1736–47) and invasion of Mughal India; resumption of civil war; emergence of Karim Khan Zand (1779–95) in southwestern Iran; continued civil war among different claimants; disruption of trade and a decline in the urban population; rise of the Qajar dynasty (1794–1924).

Women in Iran from the Rise of Islam to 1800

INTRODUCTION
Guity Nashat

THE INSPIRATION FOR THIS VOLUME derives from people's interest in Iran's revolution in 1978–79. The role that chadur-clad women played in toppling one of the seemingly most stable regimes in the region was surprising because of long-held perceptions about the veil and seclusion of women in Iran and the rest of the region, where Islam has been the predominant religion. Since then, many popular and scholarly books and articles have been written about women and the revolution. Some authors praise the revolution's impact on women, while others condemn the government that came to power for the treatment women received. The point of departure in many of these works is the teachings of Islam, which some writers extol as elevating women and others criticize as being patriarchal and restrictive.

A closer examination of the historical evidence reveals that many features associated with women in Iranian society and other Islamic countries, such as seclusion, the veil, and the division of society along gender lines, predate Islam by many centuries. The association of these practices with Islamic teachings stems in part from the periodization of the history of the Nile-to-Oxus region, which embraced Islam soon after its rise.[1] This periodization was adopted first by Arabian Muslims, who believed their pre-Islamic traditions belonged to the time of ignorance. Subsequently, many people of the region adopted this attitude toward their pre-Islamic past as they converted to Islam following the conquest of non-Arabian territories within a few decades after the Prophet Muhammad's death. Although people in the Iranian highlands retained memories of their pre-Islamic history, most were not aware that many of their practices and institutions were legacies of the Sasa-

nian empire, which became the heartland of the Muslim empire after the rise
of the Abbasid caliphate. Many scholars of early Islamic history also adopted this periodization and searched for Islamic antecedents in pre-Islamic
Arabia rather than strands of continuity with non-Arabian traditions in regions conquered by early Muslims.[2]

Such a sharp division between pre-Islamic and Islamic practices is particularly unsuitable for the study of women, whose status and treatment in
Iranian and Islamic society were influenced by economic, social, and cultural
conditions that began to develop in the Nile-to-Oxus area about two millennia before the rise of Islam. Practices adopted by women and perceptions
affecting their status were shaped primarily by people's experiences in urban centers even before the emergence of a formal state in the Iranian highlands during the Achaemenid period.

The influence of non-Arabian practices and attitudes explains the virtual disappearance of women from formal Islamic historical texts shortly after the first century of Islam. The problems posed by the invisibility of women
in Western history have been discussed since the 1960s, and women are also
not often found in formal historical records of other parts of the world.[3]
Women's lives in a Muslim country such as Iran, with societal rules of seclusion and the veil, raise special questions. What were women's lives like in
societies whose social and religious norms and the public rhetoric derived
from them dictated invisibility for much of the female population? Did the
exclusion of many women from the public sphere constitute the eradication
of their influence on society as a whole? How closely were these strictures
against women followed through time? If women did have influence after all,
where was it wielded? Where do we look for evidence of women in societies
that often seemed to require their removal from the public gaze?

To understand women's roles in Iran, we must probe the emergence and
persistence of practices that place women predominantly in the private sphere
and seemingly give control over their lives to fathers, brothers, husbands, and
older sons. This task is not easy because the very separateness of women's
lives seems to exclude them from the formal accounts that create recorded
history. Yet despite the virtual absence of concrete, detailed information about
individual women in official sources, images of women abound in other kinds
of sources. In order to delineate women's roles and influence, we must cast
a wider net. It is necessary to consult official chronicles but also works of
theology, biographical dictionaries, literary works (including poetry, prose,
epics, and folktales), manuals written for the edification of princes, travel
accounts, art, and architecture. Facts about women can also be deduced from

economic records. Wills and letters of women who were close to political actors and sometimes directly or indirectly involved in public events can yield information to better our understanding of Iranian history. Although knowledge about particular individuals may remain scant and may be limited to a few women in the upper socioeconomic stratum of society, this evidence can also supply clues about women of other classes.

The norms influencing women's activities evolved over thousands of years in a core area called Mesopotamia in classical times and forming the southern part of the present-day nation-state of Iraq. Obviously one cannot be certain about women's roles in the earliest stages of the history of the Nile-to-Oxus region, especially before the invention of writing. This period lasted over five millennia, and research on women in this period has begun only recently. Material evidence on this subject is minimal, and any discussion of women and their social environment must be based on sparse and fragmented archaeological data. Yet despite these constraints, it is necessary to begin with Mesopotamia, which became the core from which civilization (as defined by urbanism, written language, codified laws, a priestly class, increasing occupational specialization, monumental architecture, institutionalized trade, and so forth) radiated through the Nile-to-Oxus region. The available data do suggest the rough outlines of the gradual transformation of women's roles, from active participation in communal life to confinement within the household where child rearing, chores, and crafts were performed. Changes in women's lives included a more strict division of labor along gender lines, their gradual seclusion, the emergence of the veil as a symbol of propriety, and their eventual legal subordination to men.

Seclusion and the veil create barriers hampering the study of women by scholars, some of whom view the division along gender lines as synonymous with women's victimization and oppression. This a priori association between seclusion and oppression makes it difficult to gain a better understanding of the roles that women in fact played in different periods and under conditions that vastly differed from those in which many women live today. A dispassionate approach is essential for the study of distant periods and the people whose options and preferences were radically unlike those in modern times. We can try to discover the values by which people in the past lived and the ways these norms succeeded in achieving various ends.[4]

When one examines the evidence, as sparse as it is at present, one realizes that Iranian and other women in this region did not form a monolithic group. They led varied lives determined by their era, location, socioeconomic class, livelihood, and specific society and culture. Despite many of them being excluded from the public sphere, they must have contributed to society as a whole. Their influence can be detected in the survival of institutions with deep roots in the region's history. Although more is said about this issue in *Women in Iran from 1800 to the Islamic Republic,* suffice it to say here that the role that many women played in the 1978–79 revolution was in line with the types of roles women played in Iranian society for many centuries.[5] That Iranian women were aware of ways to promote their interests and protect their welfare was also demonstrated during presidential elections in 1997 and again in 2001. The majority of women voted for Muhammad Khatami, who promised greater civil liberties, instead of for candidates who wanted to impose greater restrictions in the name of religion.

Despite many studies of women and the revolution, and the antecedents of that event, little attention has been paid to continuity in women's roles over time.[6] One reason is the virtual absence of women in official sources. Another is that many writings on women in Iran and the Muslim world come from indigenous and foreign scholars using standards developed in the West since the 1960s. While contributions of women to society throughout recorded history have not been adequately recognized, and women have experienced discrimination no matter where they lived and regardless of their socioeconomic status, their treatment has varied greatly. For this reason, methodologies and categories developed for the study of women and gender in the West must be modified to explain women's position in Iran and the wider region. One reason for creating the present volume is to learn more about the roles that women played historically. Its contributors offer evidence that many women, despite their frequent absence from public life, played vital roles in their families and communities.

The social paradigm that began about two millennia before Islam maintained that women should devote themselves to motherhood and work within the home, while men should pursue activities outside it. It was at that time that agricultural production expanded, a food surplus allowed the human population to increase and to specialize, and urban centers grew. By the time Indo-European tribes entered the Iranian plateau in the late second millennium B.C.E., features characterizing women's roles were already established practices in many urban areas. A more strict division along gender lines probably occurred slowly, perhaps in response to economic and social realities in a region where the rise of urban life and trade helped expand resources. The separation between men and women increased and was enforced by seclusion, the veil, and women's legal subordination to men. Women's unequal status compared to men was bolstered by moral and religious teachings long before the rise of Islam.

These norms were implemented most faithfully among well-to-do people in urban areas, because wealthy men desired to ensure the purity of their progeny. The possibility of contact between women and male strangers was greater in urban communities where anonymity could also be maintained. In rural areas, division along gender lines was not as stringent because of a higher degree of trust. These communities were smaller, and many people there were either related by kinship or acquainted since childhood. Furthermore, although the inhospitable climate and the need to marshal water resources for irrigation left much of the difficult physical labor to men, many rural women participated in agriculture and animal husbandry.

Until the nineteenth century, Iran and the rest of the Nile-to-Oxus region had a large tribally organized, pastoralist, often nomadic, population. Women's participation in communal life there was influenced by differences in the size of groups, the frequency of migration in search of pastures for flocks, and the importance of agriculture. The observations of classical authors such as Herodotus in the fifth century B.C.E., historians of pre-Islamic Arabia, and Muslim travelers such as Ibn Battutah indicate that women pastoralists were not secluded as much as urban or other rural women.[7] Women were active in many aspects of public life, sometimes including warfare.

The normative standards that regulated and restricted women's activities most probably developed in urban areas. Gradually these standards were codified and became the guidelines of behavior for many women. Frequently, throughout the region's history, as tribal and other rural people conquered or moved more peacefully into urban areas, they began to adopt patterns and practices they saw there. Norms relegating women to domesticity were enshrined in moral and religious teachings, yet the very separateness of women's lives excluded them from the formal accounts that create what we typically consider history. Despite the gender division along vertical lines, with women occupying predominantly private domains and men public ones, women in Iran and neighboring regions continued to play vital roles in many activities, which facilitated the transmission to future generations of certain attributes of the urban societies we associate with the region. Difficulties arise when we try to delineate this vital task, because official sources have tried to avoid mentioning women or elaborating on their deeds even when they occupied influential posts.

Women's contributions are expressed and acknowledged by the thirteenth-century philosopher Nasir al-din Tusi (d. 1274 C.E.). In recommending the qualities a man must consider when choosing a wife, he states: "A virtuous wife is the man's partner in property, his colleague in housekeeping and the regulation of the household, and his deputy during his absence.

The best of wives is adorned with intelligence, piety, continence, shrewdness, modesty, tenderness, a loving disposition, control of her tongue, obedience to her husband, self-devotion in his service, and a preference for his satisfaction, gravity, and the respect of her own family. She must not be barren, and she should be both alert and capable in the arrangement of the household and in observing a proper allotment of expenditure. In her courteous and affable behavior and in her pleasantness of disposition, she must cultivate the companionship of her husband, consoling him in his cares and driving away his sorrows."[8] We need not accept Tusi's opinion about what constitutes a good wife, but we can hardly doubt his awareness of the importance of a woman's place in society.

The present work focuses on women's roles and activities and attitudes about them in the premodern period. The chapters cover a range of topics concerning women as they have appeared in chronicles, religious treatises, theological tracts, literature, myths, folktales, and art and their contributions to these fields. Women's participation in economic life and their roles in politics, particularly as members of Turkic and Mongol dynasties, are also studied. In another volume, *Women in Iran from 1800 to the Islamic Republic*, we examine women's roles and activities in the nineteenth and twentieth centuries and the degree to which Iran's encounter with the West influenced their lives.

· · ·

The chapters in this book open with an overview about women prior to and just after the rise of Islam. Much of what has affected women in Iran and other parts of the wider region has deep roots in the area's history. To bring out continuity in women's roles and activities, I provide in chapter 1 an outline of changes affecting women before and just after Islam emerged in the seventh century A.D. Despite the widespread perception both in the West and among many Muslims, the position of women had little to do with Islamic teachings and was instead the result of millennia of practices and attitudes. My essay supports an interpretation of women's roles that leads away from the Qur'an and religion per se and toward the economic and social conditions of a changing, vibrant, expanding society. Nomadic life and its focus on group welfare required the public participation of women. Not surprisingly, both in the Meccan society of the Prophet Muhammad's day and among the Turkic and Mongol peoples who migrated to the Iranian plateau, women had opportunities that were lost over the next few centuries. Although the spread of Islam throughout and beyond the Middle East is contemporaneous with the decline of women's public participation, other factors, such as the rise of urban life and the expansion of leisure time that accompanied the region's growing wealth, provide competing explanations for the changing place of women in society.

In chapter 2, Jamsheed K. Choksy describes the impact of the rise of Islam on women in Iran and shows that it brought them an alternative to the restrictive codes of Zoroastrianism, a belief system stipulating that females are ritually unclean and requiring women's strict observation of complex laws governing such everyday acts as eating, bathing, and selecting clothing. According to Choksy, women's status is crucial to understanding the conversion of the Sasanians to Islam. The cumbersome rules in late Zoroastrian teachings and the erosion of the property rights and social status of women whose family members were apostates surely hastened women's own conversion and thus contributed to the ever-growing Muslim population. Although often ephemeral in the official record, women participated actively in defining the history and culture of early Islamic Iran.

In chapter 3, Richard W. Bulliet views women in Iranian society through the lens of Islam. He examines specific sources—medieval biographical dictionaries from Baghdad, Nishapur, and Gorgan—that attest to learning in the community. These sources are important for understanding the emergence of the ulama (religious scholars) in the pre-Mongol period and the public esteem bestowed on them. He relates the paucity of entries about women in these sources to a general tendency in the genre to focus on men, but he suggests two mechanisms for that gender exclusion. First, having little or no public role, women had no need to accumulate certificates as proof of their learning; second, the compilers of these records, having little contact with women outside their own circle, were most likely uninformed about the education of elite females. Yet as Bulliet's evidence shows, little in contemporary teachings and attitudes prohibited women from pursuing knowledge and obtaining an education. Perhaps the emphasis that society placed on the merits of marriage and procreation encouraged more women to marry than to pursue knowledge.

In chapter 4, Julie Scott Meisami also uses text to create a picture of women in Islamic medieval society. She cautions that in reading the *Tarikh-i Bayhaqi*, the work of the eleventh-century Ghaznavid historian Abu al-Fazl Bayhaqi, we must also consider its ethical-rhetorical intent. While Bayhaqi informs us about women—at least of the ruling class—and the rules governing their education, marriage, and legal standing in society, Meisami advises the reader to set aside Western prejudices about women during this period and to understand that Bayhaqi is weaving a moral tale as much as he is accounting for facts.

In chapter 5, Carole Hillenbrand examines the lives of women during Iran's Seljuq sultanate (1030–1194) and takes evidence from Seljuq legal and literary works, historical chronicles, biographical dictionaries, monumental inscriptions, and works of art. Even after considering a broad array of sources, she warns that the picture emerging will remain impressionistic because evidence about some aspects of women's lives is scanty. Despite evidentiary problems, the period is intriguing. Did the less-restricted lives of Turkic nomadic women influence other women in the region? How can one account for the influence and prestige accorded to royal Seljuq women in light of the constraining social codes applied to women in urban areas? Hillenbrand compares the formal limitations on women, as reflected in the period's legal and religious works, with the circumstances that were more likely to have affected women's actual, daily lives. To illustrate the latter she draws on travelers' testimony, images of women in paintings, and women's architectural patronage. She points to the gap between society's prescriptions for women—as reflected in the ulama's writings and the recorded laws of the day—and the lives that women were likely to have led, which find their reflection in less idealized, less formal sources.

In chapter 6, Beatrice Forbes Manz engages the issue of women and politics during the Timurid period (1370–1507). To determine accurately the situation of women, she maintains that one must take into account the dynamics of the social order that governed them. Without such an approach, it is not possible to determine the function women fulfilled in political life and to know whether or not that participation was considered legitimate. The Timurid dynasty emerged from a tribal society in part through a careful strategy of marriage for allegiance; this practice placed women in crucial roles not only as wives but also as mothers of future rulers and other elites. Manz relates the stories of two women—Shad Malik, a person of lowly birth who attained great influence, and Gawharshad, a high-born wife of Shahrukh—in order to examine the social legitimacy of women's power.

Issues of status and marriage are likewise visited by Maria Szuppe in chapter 7 on the Safavids (1501–1724). She finds that women, such as Pari-Khan Khanum and Khayr al-Nisa Begum, exerted influence in politics and were present at public events including the battlefield. She shows that royal princesses enjoyed many privileges including an education similar to that of princes. Although the focus of Szuppe's article is the sixteenth century, her discussion of the role that Safavid women played in court politics confirms one of the perennial themes of Iranian history: the gradual weakening of tribal customs as a result of exposure to urban culture, whose practitioners viewed women acting in politics as a breach of propriety. As Szuppe states, by the end of the Safavid period, royal women's activities became more circumscribed.

The authors of chapters 8, 9, and 10 examine creative, aesthetic works—as opposed to chronicles and legal texts—to explicate the image of women in Iranian society. In chapter 8, Mahmoud Omidsalar discusses the salience of feminine imagery in the ethnopoetry of the *Shahnama*, Iran's national epic, while Fatemeh Keshavarz in chapter 9 looks to Nizami's *Khusrau u Shirin* for a startlingly heroic image of a woman in premodern society. Omidsalar notes that, while the central actors in the *Shahnama* are men, the epic's transcendent moments are dominated by women or feminine symbols; through these moments of conflict or discovery, the invisible (woman) is made visible. Keshavarz offers the intriguing idea that the presence of a strong, dynamic, and complex figure in the person of Shirin deserves attention for reasons other than those exclusive to literary inquiries. The creation and acceptance of Shirin demonstrates that the necessary cultural space existed for a female character of her magnitude and complexity. In both chapters, the power of women's presence in society through relationships with others—as mothers, wives, and lovers—is strongly drawn.

In chapter 10, Layla S. Diba surveys Iranian painting from the thirteenth century to the early twentieth century to glean images of women from the perspectives of power, love, and society. Not surprisingly, she shows that the powerful images of women in Persian literature reoccur in painting, which allows us to deflate the stereotypical image of Iranian women as dominated and barely visible. She maintains that, despite their idealized representations, paintings sometimes offer realistic glimpses of contemporary life.

. . .

This volume informs readers about women not only in Iran but also in other parts of the region, because until the last century the larger area had a shared history and culture. Because political and cultural demarcations within the Islamic Middle East were not distinctly drawn, the discussion of Iranian women sheds light on women's circumstances elsewhere. The broad scope of this work also provides new perspectives for those interested in comparative studies of women and gender by offering information and analysis that vary from recent perspectives on changes in women's statuses and roles in the West. Learning more about women and their impact on society in various periods and different settings enhances our knowledge of social history, a neglected field in Middle Eastern and Islamic studies.

NOTES

Lois Beck offered comments on and suggestions for this introduction.

1. I use the phrase "Nile-to-Oxus" from Marshall Hodgson's work because it is devoid of the Eurocentric and modern nationalistic associations suggested by the term "Middle East."

2. An exception is Marshall Hodgson, who begins his work on Islamic civilization by discussing continuities between pre-Islamic and Islamic traditions and institutions of the Nile-to-Oxus region; *The Venture of Islam* (Chicago: University of Chicago Press, 1974), 1.

3. For an overview of the problems of women in the history of the West, see Bonnie Anderson and Judith Zinsser, *A History of Their Own: Women in Europe* (New York: Harper and Row, 1988).

4. Before critiques of "Orientalism" became common, Hodgson conveyed the point extensively; see *The Venture of Islam* 1:22–45. Western misconceptions and misrepresentations of women in the pre-Islamic and Islamic periods have deep roots. See Maria Brosius, *Women in Ancient Persia (559–331 B.C.)* (Oxford: Oxford University Press, 1996); Aryeh Grabois, "Islam and Muslims as Seen by Christian Pilgrims in Palestine in the Thirteenth Century," *Asian and African Studies* 20 (1986): 309–27; David Waines, "Through a Veil Darkly: The Study of Women in Muslim Societies," *Comparative Studies in Society and History* 24 (1982): 642–59; Leslie P. Peirce, *Imperial Harem: Women and Sovereignty in the Ottoman Empire* (Oxford: Oxford University Press, 1993); Judy Mabro, *Veiled Half-Truths: Western Travellers' Perceptions of Middle Eastern Women* (London: I. B. Tauris, 1991).

5. See *Women in Iran from 1800 to the Islamic Republic,* ed. Lois Beck and Guity Nashat (Urbana: University of Illinois Press, forthcoming).

6. Scholars are becoming more interested in the historical study of women in Iran. See *Women in the Medieval Islamic World,* ed. Gavin R. Hambly (New York: St. Martin's Press, 1998), which contains several studies on Iran.

7. Abu Abd-Allah Muhammad Ibn Battutah, *Rihlat Ibn Battutah* (Travels of Ibn Battutah), 2 vols., ed. Ali al-Kattani (Beirut: Mu'assat al-risalah, 1395/1977), 1:365; 2:777.

8. Nasir al-din Tusi, *Nasirean Ethics,* trans. G. M. Wickens (London: George Allen and Unwin, 1964), 161.

1 Women in Pre-Islamic and Early Islamic Iran

GUITY NASHAT

DESPITE PERCEPTIONS about how Islamic teachings regulated gender roles, many practices and values such as the seclusion of women, the veil, the legal subordination of women to men, and societal attitudes enforcing a division of labor along gender lines are rooted in the pre-Islamic history of the inhabitants of the Iranian plateau and their neighbors in the Nile-to-Oxus region.[1] The basic features that characterized the roles and statuses of women had already become accepted in most urban centers during the second millennium B.C.E.—before the arrival of Iranian (Indo-European) tribes on the plateau that bears their name.

The norms determining women's roles developed over several millennia in Mesopotamia, in the southern part of present-day Iraq, especially during the Sumerian period (3500–2000 B.C.E.), where urban life and institutions that governed society developed. Urban life fostered the expansion of various crafts, greater division of labor, flourishing trade within each town and with the outside world, an increase in wealth, and complex political and religious institutions. Population growth and the rise in prosperity encouraged specialization and further division of labor. As urban life expanded and became more complex, women gradually focused on producing and raising children, and men emphasized work outside the home.

The importance of children in these societies made reproduction a highly valued activity and rewarded women who devoted most of their time to child rearing with social status and greater security in old age. At the same time, as some elite families became wealthier, the desire to pass their assets to their children led to efforts to prevent their wives and concubines from contact with male strangers. Interest in ensuring the purity of the bloodline also caused adultery to be treated as a serious offense, for which the laws dictated, "She will die by the iron dagger."[2]

As women became more involved with raising children, they became less concerned about events outside the home. Over the centuries, women's absence from public life encouraged the development of norms in Mesopotamia that placed greater restrictions on the participation of women in public activities.[3] Although it is difficult to pinpoint when seclusion was introduced and how widely it was practiced, legal texts from the mid-Assyrian period (1132–1115 B.C.E.) reveal that the wives, concubines, and even female servants within the palace lived in separate quarters and were closely watched by eunuchs and guards. The slightest suspicious contact with male strangers could cause serious repercussions, as the following law indicates: "If a palace woman [and a . . . man] are standing by themselves, with no third person with them whether [they are behaving] in a flirtatious manner [or in a serious manner], they shall kill them."[4] However, seclusion did not prevent females in the royal and princely families from influence and indirect political power. These women took advantage of their proximity to powerful men to play a role in political events and to acquire enormous property and wealth.[5]

Our knowledge about women in the lower social strata is limited and sporadic. Poorer women had to go to the market to buy goods and often had to work outside their homes, suggesting a less secluded lifestyle. Many participated in the labor force as servants, shop and tavern keepers, textile workers, bath attendants, midwives, scribes, and temple workers. Non-elite women also considered propagating children to be their major contribution, and they too aspired to the norms developed in the urban centers.[6]

The Nile-to-Oxus region had an agrarian economy, and the majority of people lived in rural areas or as pastoralists. Rural women often helped with the harvest, tended vegetable gardens, cared for and milked animals, and made butter and cheese. They baked bread, cooked meals, fetched wood and water, spun wool, wove cloth, and sewed clothing. Since some of these tasks brought them into contact with males outside their immediate family, it is unlikely that rural women observed urban standards of propriety. Rural families valued a large number of children, since extra hands helped increase economic productivity; rural women therefore had little free time. They probably did not earn an independent income for their labor and consequently became more subordinated to men.

Pastoralism as a way of life existed in the Nile-to-Oxus region for millennia and exerted enormous influence over social, economic, and political developments in the region. Pastoralists engaged in seasonal migration and were more self-sufficient and isolated than other groups. Their isolation required greater participation by women, who were responsible for preparing food and clothing. The women also performed heavier tasks, such as pitching tents and carrying children, heavy objects, and small animals during seasonal migrations.[7]

The nomadic lifestyle required men to be absent periodically, and women ran tribal affairs during the men's absence. Tribal women did not bear as many children as rural women, since young children would be a burden during seasonal migrations, so they played more public roles in pastoral society than many urban or rural women. The variety of tasks they performed would have made seclusion and the veil impractical. Whenever pastoralist groups came to power in the Nile-to-Oxus region, women in the ruling dynasties had much greater public visibility than women in the urban centers over whom the pastoralists ruled.

Throughout history, some rural and nomadic groups moved into towns and cities. Their exposure to the cultures of the settled population eventually resulted in the adoption of mores and standards of behavior that had first emerged in Sumer, where the earliest towns in the Nile-to-Oxus area had formed. As long as basic environmental and economic conditions remained the same, Sumerian norms and institutions survived even after the demise of Sumer as a distinct political and cultural entity. These cultural aspects influenced subsequent groups that came to power in Mesopotamia and radiated to regions as far away as Greece, where similar conditions existed. Although they were modified to suit local preferences and expanded to satisfy the needs of greater political entities, the basic features remained. By the time the Indo-European tribes arrived on the Iranian plateau, the value system that had first emerged in Sumer had been accepted as the standard in defining the role of women.

Women before the Arrival of Indo-European Tribes

Discussing women's roles before the rise of Islam is essential background for a better understanding of women in the Islamic period, although the lack of information often forces us to rely on conjecture. The existing material on women consists mainly of archaeological evidence, myths, legends, and religious writings of various groups. Written records follow the rise of Elam, most of them deriving from foreign and sometimes hostile sources, such as Assyrian, Greek, and Islamic writers.

The earliest people to inhabit the Iranian highlands may have arrived fifteen thousand to twelve thousand years ago, and they formed small settlements in the foothills of the mountains across the Iranian plateau, but its geography—the great distances that separated these early communities, the mountainous terrain, and the cold climate—impeded the emergence of larger centers. Undoubtedly women's contributions were vital to the survival and growth of these early communities, but we have little concrete evidence. By 4500 B.C.E., it is possible to identify at least two groups: the Caucasians in the northwest and the Proto-Dravidians in the southeast.[8] Although pottery construction and decoration suggest that different settlement groups interacted, urban life did not develop in the area until more than a millennium after its rise in Mesopotamia. By the middle of the third millennium B.C.E., the Elamites established several city-states.[9] Information about Elamite women is fragmentary, which can be gleaned mainly from religious sources, and is limited to a small group of women associated with the royal and ruling elite.

Elamite religion was characterized by "uncommon respect and reverence for womanhood."[10] During the third millennium B.C.E., the most important deity in Elam was the goddess Pinikir, "the great mother of the gods to the Elamites" and the great mistress of heaven. Later, another goddess, Kirrisha, surpassed her, but many goddesses were gradually demoted and replaced in rank by male gods. Yet Kirrisha never lost her title as the main goddess of Elam, and it is significant for later developments that she married two of her brothers who were major gods.[11] Kings often built temples to honor her and appealed to her for protection. Despite being demoted, Elamite goddesses retained a higher status than goddesses in Mesopotamia.[12]

The high position of Elamite goddesses may reflect the status of women in Elam, whose situation improved with the rise of the nuclear family by the end of the third millennium, when daughters attained equal inheritance rights with sons.[13] Sometimes fathers even preferred to pass on their entire estates to their daughters rather than to their sons. A wife's share of her husband's estate also increased considerably in the later Elamite period. An indication of women's status is found in a letter King Shutruk-Nahhunte (1190–1155 B.C.E.) sent to the Babylonians, in which he claimed the throne of Babylonia as the son of the eldest daughter of its king.[14]

Another practice pertaining to women was the system of succession in Elam, which sometimes passed from a man to his sister's son. Succession through the sister suggests that royal women had greater political power than did royal women in Mesopotamia. The evidence about the status of Elamite queens is fragmentary, but at least one queen, Nahhunte-utu, who married two sons of Shutruk-Nahhunte in succession, seems to have held some claim to the throne, which she passed to her eldest son. Did such succession occur because she had married two of her own brothers? Despite disagreement among scholars over the origins of and reasons for this type of succession, some have considered it as evidence of next-of-kin marriage within the royal family.[15] Hinz argues that even after the sister's son was no longer the major heir to the throne, brother-sister marriage did not disappear but continued until the end of the Elamite period, when "even provincial rulers followed the 'family custom' of Elamite kings in marrying their sisters."[16] The relationship of Nahhunte-utu with her second husband indicates the esteem in which she was held. Shilhak-Inshushinak describes her as "beloved wife," and her son refers to her as "gracious mother." She is commemorated in a relief carving with her husband and four of her children. Unlike any other royal portrait, she appears to be of equal height with the king.[17]

Although it is difficult to ascertain the specific influences of Elam on women in Iranian society, it may be possible to trace next-of-kin marriage in the religious teachings of the Sasanian period to this Elamite practice. Even after the decline of Elam as a political entity, its influence survived in the subsequent dynasties and groups emerging in the Iranian highlands.

Arrival of the Indo-European Tribes

In the second millennium B.C.E., the arrival of various Indo-European tribes significantly influenced the political and cultural development of the Iranian plateau. As society changed, the lives of women were also affected. A lasting legacy of these Indo-Europeans was Zoroastrianism, for its teachings became the foundation of ethical and moral values in the highlands for centuries to come. Although no historical record of Zoroaster exists, the teachings of this religion are preserved in the Gathic hymns, the earliest portions of the Avesta.[18]

The Gathic hymns provide a glimpse of society and gender roles. They portray an agricultural livestock-tending people who prized men for work and protection. Male children were valued, as the following address by Zoroaster to King Vistaspa reveals: "May ten sons be born of thy own body! Three as Athravans [priests], three as warriors, three as tillers of the ground! May one of them be like Gamaspa [the king's minister], that he may bless thee with great and ever greater happiness!"[19] The hymns reveal that women engaged in agricultural work, such as sowing seeds, harvesting corn, and milking cows, but their most important role was to provide society with children. The ethical and moral teachings of the Avesta emphasized the importance of reproduction, the survival of children, and the need to protect boys. They encouraged chastity, forbade sex outside marriage, and taught that prostitutes defiled the world and deserved to be killed as one would kill a dangerous snake. Yet because children were valued, abortion, even when pregnancy occurred out of wedlock, was a capital crime. "And if the damsel for the dread of the people shall destroy the fruit in her womb, the sin is on both the father and herself, the murder is on both the father and herself; both the father and herself shall pay the penalty for willful murder." One injunction places the responsibility of caring for a child on the community if a man refuses to support the woman he impregnated.[20] Preventing the marriage of women was considered a high sin, "the worst deed that men and tyrants do, namely, when they deprive maids, that have been barren for a long time, of marrying and bringing forth children."[21] Marriage with non-Iranians was discouraged. The absence of mention of next-of-kin marriage is striking, given the importance this practice attained in later Zoroastrian teachings.

Ambivalence toward the power of women is manifested in the roles attributed to female deities. While some major female deities, such as Kisti (or Chisti), the personification of religious wisdom, and Daena, the personification of religion, are benevolent, the incarnation of evil and deceit, Drug, is also female. She appears as a counterpart to Asha, or righteousness. "The Gathas give her greater prominence than to any other evil being."[22]

Parallel to the fear of women's power was fear of dead objects, which followers of the Gathas considered controlled by demons and which accounts for attitudes about blood and menses, considered dead material. Although this fear was not unique to these followers, the Avestan attitude represents one of its more extreme manifestations. Menstruating women were considered polluted and polluting because they were thought to be possessed of

Angra Mainyu (later Ahriman), the incarnation of evil. Even the touch and look of menstruating women were considered polluting. During the menstrual cycle, women were restricted to rooms with no view of the sky, moon, water, fire, or any other sacred object that they could pollute. Those who brought them food were to stay a distance away. Their food was served in "vessels of brass, or of lead or of any common metal" and not of pottery, which could not be properly cleansed.[23] The same precautions were taken when a woman gave birth, for fear that bleeding would pollute her surroundings, because any emission from her body was considered to be dead matter and the property of demons.

Perhaps because of this periodic isolation, women were in effect disqualified from performing ritual duties. Men and not women were responsible for keeping the fire continuously lit in the hearth, a requirement in every household that followed the religion. Women's lesser status is also revealed in their absence from any descriptions of paradise, which mention only the rewards that await righteous men. There a man would encounter "a maiden fair, bright, white-armed, strong, tall-formed, high standing, thick breasted, beautiful of body, noble, of a glorious seed, of the size of a maid in her fifteenth year, as fair as the fairest things in the world."[24] Despite these limitations, the Gathic woman could be entrusted with propagating the faith, as Zoroaster's prayer indicates: "Grant me this boon, that I may bring the good and noble Hutaosa [King Vistaspa's wife] to think according to the law, to speak according to the law and to do according to the law, that she may spread my Mazdean law and make it known."[25]

One of the earliest Indo-European groups to form a political entity was the Medes. Initially establishing several embryonic states, they eventually conquered Elam and Assyria in 612 B.C.E.[26] The Medes adopted some customs of older societies, including employing eunuchs. Although it is uncertain when they adopted Zoroastrianism, its teachings and moral and ethical values regarding women influenced the attitude of people in the Iranian highlands.[27]

Women in the Achaemenian Empire

The Achaemenian empire was founded by Cyrus the Great (r. 559–530 B.C.E.), a descendant of a Persian ruling house from Fars, who first conquered Media and then united much of the Nile-to-Oxus region in one political entity.[28] Although Persians were a minority in the vast empire they ruled, their culture and identity survived, which may be explained in part by the adoption of Zoroastrianism as the state religion during the Achaemenian period. The inhabitants of the Iranian plateau, who spoke different dialects of Iranian languages by this time, adopted the accounts and values reflected in the Gathas as their common heritage and acquired an identity that separated them from their neighbors. The culture of the Iranian highlands was a synthesis combining various traditions: the worldview reflected in the Gathas, the cultures of the Elamites and Medes and others who had inhabited the Iranian highlands, and the urban traditions of Mesopotamia from the Sumerian to the Babylonian periods.

Like earlier inhabitants of the Iranian highlands, the Achaemenians interacted with their subjects and were influenced by the older cultures of Elam and the Medes. But the urban-based culture of Mesopotamia exerted the strongest influence on them.[29] The Mesopotamians were heirs to the oldest, most complex society in the Achaemenian empire, and the Achaemenians tried to emulate them. Channels of transmission from Mesopotamia were varied and extensive. Many Persians, including members of the dynasty, settled in Babylonia, and some Babylonians moved into the Iranian highlands. Some Achaemenian kings and noblemen had Babylonian concubines and children by these women. Although rules of succession required that both parents of the heir apparent be of Persian ancestry, Darius II (r. 424–404 B.C.E.), whose mother was a Babylonian, ascended the throne after the brief reign of his brother Xerxes II (d. 424).[30]

Influence of Mesopotamian culture on the treatment of women and their roles in Achaemenian society developed slowly, perhaps because the Achaemenians and their Persian followers did not totally abandon their own traditions, which survived within the royal household and Persian nobility and among commoners. But exposure to other cultures began to modify the role of women, at least within royal and noble households, as suggested by the introduction of women's seclusion, some type of veiling, and use of eunuchs to ensure that rules of seclusion were observed. Women were not as restricted in the Iranian highlands as they were in the more urbanized areas of the Achaemenian empire. Women's participation in activities that defied urban norms was greater at the beginning of the Achaemenian period, but their visibility still shocked many urbanites, who reflected their disapproval in their accounts of the period.

Like the Medes who preceded them, the Persians were not literate before coming to power; hence information about their early history derives from the accounts of their adversaries. The main sources on the Achaemenian

period are the accounts of Greek historians, whose testimony offers conflicting portraits of women in Achaemenian ruling families. Sometimes women
appear as powerless and secluded behind harem walls; at other times they
are presented as manipulative, untrustworthy, and vengeful. According to
Greek accounts, the meddling of some royal wives in the affairs of state was
responsible for the decline of the once-great empire.[31]

What may have disturbed the urbanite Greeks most was the presence of
women in the public sphere along with men.[32] Herodotus (484–420 B.C.E.),
who visited the Achaemenian empire, notes, "With us men and women are
separated." He relates that Persian men allowed their wives to participate in
public ceremonies and activities, and he reports someone saying, "We Persians
have a custom; when we put on a great feast like this one, we bring our wives
and our mistresses to sit with us."[33] This radical departure from behavior that
Greek historians considered appropriate for women may account for the historians' denunciation of royal women who took an active part in the empire's
affairs. Greek observers often commented disparagingly on royal women in
the king's entourage during his travels, hunting expeditions, and campaigns.[34]

The negative views expressed by Greek historians about Achaemenian
women stem from different social and economic conditions in the two societies and opposing norms on women's behavior. Greek society was largely
urban and sharply divided along gender lines. Respected Greek women were
mostly absent from public life. Athenians, the standard-bearers of Greek
culture, held that a woman's proper place was in the home where she could
protect her reputation and virtue.[35] The attitude of Greek authors was also
colored by the Achaemenian conquest of much of the Greek world or the
threat of invasion by its armies. With the exception of the reigns of Cyrus
the Great and Darius I (559–486 B.C.E.), the remaining years (486–330 B.C.E.)
were portrayed as a period of decline and decadence. In their search to explain the causes of the waning, they singled out the role of Achaemenian
women and their depravity.[36]

Despite these drawbacks, the paucity of indigenous sources renders Greek
accounts valuable for learning about Achaemenian history and society and
useful for information about women. Although the material they provide is
limited to that which is associated with the ruling family and nobility, and
they mean to convey the danger that women's meddling in public life could
cause, they are still helpful because they provide glimpses of individual wom-
en and their roles. Despite their condemnation of the women they describe,
they reveal that women did have the power to engage in politics, advise the
king, and influence the course of crucial events.

Occasionally, Greek descriptions provide positive images of women, such as Phaedyme, who was married to Smerdis, a Magian who claimed to be the son of Cyrus the Great and briefly ascended the throne after the death of Cambyses II (r. 529–522 B.C.E.). To establish his true identity, Otanes, head of a noble family, asked Phaedyme, his daughter, to examine the king during his sleep to see if he had ears. Despite the threat the step posed to her life, Phaedyme discovered that the man posing as king lacked ears and was in fact an impostor. The revelation led to his removal from the throne and the elevation of Darius, a member of a minor branch of the royal family, as the next ruler. Although Herodotus may have embellished her role for dramatic effect, Phaedyme emerges as a main character in this episode. He also reveals that Otanes and other contemporaries held a high opinion of women's courage and trusted their ability to perform crucial tasks.[37]

The positive treatment that Phaedyme receives is rare, and most females discussed by Herodotus and other historians are generally presented in a negative light. Royal women—such as Atossa (daughter of Cyrus the Great, wife of Darius I, and mother of Xerxes) and Parysatis (daughter, wife, and mother to three later kings)—are often portrayed negatively by those who discuss their participation in contemporary events. According to Herodotus, Atossa instigated the disastrous invasion of Greece under Darius I. The choice of Xerxes, one of Darius's younger but perhaps less able sons, as heir was also her doing, "For Atossa had all the power."[38] Although Herodotus does not blame her directly for the decline that set in during Xerxes' reign, such a connection is implied.

The glimpse of women we get in Greek sources is limited, often fictitious, and negative; nevertheless, it does convey the impression that the power these women exerted was real and that such an exercise was perceived by society to be common.[39] If we make allowance for the negative portrayal of women, what the description of Greek authors conveys is that kings and other leaders accepted the role these women played and valued their judgment. Queen mothers and queens kept abreast of events in the empire and took sides in political conflicts, sometimes between their own children. For example, in the civil war breaking out between Artaxerxes II and his brother Cyrus the Younger from 409 to 405 B.C.E., their mother, Queen Parysatis, constantly communicated with the rebel prince and supported him with revenue from her Babylonian estate.[40] Royal and aristocratic women also received an education, which included the use of arms and horseback riding.[41] The Persepolis and Murashu archives (see below) reveal that queens and royal princesses were given vast estates and controlled the revenues they received. The power of royal women also extended to their ability to appoint judges within their estates; a certain Babylonian judge was known as "judge of the house of Parysatis."[42]

Greek sources account for the presence of women in court life and cere-monials. The king's mother and wife often accompanied him when he had dinner privately. Their special status is confirmed by their ability to appear before the king without being summoned, a privilege shared only by heads of the leading Persian clans of the realm.[43] Royal women participated in offi-cial ceremonies, such as the king's birthday, which was considered the most important feast. Queens and royal princesses may also have arranged feasts for women in their palaces.[44] An episode in the Book of Esther suggests that the participation of royal wives in public festivals and court ceremonials was part of their official duty. According to this account, Queen Vashti's refusal to join official festivities led to her downfall.[45] Although this biblical narra-tive cannot be treated as factual, it suggests that the queen could be defiant when the king did not observe royal decorum. According to custom, female members of the royal household withdrew from the scene when music and drinking began.[46]

To what extent were Achaemenian women secluded and veiled? Given the degree of women's public presence, how likely is it that royal women were shut off within harem walls? The assertion that Persians kept their wives and concubines cloistered was expressed by Plutarch (46–120 C.E.) and has been repeated by contemporary historians. Dandamaev and Lukonin, using Plu-tarch as their main source, write, "A wild jealousy was characteristic of the Persians, not only in respect to wives but also in respect to female slaves and concubines. They kept the latter under lock and key in order that outsiders not see them; during trips they carried them in closed carriages."[47] It seems naïve to accept as fact a statement by an author who lived three and a half centuries after the end of the Achaemenian period and claimed little knowl-edge of the Persian empire. The statement also contradicts the earlier obser-vation by Herodotus that Persian men liked their women to participate with them in celebrations.

Before the Achaemenians emerged as rulers of the empire, the Persians did not require women to be veiled or secluded. By the mid-Assyrian period (1200 B.C.E.), respectable women in Assyria had begun to adopt the veil. Kings of Assyria kept large harems in which royal women—wives, concubines, and slaves—lived under the supervision of eunuchs and guards. Urban Greeks, too, enforced seclusion and separation of genders.[48] Perhaps after the Achae-menians became exposed to the peoples they conquered, veiling and restric-tions on the movement of women were introduced into their society. Evidence that women did not lead completely secluded lives and were only partially veiled can be gleaned from the reign of Darius III (r. 336–330 B.C.E.), the last Achaemenian ruler. During his encounter with Alexander the Greek, his mother, wife, daughters, and other female relatives were with him. A large retinue of noblewomen accompanied the queen on horseback, and queens and princesses frequently traveled to their own estates throughout the empire.[49] Yet the presence of eunuchs and curtained carriages when women traveled with the king in the later Achaemenian period suggests that some type of veiling and seclusion had emerged. The attendance of eunuchs implies that some limits were placed on the contact of royal women with male strangers and may also indicate that the Achaemenians had adopted some of the pomp that befitted women of the royal house.

Achaemenian kings married more than one wife and had concubines—perhaps evidence that they were adopting Mesopotamian traditions.[50] The marriages of Cyrus the Great and Darius I were determined by political expediency. Both married more than one wife and entered marriage alliances with non-Persian women to consolidate their power. Because they ruled over a vaster territory than earlier dynasties, their harems contained more wives and concubines, who were often daughters of foreign rulers and nobility. They also gave their daughters and sisters in marriage to reward noblemen and to cement political alliances.[51]

Royal marriage practices suggest that women in various branches of the Iranian tribes retained some degree of power from earlier times. For example, Cyrus the Great enhanced the legitimacy of his claim to the Median throne through his mother, Mandane, the sole child of the king of Media.[52] Similarly, Darius I, the Achaemenian, created a closer link with Cyrus the Great, founder of the Persian empire, through marriage with his two daughters and his granddaughter.[53] These unions suggest that Darius took seriously women's probable right to succession and was trying to eliminate any future threat from their offspring.

Were any of the later kings monogamous? Contemporary sources mention only Parysatis as Darius II's legal wife and Stateira as the wife of Artaxerxes II. Artaxerxes II is alleged to have also married two of his daughters, but some doubt this assertion.[54] The legal wife or wives of a king were either members of the royal household or Persian nobility, because only children produced from such marriages were considered legitimate and could ascend the throne. In the absence of legitimate children, children of concubines would qualify, as did Darius II, whose mother was a Babylonian concubine.

Another uncertainty surrounds the question of concubines in Achaemenian society. Beginning with Herodotus, Greek sources mention that the Achaemenians kept many such women.[55] But determining the status of a concubine is difficult because Greek sources do not distinguish among slaves, servants, female captives of war, and even daughters of foreign kings and nobility, who could not be legal wives but with whom the king could have children. The biases of classical Greek historians against the later Achaemenian rulers as effete and decadent, as dominated by women and eunuchs and surrounded by concubines, have given rise to uncritical statements by modern historians about the marital status of this dynasty's rulers. Olmstead, citing Plutarch, claims that Artaxerxes II kept a harem of 360 concubines who bore him 115 sons.[56] What makes this account unlikely is that only one son survived, the others allegedly murdered by the son who succeeded him to the throne as Artaxerxes III, and the line passed on to a minor branch of the Achaemenian house.

To what extent did the rest of Achaemenian society emulate the rulers' marriage practices? Dandamaev and Lukonin claim that "it was permitted to have many legal wives and also concubines."[57] They seem to base their assertion on Herodotus's observation that each Persian marries many lawful wives and takes many concubines.[58] Contemporary references and practices do not support such a generalization. Although Achaemenian rulers and some noblemen did have more than one wife and perhaps concubines, it is unknown if polygyny was widespread.[59] Herodotus does mention that Cyrus the Great and Darius I were deeply attached to a particular wife, many Persian noblemen were monogamous, and some revealed love and loyalty toward their wives.[60]

The extent to which Achaemenian society at large practiced next-of-kin and other close-kin marriage has also resulted in scholarly debate. Some contemporary Western scholars indicate that such marriages were practiced widely throughout Achaemenian society, and they point to Avestan teachings and the marriages of some rulers with close relatives as proof.[61] Others view the diffusion of this practice with more skepticism.[62] Such marriages may have been more the exception than the rule. The Avestan references to the merit of this type of marriage appear not in the Gathas but in Sasanian texts almost a thousand years later. Moreover, classical Greek historians, such as Herodotus, who traveled extensively in lands under Achaemenian control, do not mention such a practice. Herodotus refers only to the marriages of Cambyses II to his two sisters and considers the unions as proof of the king's insanity, which caused him to act contrary to the practices of the Persians; he attributes the aberration to the king's exposure to such practices among

Egyptian royalty.[63] Cambyses' marriages with his sisters produced no children and may indicate his attempt to prevent the rise of competing claims
to the throne.[64] Although several other members of the dynasty married close
kin, little evidence that such marriages were common exists. Examples include Darius II, who married his half sister Parysatis, and their son Artaxerxes
II, who is alleged to have married two of his daughters.

The power of women in the royal household and nobility has been sub-
stantiated by the discovery in the late nineteenth and early twentieth centuries of three different archival documents in Elamite, Neo-Babylonian, and
Aramaic in Persepolis and Nippur, the old Neo-Babylonian capital. The Persepolis fortification texts cover the years 509–494 B.C.E. of the reign of Darius I. They contain amounts of daily, monthly, and special rations to officials,
workers, and members of royal households near Persepolis and Susa. The treasury texts, smaller in number, come from the period 492–458 B.C.E. and consist of records of payment of silver from the Persepolis treasury. The Murashu
archive, dating from 455–405 B.C.E., depicts the business transactions of a Neo-
Babylonian family by that name, whose members served the crown for several generations. These texts contain information about the administrative
practices and social and economic conditions of the Achaemenian period and
shed light on women's roles during the periods covered. We learn that royal
and aristocratic women played a greater social and economic role in the empire than had been realized and that women participated in the workforce,
but these sources do not reveal much about individual women.[65]

Women within the royal household controlled extensive estates in Fars,
Babylonia, Media, and Syria and exercised independent control over these
lands and the revenues they generated. They ran their estates with the help
of bailiffs because most of them lived elsewhere. "The lady of the palace,"
either the mother of Artaxerxes I (465–425 B.C.E.) or one of his four wives,
received rent from landed property in Babylonia, as did Queen Parysatis, the
half sister and wife of Darius II.[66] The economic control of some women over
their revenues can be measured by the support that Parysatis provided to her
younger son, Cyrus the Younger, from her Babylonian villages.[67] Women of
high rank, including the queen and royal daughters, also received large rations of grain, wine, livestock, and other food stuffs in their own right.[68]

The fortification texts provide information about women's participation
in the labor force. The data reveal only slight differences within a given rank
in the wages of men and women and indicate that women could become
supervisors over workers who included men. Female supervisors received
wages equal to those of males, and their rations were one-third to one-half

more than those of average workers. Highly skilled women received rations
of meat, grain (the basic food), or wine equal to or greater than the rations
of men, but the rations and wages of female workers on average were slightly less than men's. The workforce included boys and girls who received equal
pay. The minimum ration, given to all adolescent workers, was five quarts
of grain per month. Other data do show a preference for boys; women who
gave birth to boys received twice the allowance that those who delivered girls
received. During a thirteen-year period, women constituted 40 percent of the
total *kurtash*—an Elamite term for workers—which included 38 percent men
and 22 percent boys and girls.[69] This rate of women's presence in the workforce is high even by modern standards.

Despite disagreement among scholars about the legal status of the workforce, most concur that the kurtash was composed largely of conquered populations such as Babylonians, Egyptians, and Greeks but that the supervisors
were mostly Persian. Participating in the building of Persepolis, the kurtash
consisted of masons, stoneworkers, woodworkers, blacksmiths, and sculptors.
Some were more skilled than others as demonstrated by their higher wages.
Women contributed along with men in many of these activities, including
heavy work; one tablet indicates that a group of stonemasons included twenty-seven men and twenty-seven women. With the exception of the group's
master who was a man, women received only slightly lower wages than men.[70]

Perhaps the desire of the rulers, Darius I and Xerxes, to finish the project
at Persepolis quickly was one reason for the many women in this particular
workforce. It is unlikely that female workers withdrew from the labor force
after the completion of Persepolis. Because the Achaemenians waged many
wars, the recruitment of men in these campaigns probably created an ongo-
ing demand for women in the labor force. The need for labor is also attested
to by the retention of women workers after childbirth. They were usually
given an extra allowance, although the length of the period is unstated.

The teachings of the Gathas, gradually disseminated during the Achaemenian period among Persians, reinforced the importance of women's
reproductive role. Persian and other Zoroastrian women were probably encouraged to spend their childbearing years in having and raising children.
According to Herodotus, Persians viewed having children as the highest good,
"For multitude, they think, is strength." To encourage reproduction, "To him
who can show most, the King sends gifts every year."[71]

The role of Persian women in agriculture was perhaps limited. Rural
women would have performed some lighter field work and tended their vegetable gardens and flocks, but they probably left the heavier work to men. As

in other plow-using farming communities, use of plows and the difficult task of building and maintaining irrigation works to compensate for the scarcity of water would have rendered women's participation in agriculture less than men's.[72] Such labor-intensive activity would have kept them from fulfilling their main duty, which was to produce and care for children.

During the Achaemenian period women gradually became less active in public life as the dynasty became more influenced by the attitudes of its urban populations and by the spread of urban life in the Iranian highlands. With the conquest of the Persian empire by Alexander in 324 B.C.E., this process became more pronounced; the tradition of greater confinement of Greek women was now added to customs already existing in Achaemenian centers such as Babylonia. Some of these traditions continued well into the Sasanian period.

Women in the Sasanian Period

Almost five hundred years separate the Sasanians (224–651 C.E.) from the Achaemenians, from whom they claimed descent. In the intervening period, Alexander and various Hellenistic rulers came to power in Iran and were followed by the Iranian Parthian dynasty (67 B.C.E.–224 C.E.). Despite nearly three hundred years of rule, the Parthians failed to establish firm control over the entire territory for long periods. The expansion of international trade over a vast region from China in the east to the Roman empire in the west boosted trade within the Parthian state, to which leaders of this dynasty contributed. They improved commercial roads, built new towns, and encouraged expansion of agriculture. Consequently, the trend toward greater social and economic complexity in the Iranian plateau continued during this half millennium.[73]

Zoroastrianism spread as the dominant religion of people in the Iranian highlands, who adopted the Middle Persian, or Pahlavi, language. As the religion consolidated, its representatives, the *magi* class, became more powerful. These developments may have contributed to a sense of common identity among some of the plateau's inhabitants and the rise of a more effective centrally controlled state under the Sasanians.

Mesopotamia, or Eragh (as the region was called in Pahlavi), was integrated in the Sasanian world.[74] The new dynasty chose Ctesiphon, a city founded on the Tigris river by the Parthians, for its winter capital. The importance of some cities such as Babylon declined, but Mesopotamia constituted the heartland of the Sasanian empire and attracted a stream of new settlers from the Iranian highlands. Although the Aramaic inhabitants of Mesopotamia did not adopt the language or religion of the Sasanians, their values affected Persian culture and became more fully integrated into Sasanian society. The synthesis between the Mesopotamian and Iranian elements "enabled them to penetrate the cultures of neighboring countries in all subsequent ages" and resulted in "the vast world-historical perspective that is still evident on all sides."[75] One culture that fell under the influence of this Mesopotamian-Iranian synthesis is the Islamic one that emerged after the rise of Islam.

The influence of Sasanian practices on the way women were perceived and treated in Islamic Iran and areas within the Iranian cultural sphere has not been sufficiently recognized. This neglect stems mainly from the dearth of sources and their fragmentary and narrow scope, which make a systematic study of women in the Sasanian period difficult. Yet circumstantial evidence suggests continuity in some practices and attitudes affecting them.

One source of information consists of rock reliefs commemorating the deeds of the dynasty's rulers and providing references to the dynasty's women. More significant is the *Matakdan-i hazar datastan* (Book of a thousand judicial decisions, the Sasanian law book), which contains legal cases covering private law. The cases were inspired by the ethical and moral teachings of the Avesta and were designed to be used as a guide by Zoroastrians. Although, in theory, religious writings and the legal system that derived from them were grounded in the teachings of Zoroaster, at least a millennium separated him from his followers and those who claimed to speak for him in the Sasanian state. During much of this period, liturgical literature and legal ordinances were transmitted orally by the Zoroastrian clergy, and only from the mid-Sasanian period did they begin to be written down. Some legal rulings even belong to the period after the Islamic conquest.[76]

Like most legal systems, Sasanian religious writings and law reflected the moral standards and practices of that society. The gap between the agricultural and pastoral environment of the Gathas and the more complex society and imperial conditions was bridged by extensive interpretation in the intervening centuries. The Sasanian clergy often justified the later religious injunctions and practices by attributing them to the teachings of Zoroaster. A comparison of the earliest portions of the Gathas with later works provides insight into the causes of change occurring in these two periods, especially in women's roles. To be sure, the ethical and legal edicts that were being codified dealt with conditions that affected a limited group of women who had access to wealth and property, but they also reveal society's normative standards and perceptions. The religious texts show an unmistakable effort to convince women that their highest duty in this world, on which their salvation in the next is based, is submission to their husbands and reproduction, but we should not interpret the normative standards as an accurate portrayal of how women were actually treated or how they behaved.

The Sasanians derived from a minor dynasty in Fars, and some of their practices reveal traces of their origins, such as the high status royal and aristocratic women enjoyed. Rock reliefs indicate their prestige during Sasanian rule. Some women's privileges were equal to those of male members of the dynasty. Initially, women belonged to the highest council of state, which was headed by the king's mother, followed by his brothers and sisters and his children, regardless of gender, from his principal wife.[77] While restrictions may have been placed on royal women as the dynasty consolidated its power over areas where people held other kinds of perceptions about women, the right of women to ascend the throne was not undermined. Bistam, the maternal uncle of Khusrau II (r. 590–628), who challenged his nephew and set up a rival capital in Rayy, based his claim to the throne on his descent through the maternal line.[78] In the absence of a male heir, female members of the Sasanian clan could be elevated to the throne, as indicated by the brief rules of Purandukht (630–31) and Azarmidukht (631–32), daughters of Khusrau II.

Royal women exercised independent control of great wealth. Queens and queen mothers constructed several towns and renovated older ones.[79] The courageous role and political acumen of at least one woman are suggested by a possibly fictionalized story about King Kavad (r. 488–96, 499–531), who was deposed and imprisoned by the chief religious authority (*mubad*) and some grandees, who believed he had embraced Mazdak's creed. He was restored to the throne when his sister used her charm with the prison warden, rolled her brother in a carpet, and had the carpet carried out of jail by a prison guard.[80]

Sasanian legal and religious literature reveals similarity to attitudes toward women that had emerged in urban centers of Mesopotamia. While women enjoyed certain rights, such as inheritance and dowry, they were subordinated to male members of their family and fell under their legal authority. Men controlled the resources of society and devised its moral code. Laws regulating sexuality, marriage, and divorce increasingly tended to cater to men's preferences. The power of fathers, husbands, and other males over women is a salient feature in the literature.

While Sasanian sovereigns prided themselves on building towns, the Iranian highlands maintained their rural character. Ties to land and agricultural activity shaped social interactions and the political institutions of the realm. The nuclear agnatic family constituted the foundation of society. Women's membership in an agnatic group derived from their relationship to males; before marriage a woman belonged to her father's group, while after marriage she joined her husband's group. Thus she was entitled to support from one or the other group in the event of her father's or husband's death.[81]

Marriage was so highly regarded that locating a suitable mate for a daughter was considered a father's religious duty. He was advised to "find an intelligent and well-brought-up husband for your daughter. Such a man is akin to a fertile land, if you till wheat in such a land it will yield rich produce."[82] Girls were considered ready to marry at fifteen, or even younger, and often had many suitors. The woman's father or guardian represented the bride and negotiated the terms of the agreement on her behalf, including the bride-price consisting of cash and property that belonged to her and could not be alienated. In case of divorce, she received her entire property as stated in the marriage contract. Another parental responsibility was defining the limits of the husband's authority and the types of restrictions he could place on his wife, because he would acquire legal authority over her.

These negotiations were conducted on behalf of a woman who was to be a privileged (*patikhsahi*) wife, which placed her in the highest form of marriage, required a contract, and specified the mutual obligations and rights of a husband and wife. She and the children produced in this type of union were entitled to inherit from him and to full membership in his agnatic group. A daughter received only half of a son's share, but the wife's share from her husband's estate equaled her son's. If her husband died, she became her children's guardian until her eldest son attained majority at the age of fifteen. A man could have only one privileged wife, and any other woman he married was considered a subordinate (*chagar*) wife, who lacked the same rights as the principal one. She was not entitled to any of her husband's wealth after his death, and neither were her children, over whom her authority was limited.

An unmarried female was obligated to marry in order to produce an heir for a dead relative, but she could become only a subordinate wife when she married to fulfill that obligation. Technically she was considered the privileged wife of the dead relative, and her firstborn male child was his too. The dead man was entitled to half of the children she bore the actual husband.[83] The responsibility to provide an heir for a dead relative hampered a woman's chance of marrying the most suitable husband because of these restrictions. Although this type of marriage ensured the dead man's salvation, it put the woman at a decided disadvantage. She was considered only a secondary wife of whomever she married and lacked the advantages of ever becoming a privileged wife. The remaining children were also disadvantaged, because children of a secondary wife were not members of their actual father's agnatic group and did not inherit from his estate. Although some husbands and fathers provided for their subordinate wives and children prior to their death, the absence of legal provision left some of them at the mercy of the male who succeeded as the family head when no provision had been made.[84] Whereas a male child could be adopted because he could become an heir, prospects for the adoption of a female infant were slim. A secondary wife did not have a secure means of support, and the main hope for a female child was for her father to provide for her and her mother in his will.[85]

A young woman could refuse to marry her father's choice and would not be penalized. If a father failed to find a suitable husband for his daughter by the time she reached fifteen, the daughter could marry without his consent, and he could not disinherit her. But the husband was not obligated to support her, because she was only a self-entrusted, self-dependent wife (*khwas-ray*). Her status would change to that of a principal wife after she gave birth to a son and he reached fifteen.[86]

A woman was entitled to a share of her father's estate when she married but not to any additional inheritance when he died. Both dowry and bride-price were hers, but a husband had a right to her property unless he was restricted by her marriage contract. He could not refuse to pay the bride-price if he divorced her. A woman could inherit property from her father, but she could be only a temporary heir (*ayoken*) until a suitable male heir appeared. What rendered women unfit for that role was the attitude toward menses, which barred them from performing daily religious rituals during that time. Sasanian religious doctrine emphasized life after death and considered salvation in the next life dependent on the uninterrupted performance of the religious liturgy and rituals in every household. Having a male heir who could perform these daily obligations ensured the salvation of the deceased's soul.[87]

Reproduction continued to be the primary purpose of human sexuality, and religious literature emphasized women's obligation to raise healthy, well-fed children. In *The Book of Arda Viraf,* a religious work from late Sasanian times, mothers who neglected to feed their infants sufficiently were told that they would be punished in the next world by ever digging "a hill with their breasts and by being kept perpetually thirsty and hungry." Women were discouraged from working as wet nurses lest this leave inadequate milk for their own infants. They were told that those "who gave their own infants no milk and gave milk to infants of others" would have "their breasts placed upon a hot frying pan by their own hands and were ever turned from side to side."[88] The rate of child mortality may have been high, and thus fertility was encouraged. Warnings to women who neglected their children imply that population growth was important.

A shortage of available women is implied by a doctrine of Mazdak's movement, which occupied most of Kavad's reign. The duration of this movement indicates that Mazdak's teachings had wide support. He advocated redistributing wealth, sharing wives, and even abolishing marriage.[89] The adoption by Zoroastrian religious authorities of a similar idea about sharing wives suggests that the shortage was real and was one reason for Mazdak's appeal. Perikhanian states, "The Sasanian jurists regarded this form of marriage as an act of solidarity with a member of one's community, which was sanctified as a religious duty."[90] It is doubtful that Zoroastrian religious teachings, which condemned adultery and threatened offenders with death in this world and perpetual suffering in the next, would have supported such an idea if the dearth of women was not a critical issue.

Another factor possibly contributing to the shortage of women and perhaps also the loss of appeal for Zoroastrianism may have been the practice of next-of-kin marriage (*khevtuk-das*). The meaning of the term in Sasanian religious texts suggests actual marriage with a parent or sibling. The *Dinkard,* a rendition of some Gathic materials compiled in late Sasanian and early Islamic times, attributes the practice to Zoroaster by saying that he married his daughter Porukast, who presumably after his death married Gamasp. But according to the earliest texts, the Gathas, Zoroaster merely gave his daughter in marriage to Gamasp.[91]

Next-of-kin marriage assumed increasing importance in Zoroastrian teachings during later Sasanian and early Islamic periods. Religious leaders encouraged this form of marriage on the grounds that it emulated the act of creation, when the seed of Gayumard, the first male, fell on earth and produced the first male and female—a brother and sister—who became the progenitors of all humanity. Priests argued that marriage within the family produced stronger males, more virtuous females, and higher quality and quantity of children, and it protected the purity of the race and propagated it.[92] Even if only a small fraction of males chose to enter such an alliance with a close female relative, that would have aggravated the shortage of women, because a male who married a close kin could still marry another woman, but his female relative could not.

The defense of khevtuk-das by religious leaders, the increase in rewards promised to anyone who practiced it, and the rise in conversion of Zoroas-

trians to Christianity may indicate the unpopularity of this marriage practice among the public. Resistance may also be reflected in rulings of the chief
religious authority in a post-Islamic law book, who allows the pious to be
rewarded for khevtuk-das through payment for a proxy marriage. He recognizes the merit of a formal marriage without insisting on its consummation, as some earlier authorities had done.[93]

Religious literature demonstrates that the norms developed in this period by the priesthood reinforced millennia-long attitudes toward women. This
trend was boosted by the exposure of Sasanian ruling and priestly classes to
Mesopotamian values regulating gender relationships. Women were told that
their salvation depended not on good works but on total obedience to their
husbands. A typical example stated that those women "who practiced acquiescence and conformity, reverence and obedience to their husbands and
lords" would be rewarded with eternal salvation.[94] Women who were defiant
or disobedient were threatened with eternally "licking a hot oven with their
tongues, and having their hands perpetually burnt under an oven in hell."[95]
Similar punishment awaited women who refused the sexual demands of their
husbands. Preventing adultery occupied part of the ethical and religious
teachings of the Zoroastrian clergy and much of the wisdom literature, and
the effort is revealed in the severe and graphic punishments now and in the
hereafter.[96] Women were told that they lacked wisdom and that their judgment was weaker than men's. For this reason, women's testimony in a court
of law was not acceptable.

If we judge women's status only on the basis of religious teachings and
legal ordinances in the late Sasanian period, it would appear that they occupied a low position in society, had few rights or privileges, and lived in perpetual fear of terrible punishments lest they fail in their duties toward their
husbands or children. A closer examination of the same body of writings
reveals a different picture. Social efforts to mold women did not correspond
to how women behaved or were treated. How else can we explain the graphic references to sanctions in the next world if women never committed adultery? Women "who ever shed and sucked and ate the blood and filth of their
ten fingers" because "they beautified their faces" or those whose eyes crawled
with worms because they "curled their hair" suggest that in reality many
women ignored the warnings of religious leaders and were not deterred by
the threat of punishment in the afterlife.[97]

Other glimpses of women suggest that they could be assertive, lively, and
well informed. Bartholomae recounts an episode in which five young women encountered a learned judge on a country road and questioned him on

the finer points of law. At first he was able to answer with ease, but as he began to falter, one of the women said, "Master, do not trouble your brain, and say, 'I do not know.' You can find the answer in such and such a work."[98] The incident reveals that at least some women received an education.

Passages in the Sasanian law book indicate that women's clothing reflected social distinctions. Aristocratic women "are attired in silk garments, live in magnificent palaces, wear headgears, go hunting, and follow all the other manners of the aristocracy."[99] Some type of veiling and seclusion probably upheld social and economic codes. Elite women were perhaps more strictly veiled and secluded to protect them from contact with non-elite men, but it is uncertain whether other categories of women were also veiled. Because many aspects of women's roles in Sasanian society derived from earlier practices in the region, where wealthy women in urban areas did not appear in public and wore some type of veil, this pattern probably also existed for Sasanian women, especially in Mesopotamia.

We know little about women in the labor force. Although towns were expanding in the Iranian plateau, it is unlikely that many women of childbearing age worked outside the home because of the emphasis society put on reproduction. Also, husbands would not have encouraged their wives to work outside, for fear that they would come into contact with male strangers. Richer and middle-income families likely relied on the services of servants and slaves for domestic work. Injunctions in the law book state that when a pregnant female slave is sold, so is her fetus, and when the female slave is manumitted, so are her children. Poor women probably worked before marrying, as the use of the Pahlavi term *kar-windisn* in the law book, in reference to wages, indicates. Some may have continued to work after marriage. The terms of a marriage contract entitled a woman to keep her wages for her own use after she married and stipulated she should share her husband's income.[100] Some poor women worked in the service sector because elite women relied on servants and slaves and used nursemaids for childcare. Midwifery offered women a suitable profession.

Most rural women were probably active in agriculture and pastoralism. Their economic contributions were encouraged by the rewards they were told they would receive in the next life for caring for flocks of sheep and cattle.[101] One reason for their participation may have been the recruitment of men for the army. During much of its history, the Sasanian state engaged in wars with the Byzantine empire in the west and various tribal confederations in the east. The rural population provided the manpower for the army under the landed nobility's leadership. The state relied on revenue from land tax in the lowlands

of Iraq and the Iranian highlands to pay for these wars and was forced to increase taxes on rural peoples—one of the main factors behind the Mazdakite
rebellion. The recruitment of rural males and the need to pay higher taxes
probably forced rural women to engage in other than domestic activities. The
strength of such women was celebrated in many tales from the period.[102]

Rural and poorer urban women also contributed to the economy by spinning wool; wool was widely used in the production of carpets and clothing.
These women probably played a role in the expansion of handicrafts, which
fostered the growth of towns and trade across the Iranian plateau.

Between 637 and 651 the Sasanian empire (and the religious hierarchy that
supported it) collapsed as a result of campaigns launched by Arabian armies,
and it was incorporated into a newly formed Arabian Islamic state.[103] Within the next two centuries, the Zoroastrian religion was reduced to the status
of a creed for a small minority scattered in towns and villages across the Iranian highlands. Despite this development, much of Sasanian culture and the
teachings of the religious hierarchy survived, albeit under a seemingly new
guise. To gain a better understanding of the causes of their endurance, including attitudes toward women, we must compare women's roles in the pre-
Islamic and early Islamic periods.

Women in Arabia and Early Islam

Islam was revealed to Muhammad in Arabia, through a series of revelations
from god, and by the time of his death in 632, most of Arabia had converted
to the religion. Within two decades the heartland of the Sasanian empire was
conquered by the newly founded Muslim state. After the conquest, many
leaders of the new state left Arabia and made the former Sasanian territories
their new home. Soon a process of assimilation was under way as the conquerors began to be influenced by the cultures of the conquered peoples. The
synthesis emerging from the interaction of the new rulers with their numerous subjects gave rise to a seemingly new society and culture but one that
was now Islamic. Yet it was deeply steeped in the earlier cultures of the region, particularly Mesopotamian-Iranian traditions. The reasons are not hard
to find. The number of Arabians who moved into the new regions was much
smaller than the conquered population, and their unfamiliarity with conditions outside Arabia forced them to rely on their subjects to run the empire.
Despite avowing allegiance to their own culture, the Arabians gradually
adopted many customs of the conquered areas. Practices meeting the needs

of Arabia and surviving during the prophet's time did not answer the demands of a different kind of society.

Before the rise of Islam, most Arabians were nomadic and tribally organized, and women's economic and social contributions to their communities were essential. Arabian women were not secluded or veiled, because confining women was not compatible with their way of life. They could divorce and remarry without being socially ostracized. Sometimes accompanying men on raids, women attended the wounded, provided water and provisions, and occasionally put a wounded captive to death. Some women became famous as poets and critics of poetry, a popular activity among Arabians. Even though Mecca, Ta'if, and Yathrib (later named Medina) held sedentary people, and Mecca was emerging as a small commercial town, the values of society were set by tribal, non-urban standards, and women's participation in social life was not discouraged.[104]

Although Islam was revealed in Mecca and Medina, which had been undergoing change before the religion's rise, attitudes toward women had not changed dramatically. The prophet believed he had been sent to correct existing problems rather than to overhaul society. Many statements in the Qur'an, such as, "Thou art a warner only, and for every community a guide,"[105] suggest that Muhammad viewed himself as one prophet in a long line of prophets. Qur'anic teachings did not refute former attitudes; they aimed mainly toward ameliorating existing practices. For example, the Qur'an did not forbid polygyny but limited the number of wives and stipulated that each wife must be treated equally.

The Qur'an contains some legal injunctions, but the primary focus of its teachings, particularly in the Meccan period, is moral. Legal provisions were revealed in response to specific situations faced by the newly established sovereign community after the prophet emigrated to Medina in 622. Proving to be a blessing, the emigration (*hijrah*) had momentous consequences for the newly founded community. In Mecca, Muslims were a small minority, but in Medina, the majority of Arabians submitted to Islam and accepted Muhammad's leadership. This circumstance made it possible for the practical implications of the new faith to unfold gradually. Beginning in this period, members of the community turned to the prophet for temporal as well as spiritual guidance. Most legal ordinances aimed to solve ambiguous situations or meet urgent needs. They were the by-products of the day-to-day life of this community and were oriented toward ending existing inequities.

Legal pronouncements in the Qur'an on women demonstrate the same tendency. Most injunctions affecting women were revealed in connection with specific situations Muhammad or the community faced. One example is the Qur'anic sanction of polygyny. Coming in Medina following the battle of Uhud, this revelation was intended to resolve the problem created by the widows and children of fallen soldiers.

The teachings of the Qur'an reflect social and economic changes in Mecca and Medina during Muhammad's time. Many Qur'anic injunctions affecting women, such as allocating specific shares in bequests to wives and children, reflect the growing importance of family bonds. Refraining from adultery became a condition of conversion because adultery left children's status uncertain. But the punishment for adultery—giving offenders one hundred lashes—was in keeping with prevailing Arabian attitudes.[106] The penalty is mild compared to the sanction for adultery in the Mesopotamian tradition, which demanded death for the culprit.[107]

The aim of the Qur'an, to improve prevailing practices, is discernable in provisions concerning marriage and divorce. It highly recommends marriage for everyone, approves polygyny, and allows men to marry up to four wives. Men are made responsible for the support of their wives, while wives are not obligated to share their wealth with their husbands. Islamic teachings affected women's economic status by changing the payment of the marriage fee (mahr) to the bride herself rather than to her father. The Qur'anic injunctions on divorce reveal a similar approach. Although men have unconditional ability to divorce their wives, in practice they cannot take divorce lightly. Husbands are forbidden to reclaim gifts they had given to wives. If the husband pronounces the divorce formula three times, he is not able to remarry the same wife unless she marries another man, is divorced by him, and observes the waiting period (iddah) of three months and ten days between each divorce and remarriage. He must also support her and their children while they live with her. The law of inheritance provides a woman with half the male share of the estate of her parents, siblings, spouse, and children. These provisions became important assets to women in later periods when many of their other rights were circumvented.

Although women are not equal to men in some legal injunctions of the Qur'an, they enjoy equality in religious obligations and duties. The notion of gender equality was a major departure from prevailing Arabian attitudes. The Qur'anic concern with individual worth accounts for the banning of female infanticide, which was perhaps how pastoralist Arabia handled population control. The Qur'an does not mention abortion.

During the prophet's lifetime, the growing prosperity of Mecca had strengthened patriarchal tendencies in that city; nevertheless, women enjoyed greater social freedom than those in the contemporary Sasanian or Byzantine empires. The Qur'an defines a good wife as one who obeys her husband and keeps his secrets. The mores of Arabia concerning women's behavior can be inferred from the Qur'anic recommendation that the husband of a disobedient wife should punish her by sleeping in a separate bed or beating her. These actions are mild compared to punishments found in Mesopotamian and Zoroastrian codes of law for disobedient wives.

By defining some aspects of women's legal rights, such as inheriting as well as owning and disposing of their own property, Qur'anic teachings granted women valuable protections. This positive attitude was reinforced by the prophet's treatment of women. He relied on their counsel and friendship. Khadijah, his first wife, was the one who reassured him about the validity of his initial revelation and was the first convert. During his time, Muslim women continued to be active in public life as they had been before Islam. For example, women, including his aunt Safiyyah, accompanied the prophet on his campaigns and occasionally suffered injury.[108] They also participated in communal religious rituals and memorized and collected parts of the Qur'an. Subsequently, some of their recollections concerning the prophet became recognized sources of hadith (reports of his sayings and actions).

Muhammad died in 632. Within the next few decades, in a succession of swift campaigns, his followers defeated the rulers of the Sasanian empire and wrested control of the eastern Mediterranean from the Byzantine empire. These conquests had a profound impact on the development of Islam and on many aspects of the life of those Arabian Muslims who settled in the newly conquered regions and constituted a military ruling class. Because they lacked adequate knowledge to run the complex administration and economy of the conquered territories, the new rulers left existing Persian and Byzantine officials in charge. Mu'awiyah (r. 661–80), founder of the Umayyad dynasty, moved the capital from Medina to Damascus, the capital of Byzantine Syria. Steeped in Byzantine and Christian tradition, Damascus became the earliest channel for transmission of the practices and attitudes of the conquered empires to the new rulers.[109]

Women's lives changed slowly at first, but by the end of the first Islamic century, they became gradually less visible. The change is reflected in the discrepancy among Qur'anic teachings, the prophet's treatment of women, and their position in Islamic law (shari'a). An obvious example is the spread of seclusion and the veil. Although a Qur'anic revelation addressed to the prophet's wives recommended seclusion to them, contemporary women seem to have treated it as a special ordinance. The absence of veiling is confirmed by the essayist al-Jahiz (776–869), who states, "Noble ladies used to sit and talk to men; and for them to look at each other was neither shameful in Pre-Islam nor illicit in Islam."[110] Another revelation recommended that women dress modestly and not display their ornaments. It is unlikely that the purpose of this revelation was the type of veil that enveloped women later in Islam, because women who participated in the pilgrimage to Mecca (hajj), which began during the prophet's time, would have adopted such a practice. In fact, women do not cover their faces during the hajj. When Mansur (r. 754–75), the second Abbasid caliph, built Baghdad as his capital, he ordered a separate bridge built over the Tigris for women.[111]

The veil, seclusion, and the withdrawal of women from the public sphere derived not from the Qur'an nor from practices of the Muslim community during the prophet's time but rather from the Arabians' exposure to the societies of the territories they conquered soon after the prophet's death. These territories included Iraq, which had been the heartland of the Sasanian empire and the home of the first urban society in the region. Customs there had initially emerged in response to the demands of existing social and economic conditions, particularly those of the first towns, but they had changed because of their exposure to millennium-long needs of the Persian empire. By contrast, Arabian culture had developed in response to conditions of the desert and its largely tribally organized, nomadic, pastoralist population. The former Arabian ways neither suited the lifestyle of rulers of a prosperous and mighty empire, nor could they be easily adapted to the complex and vastly different conditions of the conquered regions. Consequently, shortly after the conquest, Iraq became a major center of transmission of Irano-Mesopotamian culture and institutions to the new settlers from Arabia.

Also important was the number of Arabians compared to the conquered peoples. Although we lack demographic information about the Arabians who came to reside in the conquered territories, we can assume that they were a small minority, and they settled in the midst of a relatively vast non-Arabian population.[112] Despite being the ruling class, these relatively few Arabians did not affect the basic economic and social conditions or the political structure of the Sasanian empire. The conquest unified a large geographic area—the eastern portion of Byzantine, the entire Sasanian empire, and Spain—and thereby facilitated communication and trade. In this way, during the first century Arabian men and women, who initially had stayed aloof from mixing with the conquered, gradually absorbed their practices and attitudes.

A further factor was the desire of increasing numbers of Arabian leaders and notables to emulate the lifestyle of the former Sasanian aristocracy and the landed gentry. Many gentry continued to live in Iraq, some converted to Islam either out of conviction or convenience, and large numbers were retained in their posts because Arabians were unfamiliar with the ways of the newly acquired territories. The Arabian elite adopted many symbols of social distinction, such as cuisine, clothing style, and riding with a large retinue. Assimilation of the Irano-Mesopotamian culture was reinforced by the presence of many Persians who had moved into the newly established garrison towns at Kufa and Basra. The number of Persian-speakers was so large that the language was spoken along with Arabic in both towns.[113]

Another channel of transmission of Persian culture was the many Persian women and children who were captured by Arabians during wars between the two armies. The captives were considered war booty and distributed among soldiers and military officers. Some were sent to the Hijaz, others to garrison towns. Initially, Arabian men did not marry non-Arabian women but used them as concubines who bore their children. Despite their low status as concubines, servants, and slaves, these women introduced Persian domestic culture among Arabians.[114]

The influence of non-Arabian practices at the court of the Umayyad caliph Walid (r. 705–15) and his preference for non-Arabian wives prompted his banning harem women from mixing with outsiders. Another caliph, Hisham (r. 724–43), revived imperial Sasanian traditions and had manuals of government translated from Pahlavi into Arabic. His son from a Persian princess, Yazid III, followed him as caliph (r. 743–44). The first ruler from a non-Arabian mother, he took pride in his descent from two royal houses.[115]

The change of attitude toward the values of the conquered peoples also affected Arabian Muslim women; their less-restricted lifestyle was gradually transformed by urban traditions, which confined women mainly to home-based activities and childcare. By the time the Abbasids became leaders of the Islamic world, wearing the veil became mandatory for urban Arabian women as well.

Persian influence became more pronounced during the Abbasid period (750–1258), when Iraq was made the empire's center, and Baghdad, the new capital, was built near Ctesiphon, the old Sasanian capital. The reliance of the Abbasid movement on Khurasanians, under the leadership of Abu-Muslim, enhanced the prestige of Persian converts who occupied influential posts in the new capital. Members of the dynasty acknowledged their Arabian origin and their relationship to the prophet, but under an Islamic guise they revived many aspects of the pre-Islamic non-Arabian culture.

The gradual conversion of the masses in the conquered territories to Islam also affected the survival of older traditions, particularly those of the Sasanians. Indigenous peoples from Egypt to Khurasan began to adopt the religion of the Arabian conquerors, but they preserved their customs under an Islamic veneer. First- and second-generation male converts had grown up in an environment where women, not active in public life, occupied themselves with child rearing and home-based activities. Some of these converts may have been aware of women's lives in Arabia before Islam and the range of freedom they had enjoyed in early Islam, but their attitude about women was shaped by the social and economic circumstances of the urban environment in which they lived rather than Arabia. They began to reinterpret the past in the light of what in their view were standards of propriety.

What eventually legitimized many of these older traditions, including the Sasanian components, was their infiltration into the shari'a, which was developing simultaneously. The shari'a, a guide for Muslims along the path of a proper Islamic lifestyle, developed in a context in which Arabian Muslims, many of whom had only recently converted, had conquered vast territories and dispersed over a large area. At the same time, growing numbers of non-Arabians, following the conquest of the Nile-to-Oxus region, converted to Islam.[116]

Initially, the Qur'an and the prophet had guided the small Muslim community in Mecca and later in Medina. Muslims considered the Qur'an to be the word of god and followed its dictates as a sign of their submission. The prophet supplemented Qur'anic teachings in a manner he believed to be in agreement with god's will. After his death in 632, pious Muslims referred to the judgment and decisions of the prophet's close companions whenever the Qur'an and his teachings did not provide the answer to new questions, because it was assumed that they also conformed to the prophet's behavior and intentions.[117]

As Muslims from Arabia settled in new environments, teachings of the Qur'an and the prophet's example (sunnah) could no longer provide the necessary guidelines for the different conditions existing outside Arabia. This problem was partly resolved by following the prophet's precedent. He had retained the pre-Islamic Arabian practices that he believed were in keeping with the teachings of the Qur'an. This became the method by which Muslims established newly needed guidelines. Before a given practice could be sanctioned, it had to prove compatible with Qur'anic teachings and the prophet's sunnah. In an effort to integrate newly conquered territories into an Islamic empire, practices from those regions were sanctioned that had little or nothing to do with Qur'anic teachings, the sunnah, or pre-Islamic Arabian norms and traditions.

During the second and third centuries, the rate of conversion of non-Arabian peoples accelerated and so did the incorporation of older norms and traditions. The development of the shariʻa was stimulated by the "religious zeal of a growing number of Muslims which demanded the application of religious norms to all problems of behavior."[118] Many Muslim jurists and theologians in this crucial period either were of Iranian background (like Hasan al-Basri, Abu-Hanifah, Bukhari, and Tabari) or were influenced by Iranian culture. Since the Qurʼan was recorded during the time of the caliph Uthman (r. 644–56), it could not be modified, including teachings reflecting earlier roles of women. But through interpretation of Qurʼanic passages and statements attributed to the prophet, some earlier practices that seemed improper and lax by the standards of the older urban cultures began to be circumvented.[119] Furthermore, as non-Arabians gradually converted to Islam, they began to interpret the teachings of Islam in ways that were compatible with their own values and customs. One example is the radical difference in the punishment for adultery between the Qurʼan and the shariʻa. The Qurʼan ordains that adulterers be given one hundred lashes. By the time of the great legist Shafiʻi (d. 820), the standard punishment was death by stoning and was justified by hadith attributed to the prophet. Many earlier attitudes about women were given an Islamic guise and reappeared in religious and legal texts. For instance, a statement in a Sasanian work advising men not to entrust their secrets to women was later attributed to Muhammad. Likewise, some tortures that Arda Viraf, the Zoroastrian sage, observed when he visited hell were ascribed to Muhammad and other early religious figures as suitable punishments for errant and disobedient wives.[120]

In this manner, by the end of the second century, many older non-Arabian practices, including Sasanian ones, became accepted norms for Islamic behavior and were legitimized through the shariʻa. By the end of the third Islamic century, a systematized body of laws and regulations governing the daily life of individual Muslims had been devised. Gradually the entire shariʻa began to be considered by Muslims of later periods as inspired by god and therefore binding on all Muslims.

These two divergent origins of the shariʻa—the Qurʼan and the teachings of the prophet, on the one hand, and the traditions encountered in conquered areas, on the other hand—help to explain why, despite the freedoms women enjoyed in Arabia and the early Islamic period, they became restricted in Islamic society. The triumph of pre-Islamic traditions is demonstrated by the adoption of the veil and seclusion of women despite the absence of such ordinances in the Qurʼan or precedents in the prophet's sunnah.

42   GUITY NASHAT

NOTES

I thank Robert McC. Adams, Lois Beck, Gary Becker, Richard Frye, Martha Roth, and Matthew Stolper for valuable comments on and useful suggestions for this chapter.

1. I prefer the term "Nile-to-Oxus" to "the Middle East" because it is devoid of Eurocentric and modern nationalistic assocations.

2. Martha Roth, "'She Will Die by the Iron Dagger': Adultery and Neo-Babylonian Marriage," *Journal of the Economic and Social History of the Orient* 31 (3) (1988): 186–202.

3. For further discussion, see Guity Nashat and Judith Tucker, *Women in the Middle East and North Africa* (Bloomington: Indiana University Press, 1999), 10–34.

4. Martha T. Roth, *Law Collections from Mesopotamia and Asia Minor* (Atlanta: Scholars Press, 1997), 197, 201, 203.

5. See David B. Weisberg, "A Royal Woman of the Neo-Babylonian Period," in *Le palais et la royauté (archéologie et civilisation)*, ed. Paul Garelli, XIXe Rencontre Assyriologique Internationale (Paris: Librairie Orientale Paul Geuthner, 1971), 446–54.

6. For the importance of royal and aristocratic women as role models in the ancient world, see Susan E. Wood, *Imperial Women: A Study in Public Images, 40 B.C.–A.D. 68* (Leiden: Brill's Scholars' List, 1998), 1.

7. The film *Grass,* about the seasonal migrations of the Bakhtiyari in Iran, shows the type of activities women performed in nomadic society. For more on this lifestyle, see Donald Cole, *Nomads of the Nomads* (Chicago: Aldine, 1975), 18–47.

8. I. M. Diakonoff, "Elam," in *The Cambridge History of Iran,* vol. 2, *The Median and Achaemenian Periods* (Cambridge: Cambridge University Press, 1985), 1–3. (Hereafter, the abbreviation CHI is used.)

9. R. Girshman, *Iran* (Harmondsworth: Penguin Books, 1978), 42; Diakonoff, "Elam," 8–12, 23.

10. Walther Hinz, *The Lost World of Elam,* trans. Jennifer Barnes (New York: New York University Press, 1973), 41.

11. This may reflect a practice in Elamite society, which later influenced the Medes and subsequent next-of-kin marriage among the Sasanians. See Hinz, *Lost World,* 41–46; D. T. Potts, *The Archeology of Elam: Formation and Transformation of an Ancient Iranian State* (Cambridge: Cambridge University Press, 1999), 210–12.

12. Potts, *Archeology,* 209, 237; *Encyclopaedia Iranica,* s.v. "Elamite religion."

13. Hinz, *Lost World,* 108; Potts, *Archeology,* 109.

14. Potts, *Archeology,* 208, 233.

15. She was first married to Kutir-Nahhunte, with whom she had a son. After his death, she married his brother, Shilhak-Inshushinak. She had several children including two more sons with her second husband. After his death, the throne passed to Hutelutush-Inshushinak, the son she had with her first husband. See Hinz, *Lost World,* 127–31; *Encyclopaedia Iranica,* s.v. "Elamite religion."

16. Hinz, *Lost World,* 144–45; *Encyclopaedia Iranica,* s.v. "Elamite religion."

17. Hinz, *Lost World,* 130, 134, plate 17 for relief; Potts, *Archeology,* 240.

18. The Gathic hymns were passed down orally before being written down during

the Sasanian period (226–661 C.E.); *Encyclopaedia Iranica,* s.v. "Avesta"; M. Schwarts, "The Old Eastern Iranian World-View according to the Avesta," *CHI* 2:640–64.

19. *The Sacred Books of the East,* ed. F. Max Müller, vol. 23, pt. 2; *The Zend-Avesta, the Sirozah, Yasts and Nyayis,* trans. James Darmesteter (1882; reprint, Bombay: Motilal Banarsidass, 1969), 328–30.

20. *The Sacred Books of the East,* ed. F. Max Müller, vol. 4, *The Zend-Avesta,* pt. 1, *The Vendidad,* trans. James Darmesteter (1887; reprint, Bombay: Motilal Banarsidass, 1969), 175–76.

21. *Sacred Books,* 23:281.

22. Maneckji Nusservanji Dhallah, *History of Zoroastrianism,* 2d ed. (Bombay: Oxford University Press, 1963), 92.

23. *Sacred Books,* 4:181–84.

24. Ibid., 23:343.

25. Ibid., 116.

26. I. Gershevitch, "Zoroaster's Own Contribution," *Journal of Near Eastern Studies* 23 (1964): 12–38; M. Boyce, *A History of Zoroastrianism,* 2 vols. (Leiden: E. J. Brill, 1975, 1982).

27. I. M. Diakonoff, "Media," *CHI* 2:114, 134.

28. *Encyclopaedia Iranica,* s.v. "Achaemenian dynasty." See also Maria Brosius, *Women in Ancient Persia (559–331 B.C.)* (Oxford: Clarendon Press, 1996), 41–46.

29. Ran Zadok, "On the Connections between Iran and Babylonia in the Sixth Century B.C.," *Iran* 14 (1976): 62.

30. A. L. Oppenheim, "The Babylonian Evidence of Achaemenian Rule in Mesopotamia," *CHI* 2:530. Muhammad Dandamaev and Vladimir Lukonin, *The Culture and Social Institutions of Ancient Iran,* trans. Philip L. Kohl with D. J. Dadson (Cambridge: Cambridge University Press, 1989), 121.

31. See Heleen Sancisi-Weerdenburg, "Exit Atossa: Images of Women in Greek Historiography," in *Images of Women in Antiquity,* ed. Averil Cameron and Amélie Kuhrt (Detroit: Wayne State University Press, 1993), 20–23; Brosius, *Women,* 24; Pierre Briant and Clarisse Herrenschmidt, *Le tribut dans l'empire Perse: Actes de la table ronde de Paris, 12–13 décembre 1986* (Louvain and Paris: E. Peeters, 1989), 129–47.

32. Urban Mesopotamians may have been equally alarmed, but their reaction about the ways of the new rulers and their women is not known.

33. Herodotus, *The History,* trans. David Grene (Chicago: University of Chicago Press, 1987), 5:8.

34. The attitude of Greek historians toward Achaemenian women is reminiscent of the Muslim historian, Tabari, who criticized the Abbasid queen Khayzuran for her role in politics, which he considered a violation of gender roles. Tabari did not pass judgment on the public role of the prophet's wife A'isha.

35. Susan Walker, "Women and Housing in Classical Greece: The Archeological Evidence," in *Images of Women in Antiquity,* 81–83; John Gold, "Law, Custom and Myth: Aspects of the Social Position of Women in Classical Athens," *Journal of Hellenic Studies* 100 (1980): 44–49.

36. The negative treatment of Achaemenians, especially women, by classical authors seems to have influenced contemporary historians, such as Dandamaev, Luko-

nin, and Olmstead, who accept the judgment of the Greeks uncritically. A more recent development in Achaemenian historiography treats classical sources more cautiously; Briant, Brosius, Kuhrt, Sancisi-Weerdenburg, and Stolper exemplify this new approach.

37. Herodotus, *History* 3:68–69. Brosius (*Women*, 51–56) doubts the authenticity of Phaedyme's role and suggests that the account was fabricated later to legitimize the events that led to Darius's accession to the throne. Even if Darius's supporters created the story to cover up the regicide, Herodotus's account suggests that women's role in such a crucial event might have seemed normal to contemporary Persians. Perhaps the reason Phaedyme is treated positively is that she participated in this crucial event to obey her father's instructions.

38. Herodotus, *History* 3:133–34.

39. Sancisi-Weerdenburg, "Exit Atossa," 20–34.

40. Dandamaev and Lukonin, *Culture*, 109.

41. Pierre Briant, *Histoire de l'empire Perse* (Paris: Fayard, 1999), 296–97.

42. Dandamaev and Lukonin, *Culture*, 123.

43. Brosius, *Women*, 94; Dandamaev and Lukonin, *Culture*, 119.

44. The Persepolis archives refer to allocations of quantities of wine and foodstuff to Artystone, the favorite wife of Darius I, which might indicate she was holding banquets; Brosius, *Women*, 97.

45. Esther 1:9–12, King James Version. The story concerns Parthian times but was set back to an earlier era.

46. Brosius, *Women*, 94.

47. Dandamaev and Lukonin, *Culture*, 119.

48. Amélie Kuhrt, *The Ancient Near East c. 3000–330 B.C.*, vol. 1 (London: Routledge, 1995), 364–65.

49. Pierre Briant, "Le nomadism du grand roi," *Iranica Antiqua* 23 (1988): 264; Brosius, *Women*, 87; Briant, *Histoire*, 296.

50. According to Kuhrt (*Ancient Near East* 1:363), by the mid-Assyrian period the average man could have more than one wife and concubine.

51. Brosius, *Women*, 36, 47–50, 82.

52. Herodotus, *History* 1:107.

53. Brosius, *Women*, 66–67; Sancisi-Weerdenburg, "Exit Atossas," 26.

54. Brosius, *Women*, 66–67, 74.

55. Herodotus, *History* 1:97.

56. A. T. Olmstead, *A History of the Persian Empire*, 2d ed. (Chicago: University of Chicago Press, 1948), 424; see also Briant, *Histoire*, 292–93.

57. Dandamaev and Lukonin, *Culture*, 121–24.

58. Herodotus, *History* 1:135.

59. For biases in Greek sources toward Achaemenians, particularly their women, see Sancisi-Weerdenburg, "Exit Atossa," 20–34; Brosius, *Women*, 198–200.

60. Herodotus, *History* 9:111.

61. See Schwarts, "World-View," 656; and Dandamaev and Lukonin, *Culture*, 121.

62. Richard Frye states that next-of-kin marriage originated with the Elamites and Egyptians, attributes the allegation of its prevalence to hostile Greek and Roman

sources, and speculates that its adoption by Zoroastrian religious authorities occurred in late Parthian and early Sasanian periods; "Zoroastrian Incest," in *Orientalia Josephi Tucci Memoriae Dicata* (Rome: Istituto Italiano per il Medio ed Estremo Oriente, 1985), 445–55. For similar opinion, see Brosius, *Women,* 80–81.

63. Herodotus, *History* 3:25–27.

64. Briant, *Histoire,* 113–18; Brosius, *Women,* 45–47.

65. R. T. Hallock, "The Evidence of Persepolis Tablets," *CHI* 2:588–609; Matthew Stolper, *Entrepreneurs and Empire: The Murašu Archive, the Murašu Firm, and Persian Rule in Babylonia* (Leiden: E. J. Brill, 1985); Amélie Kuhrt, "Non-Royal Women in the Late Babylonian Period," in *Women's Earliest Records from Ancient Egypt and Western Asia,* ed. Barbara Lesko (Atlanta: Scholars Press, 1989), 215–43.

66. Stolper, *Entrepreneurs,* 53–54.

67. Xenophon, *The Persian Expedition,* trans. Rex Warner (London: Penguin, 1972), 122.

68. Brosius, *Women,* 25–27, 122–46.

69. Hallock, "Evidence," *CHI* 2:588–94, 600–660.

70. Dandamaev and Lukonin, *Culture,* 160, 169–70.

71. Herodotus, *History* 1:136.

72. Ester Boserup, *Women's Role in Economic Development* (New York: St. Martin's Press, 1970), 24–27.

73. N. Pigulevskaja, *Les villes de l'état iranien aux époques parthe et sassanide* (Paris: Mouton, 1963), 159–94; M. Diakonoff, *Ashkaniyan,* trans. (from Russian to Persian) K. Kishavarz (Tehran: Payam, 1350/1972), 57–75.

74. The term "Eragh" meant "lowland." Iraq is the Arabized version of this Pahlavi name. See Wilhelm Eilers, "Iran and Mesopotamia," *CHI* 3, *The Seleucid, Parthian and Sasanian Periods* (Cambridge: Cambridge University Press, 1983), 481.

75. Ibid., 501.

76. A. Perikhanian, "Iranian Society and Law," *CHI* 3:627–31; Nizhat Safa-Isfahani, *Rivayat-i hemit-i Asawahistan: A Study in Zoroastrian Law* (Cambridge: Harvard University Press, 1980), i-xi; Jenny Rose, "Two Queens, Two Wives, and a Goddess: The Roles and Images of Women in Sasanian Iran," in *Women in the Medieval Islamic World,* ed. Gavin Hambly (New York: St. Martin's Press, 1998), 29–55.

77. V. G. Lukonin, "Political, Social, and Administrative Institutions: Taxes and Trade," *CHI* 3:712–13.

78. Ibid., 693.

79. Katayun Mazdapur, "Zan dar a'in zartushti (Women in Zoroastrian religion)," in *Hayat-i ijtima'i-yi zan dar tarikh-i Iran* (Women's role in Iranian social history) (Tehran: Amir Kabir, 1369/1992), 95.

80. Muhammad ibn Jarir Tabari, *The History of al-Tabari,* vol. 5, *The Sasanids, the Byzantines, the Lakmids, and Yemen,* trans. C. E. Bosworth (Albany: State University of New York Press, 1999), 135.

81. Perikhanian, "Iranian Society," 641–44; Safa-Isfahani, *Rivayat,* 290, which is a post-Sasanian source.

82. Christian Bartholomae, *Die Frau im Sasanidischen Recht* (Heidelberg: Carl Winters Universitätsbuchhandlung, 1924), 10.

83. Perikhanian, "Iranian Society," 655; Safa-Isfahani, *Rivayat*, 16, 47–53.

84. Arthur Christensen, *L'Iran sous les sassanides* (Copenhagen: Ejnar Munksgaard, 1944), 322–23.

85. *Shayist nashayist* (Proper, improper), trans. (from Pahlavi to Persian) Katayun Mazdaparast (Tehran: Muassisiyeh mutaliat va tahqiqat-i tarikhi, 1369/1990), 156; Christensen, *Iran*, 323.

86. Safa-Isfahani, *Rivayat*, 288–90.

87. Ibid., 208–16.

88. *The Book of Arda Viraf*, trans. Martin Haug and E. W. West (Bombay: Government Central Book Depot, 1872), 200, 197.

89. Tabari, *History of Tabari*, 5:132–35, 148–49; Pigulevskaja, *Villes de l'état iranien*, 195–230.

90. Perikhanian ("Iranian Society," 650) does not mention sources for this marriage. Even if it was an archaic practice, it was revived by priests in response to Mazdakite demands and the dearth of women.

91. *The Sacred Books of the East*, vol. 37, *Pahlavi Texts*, pt. 4, *Contents of the Nasks*, trans. W. E. West (1892; reprint, Bombay: Motilal Banarsidass, 1969), 298–300; *The Sacred Books of the East*, vol. 31, *The Zend-Avesta*, pt. 3, trans. L. H. Mills (1887; reprint, Bombay: Motilal Banarsidass, 1969), 191–92.

92. *The Sacred Books of the East*, vol. 18, *Pahlavi Texts*, pt. 2, trans. E. W. West, *The Dadistan-i Dinik and Epistles of Manuskihar* (1887; reprint, Bombay: Motilal Banarsidass, 1970), 199–201, 414–20.

93. *Sacred Books*, 37:364–67, 381–83; *Sacred Books*, 18:389–92; Safa-Isfahani, *Rivayat*, 190–93. West argues that the term "khevtuk-das" does not originate in the Gathas and that it is a later addition to Pahlavi religious works; *Sacred Books*, 18:427.

94. Mazdapur, "Zan," 85; *Arda Viraf*, 167.

95. *Arda Viraf*, 187.

96. Ibid., 171, 194, 195, 197.

97. Ibid., 192.

98. Bartholomae, *Die Frau*, 7.

99. Mazdapur, "Zan," 95.

100. Ibid., 98.

101. *Arda Viraf*, 162.

102. A popular story relates the encounter of Shapur, the Sasanian king, with a peasant girl who raised pails of water from a well more easily than all his officers and the king himself. Her strength taught the king humility; Mazdapur, "Zan," 96.

103. I use the term "Arabian" to refer to inhabitants of Arabia, to distinguish them from the term "Arab," which is used today for Arabic-speaking peoples.

104. W. Robertson Smith, *Kinship and Marriage in Early Arabia* (Boston: Beacon Press, 1903), 156–75.

105. Qur'an 13:7. Although the renditions are my own, I consulted *The Koran Interpreted*, trans. A. Arberry (London: Allen and Unwin, 1955).

106. Qur'an 24:2, 3; Ibn Ishaq, *The Life of Muhammad*, trans. A. Guillaume (Oxford: Oxford University Press, 1982), 493, 495.

107. Roth, "'She Will Die by the Iron Dagger.'"

108. Ibn Ishaq, *Life*, 212, 358–66, 374–89.

109. Albert Hourani, *A History of the Arab Peoples* (Cambridge: Harvard University Press, 1991).

110. Amr al-Jahiz, *The Epistle on the Singing Girls of Jahiz,* trans. A. F. L. Beeston (Warminster, Wilts: Aris and Phillips, 1980), 17. For passages addressed to the prophet's wives and on modest dress, see the Qur'an 33:32, 24:31.

111. J. Lassner, "Why Did the Caliph al-Mansur Build ar-Rusafa?" *Journal of Near Eastern Studies* 24 (1965): 97.

112. I use Charles Issawi's study of the eighth century to arrive at estimates for the first part of the seventh century: the entire Arabian peninsula (about two million), Iraq (about five million), and the Sasanian empire (about twelve million); "The Area and Population of the Arab Empire: An Essay in Speculation," in *The Islamic Middle East, 700–1900: Studies in Economic and Social History,* ed. A. L. Udovitch (Princeton: Darwin Press, 1981), 380–82.

113. Michael Morony, *Iraq after the Muslim Conquest* (Princeton: Princeton University Press, 1984), 209.

114. Ibid., 197–98, 209, 258–60.

115. M. Sprengling, "From Persian to Arabic," *American Journal of Semitic Languages* 55–56 (1938–39): 175–225.

116. In discussing non-Arabian influences on the development of the shari'a, I focus on the impact of Iranian practices and the continuity between pre-Islamic and Islamic attitudes toward women in the Iranian highlands; see *Encyclopaedia of Islam,* 2d ed., s.v. "Shari'a."

117. H. A. R. Gibb, *Mohammedanism,* 2d ed. (London: Oxford University Press, 1972), 49–73; Joseph Schacht, *An Introduction to Islamic Law* (1964; reprint, Oxford: Clarendon, 1984), 68–85.

118. Schacht, *Introduction,* 209.

119. Joseph Schacht, *The Origins of Muhammadan Jurisprudence,* 2d ed. (Oxford: Clarendon, 1950), 73.

120. S. Mudassir Shah Moosavi, *Life after Death* (San Jose, Calif.: Islamic Guidance Center, n.d.), 43–45.

2 Women during the Transition from Sasanian to Early Islamic Times

JAMSHEED K. CHOKSY

TRACING THE HISTORY of Iranian women who witnessed their lives reshaped by the Arab conquest of the Sasanian kingdom or molded by the subsequent incorporation of Iran into the Islamic world, during Late Antiquity and the early Middle Ages, is at best a daunting task. Unlike the men involved—particularly those who served as rulers, generals, preachers, scholars, authors, and bureaucrats—the women received limited notice even though they must have performed daily actions that bridged the political, religious, and social changes taking place. Literacy in those days was very much an upper-class male domain. The lives, struggles, and contributions of women were recorded when judged to be significant by the men who inscribed the historical record of the Sasanian empire's fall and the Islamic caliphate's rise. By and large, references to women tended to be tangential—that is, parts of larger narratives or issues rather than for their own sake. Another difficulty in reconstructing the roles of women in Iranian society arises directly from the Arab invasion of the first century A.H./seventh century A.D. Specifically, the historiographical tradition was temporarily disrupted. As a result, the actions and experiences of women, like those of men, were retrospectively recorded and often distorted two or more centuries later when written historiography recommenced in the region.

Nonetheless, historical and legal registers in the Arabic and New Persian languages when combined with Middle Persian or Pahlavi writings yield fleeting insights into the lives of women during the decades when Iran became an Islamic country. Some of those records refer directly to Iranian women, others to non-Muslim women within the caliphate broadly, and still others to the overall position of non-Muslims, but in contexts applicable to women. Consequently, documented incidents have to be combined with a degree of extrapolation to obtain glimpses into Iranian women's lives between the first century A.H./seventh century A.D. and the fourth century A.H./ tenth century A.D.

Generally speaking, cultures tend to be conservative when it comes to attitudinal change. This notion is especially true for gender-related issues. It is now accepted that Sasanian culture, which extended geographically from the Tigris river to the Oxus (Amu Darya) river, contributed significantly to early Islamic society. Women's lives, and the recording of their achievements and tribulations, remained under the influence of trends previously established. Thus, before probing later situations, brief attention must be paid to how pre-Islamic Iranian mores had an impact on women prior to the caliphate's establishment. Only then can features of Iranian women's experiences during early Islamic times be placed within a meaningful cultural context. In so doing, this chapter focuses on women who were part of societal transformation from Sasanian Iran, with its Zoroastrian-dominated socioreligious culture, to Iran within the caliphate, with its emerging Muslim-dominated culture, rather than on the frequently debated issue of women's statuses and roles in Islam.[1] Moreover, given the broad nature of the topic at hand, only select issues and instances can be examined herein.

Overview of Sasanian Times

Not surprisingly, Sasanian-era records include accounts of the actions of elite women, for their lives often served as role models of socially acceptable behavior. Documentary and numismatic evidence helps reconstruct an outline of the life of the Zoroastrian queen Borandukht (Boran), who reigned for one year from A.D. 629 to 630. Royal tradition ensured that her legacy survived, together with that of her sister Azarmigduxt (Azarmedukht).[2] The life story of Shirin, a Christian queen of Khusro II (r. A.D. 591–628), combining fact and fiction, was recorded in a range of textual sources including ones written in Syriac and New Persian. Involvement with Nestorian versus Monophysite church politics, coupled with popular romantic notions, kept her

memory extant.[3] There also are accounts of a purported marriage between
the same Sasanian ruler and Maria, a daughter of the Byzantine emperor
Maurice.[4] Women's lives changed once they were taken into the royal court
or other princely ones. Access to the harems in which elite women and concubines dwelt was largely restricted to kings, princes, eunuchs, and female
servants, and women inside harems experienced only indirect contact with
people on the outside.[5] But when venturing outside, these women were not
the only members of Iranian imperial households to veil themselves from
public view. Sasanian kings also wore veils that draped down from their
crowns so as to separate them from, and denote their superiority over, commoners.[6] It is unclear if veiling was ever commonplace in ancient Iranian
society. Zoroastrianism never placed such a restriction on either women or
men, and the Parsis (Zoroastrians who immigrated from Iran to India in the
tenth century A.D.) have not practiced either veiling or general seclusion of
women. Therefore, these practices may have been confined to the ruling
group of pre-Islamic Iran.

Other women became well known because their actions violated social
guidelines. Martyrologies of female Christians such as Anahid (d. ca. A.D.
446), a former Zoroastrian, and Martha (d. ca. A.D. 341) were recorded. Those
records highlight the newfound religious convictions of these women who,
consequently, refused to follow entrenched Iranian customs such as marriage
and procreation (instead of celibacy) and rejected worship of the Zoroastrian creator deity Ahura Mazda. Here religious piety preserved hagiographies
that transformed these women into archetypes for other Christian converts
in Iran to emulate.[7]

Such women were the exception rather than the rule—the vast majority
remained nameless. Nameless they may have been, but faceless they were not.
Women were frequently depicted in royal, religious, and popular art—including sculpture, paintings, seals, and metalwork—of the Sasanian era. Previously,
during the Achaemenian period (550–330 B.C.), women were excluded from
imperial art. Representation in artwork seems to be one marker of a change
in the social position of women, probably reflecting their growing importance
in the day-to-day functioning of Iranian society under the Sasanians.

Beyond the lives of specific women, certain general aspects of female life
in Sasanian times can be identified. Using a Middle Persian or Pahlavi juridical manual dating to the early seventh century A.D., it is possible to reconstruct some avenues open to Iranian women from differing walks of life. A
Syriac law book by the Iranian archbishop Isho'bokht (Jesubocht), compiled
in the eighth century A.D. but based on Sasanian precepts, has similar value.

The Babylonian Talmud of the sixth century A.D. functions likewise.[8] From these documents it is clear that freeborn women had certain legal rights and responsibilities: they could enter into contractual agreements and commercial transactions; they had access to inheritance; they had to meet debts; and they were held responsible for violations of law. But these rights were often not on par with those of men, because women's legal capacity, like that of minors, was often passive rather than active. Therefore, in many instances their public actions such as trading would have been mediated by adult males with whom the women had statutory relationships—fathers, husbands, sons, or guardians.[9] Female slaves, constantly present in secular settings and occasionally attached to temples, had few rights. They were considered property to be bought, sold, and exchanged even when pregnant (fetuses and children were not regarded as legally theirs but belonged to the master or mistress), although in general the value assigned to them was lower than that of male slaves. Only in limited situations could a slave seek legal recourse, such as if she or he had been subject to excessively cruel punishment.[10]

Marriage was a central aspect of the social role incumbent on women. Legal stipulations circumscribed marriage in Sasanian Iran. A woman's consent had to be obtained before marriage. A marriage contract protected her legal and financial rights during the union and even when divorce occurred—for instance, it could be specified therein that assets brought by the bride at the time of marriage had to be returned to her if the marriage was dissolved. Depending upon her own social status at the time of marriage, a Zoroastrian wife could be either *padikhshay* (fully empowered main wife) or *chagar* (dependent, levirate wife). A woman could also enter into marriage without the consent of her male guardians, in which case she was regarded as a *khwasray* (self-entrusted, self-dependent wife). In certain situations, legally valid unions could arise between members of the same family. For instance, a woman whose deceased father or brother had neither a padikhshay wife nor a son could become *ayoken* (gain all rights) as though she had been the dead man's main wife.[11] Such unions fell under the category of *khwedodah* (consanguineous marriage). While references to the significance of consanguineous marriages are numerous in the writings of late Sasanian and early post-Sasanian magi (priests) and rote denunciations of it are periodic in Muslim sources, little nonsectarian evidence exists for its popularity in Iran. It appears to have begun among the Achaemenian ruling family, in particular when Kambujiya or Cambyses (r. 529–522 B.C.) married his sisters, including Atossa, as a means of consolidating power. As a royal practice, it is clearly attested in the Parthian and Sasanian periods. The whims of kings, however, are only infrequently an accurate indicator of popular or prevailing custom. There is limited indication that consanguineous marriage was adopted by Iranian commoners as a legal means (the ayoken type is noted above) of retaining assets within familial units. This became especially important when families faced the possibility of members leaving the Zoroastrian community and taking economic resources with them to the socioreligious group they had newly joined. But, unlike in Roman Egypt where census records indicate consanguinity was fairly widespread among the populace, there is no evidence it ever became a popular form of consummated marriage in Iran under either the Sasanians or the caliphs—despite certain magi even giving khwedodah the status of a religious duty.[12] Marriage between cousins appears to have been common, a practice still popular among both Iranian Zoroastrians and Muslims and also among the Parsis.

Other details emerge with regard to the religious roles of Iranian women prior to the advent of Islam. Zoroastrian ritual manuals stress the constraints regularly placed on women's activities owing to that community's fear of impurity, which was thought to result from the discharge of blood during menstruation and childbirth. Influences upon and from the Jewish community are apparent, perhaps owing to communal proximity and occasional conversions, with the Zoroastrian stipulations being on the whole more stringent and restrictive for women.[13] So women could worship at fire temples, perform basic rites such as tending the sacred fires when men were unavailable, and on occasion gain religious learning and general literacy by attending *herbedestans* (theological colleges). But they could not enroll in the priesthood, owing to their being regarded as periodically polluted.[14] Because Zoroastrians formed the demographically and politically dominant group in ancient Iran, their customs found widespread acceptance. As members of another religious community, Christian women were beyond the control of Zoroastrian jurists and magi. Ideas of individual worth, spiritual equality, and open access to religious institutions, coupled with resistance to the Sasanian dynasty's religiously based social order, initially enabled Christian women— including Zoroastrian apostates who adopted the teachings of Christ—to participate extensively within their own community as the partners of men. The fifth century A.D., however, witnessed a subversion of concepts of gender equality within the Christian churches of Sasanian Iran. As men reasserted patriarchal notions of dominance, Christian women were relegated once more to secondary positions under male supervision—roles emphasizing virginity, chastity, penitence, and monasticism.[15] Religious circumscription of life for Jewish women can be seen through the prism of rabbinical materials from the sixth century A.D. Unlike male Jews, women were expected to refrain, as far as possible, from activities outside the domestic sphere. The religious dimensions of this agenda resulted in public devotional acts, such as performing the time-related positive commandments and reading the Torah, not being encouraged.[16]

Overall, the image of Iranian society during the Sasanian era is one where function became increasingly gender specific, roles came to be divided into masculine and feminine ones, and women eventually were expected to accept domesticity as daughters, wives, and mothers rather than to seek public recognition. Even within the private domain of a household, women often could exert only limited authority when determining the upbringing and day-to-day activities of their children.[17] Yet the extent of women's actual control over the domestic sphere remains hazy because historical records granted little importance to such activities, considering these part of a biological purpose believed to have been assigned to women by god as claimed through the scriptures and exegeses of Zoroastrians, Jews, and Christians in pre-Islamic Iran.

Stress of Conquest

Arab Muslims succeeded in annexing lands of the Sasanian empire from west of the midcourse of the Euphrates river all the way to the banks of the Oxus river. In cultural terms, the Iranian world of that time reached even farther— westward close to the Black Sea, northward into Armenia, eastward to Uzbekistan and Kazakhstan, and southward along the coastline of the Arabian peninsula. Successful Arab military incursions led to considerable disruption in the lives of Iranian women, be they Zoroastrians, Christians, or Jews, for about one hundred years. For some, the Arabs may have been only a fleeting experience—armies that passed by on the way to capturing cities and garrisons. Others, however, particularly women and girls living in urban centers, routinely faced spending years if not the rest of their lives providing involuntary service to triumphant Muslim soldiers. Yet others, while retaining their freedom, lost their social or financial standing. All this occurred despite an attitude among the Arab elite, later enshrined in the form of a pragmatic edict attributed to the caliph Umar (r. A.H. 13–23/A.D. 634–644), that "maintaining the original status of Iranians" was preferable to fanning the natives' antagonism by further disrupting prevailing socioeconomic conditions.[18]

Several examples can be cited with regard to the loss of personal freedom by Iranian women at the time of the Arab conquest. For instance when the town of Jalula, in the Diyala river basin on the border between the lowlands of Iraq and the Iranian plateau, fell in A.H. 16/A.D. 637, many women there "were taken as concubines and [later] bore their Muslim masters' offspring."[19] During the bitter struggle for control of Istakhr, provincial capital of Fars and a Zoroastrian stronghold from whence the Sasanian royal family hailed, several noblewomen were killed, and others from all walks of life were forced into concubinage by Arab Muslim soldiers between A.H. 23/A.D. 644 and A.H. 29/A.D. 650.[20] When Muslim troops temporarily subdued the Transoxanian mercantile city of Baykand or Paykand in A.H. 54/A.D. 674, Iranians of both genders experienced slavery. Those female residents of Baykand who retained their freedom lost it briefly to Muslim warriors during an uprising in A.H. 87/A.D. 706 until ransomed back by their menfolk.[21] At Gurgan city, along the eastern Caspian shore, persistent rebellions against Arab rule ended only after Muslim commanders hanged the male Zoroastrian rebels and led the executed individuals' women and children away as captives around the year A.H. 97/A.D. 716.[22] Nor did peaceful capitulation alter the fate of women, as at the Khurasanian oasis town of Sarakhs where residents negotiated a treaty with Muslim forces in A.H. 31/A.D. 652. Here, and at other places farther to the west, terms of surrender provided security only for Iranian men. Again, women found themselves losing their liberty, becoming concubines and servants to the newcomers.[23] The need for concubines and servant women appears to have declined only after the wives of Arab soldiers joined their men stationed in the newly conquered regions.[24]

Wealthy Iranian women who had acquired their assets through inheritance, marriage, or commerce, like men in similar circumstances, periodically had their homes and lands confiscated by Arab commanders. Events at Bukhara are a case in point. The Sogdian residents of that Central Asian oasis settlement, led by a *khatun* (female leader) who was serving as regent for her young son, agreed to and then broke treaties with Arab Muslims. After the city was finally captured in A.H. 90/A.D. 709, the Arab general Qutayba b. Muslim had residents hand over half their property to the victors who then settled there.[25] Conversion to Islam enabled some women to retain their assets—despite the general trend until Abbasid times not to grant exemptions to converts. The infrequency of such a maneuver finding success is reflected in the paucity of documented examples; the most noteworthy was that of a woman from the *dihqan* (gentry) who dwelt in the Iraqi district of Nahr Malik.[26] The collapse of the Sasanian empire also stripped elite women of their official ranks. Yet, beyond the nascent Muslim society's bounds, upper-class Iranian men and women still found their positions respected—unless they adopted Islam, in which case they were derided—by a majority of the population who remained largely Zoroastrian by confession, with substantial Jewish and Christian minorities, until the fourth century A.H. or tenth century A.D.[27]

Motives for Conversion

It is now known that only a fraction of the indigenous people chose, voluntarily or under duress, to practice Islam during the first century A.H. or seventh century A.D. Most persons, usually as urban units, agreed to pay the Arab Muslims tribute in the form of the *jizya* (poll tax) rather than give up their beliefs. Records suggest that, following a similar Sasanian impost called the *gazidag,* in the early decades of Arab rule no differentiation was made between men and women when it came to levying the jizya.[28] So initially it may have been collected from the entire population of a locality, even though in later Islamic administrative praxis it came to be due only from adult males. What is clear about the early period of Muslim rule in Iran is that collection of the poll tax was left to local, non-Muslim, Iranian authorities—often the same individuals who had gathered the gazidag for the Sasanians—to implement. A few examples may be cited from the plethora available. At the western city of Nihavand, a *herbed* (Zoroastrian theologian, priestly teacher) paid the poll tax using funds at the disposal of a local fire temple. Residents of Rayy negotiated tribute payable "on condition their fire temples would not be destroyed nor anyone among them slain." The margrave of Merv al-Rud in eastern Iran collected the poll tax for the Arabs rather than allow any Iranians to become Muslim. Zoroastrian and Buddhist elites at Balkh did the same on behalf of all residents there.[29]

Resistance to change notwithstanding, much of Iran's population gradually converted to Islam between the second to seventh centuries A.H. or eighth to thirteenth centuries A.D. At first, confessional change was mainly an urban phenomenon. Then, as time went by, new converts and itinerant preachers brought Islamic customs to villagers.[30] Certain broad reasons for confessional change can be elucidated from the extant literature. Some were gender nonspecific. One was a desire to preserve social or financial status, as witnessed by the case of the female landowner from Nahr Malik previously mentioned. Beyond particular individuals, women of means must have numbered among the residents—male and female—of Takrit along the Tigris

river's west bank, Qazvin in Media or Jibal, and Isfahan who chose to pro-
fess the victors' faith. By so doing, they sought to retain their socioeconomic clout rather than dissipate it through taxation and confiscation.[31]

Sex and intermarriage of Arab men and Iranian women became an important gender-related path to Islam, because after marriage a woman generally was regarded by all the religious communities involved as having de facto
accepted the faith of her new husband. A few unions became especially noteworthy for medieval writers. The third Shi'i imam (spiritual leader), Husayn
b. Ali (d. A.H. 61/A.D. 680), supposedly wed Shahrbanu (d. ca. A.H. 61/A.D. 680),
daughter of the last Sasanian king, Yazdagird III (r. A.D. 632–51). Their son,
Ali b. Husayn (d. ca. A.H. 94/A.D. 712), became the fourth imam. This reputed
convergence of Arabian prophetic lineage with Iranian imperial genealogy
would have associated early Islam, particularly its emerging Shi'i version, with
the cultural identity of those among the conquered who had hitherto regarded
the Arabs' faith as an alien one. A similar marriage across Arab and Iranian
ethnoreligious lines occurred between the Umayyad caliph al-Walid I (r. A.H.
86–96/A.D. 705–15) and Shahfarand (Shah i Afrid), daughter of a Sasanian
prince named Peroz. Their son, in whose personage Arabian and Iranian royal
lines were united, eventually reigned as Yazid II (r. A.H. 101–5/A.D. 720–24).
These women, and others like them who entered the caliphal courts, would
have transmitted Iranian customs such as *nav ruz* (new year's celebration) and
mihragan (feast of Mithra) to their Muslim spouses.[32]

Following in the footsteps of Shahrbanu and Shahfarand, nondescript
Iranian women frequently found husbands among Arab settlers or among
Iranians who had adopted Islam. Magi tried desperately to halt this habit by
condemning it as a grievous sin—irrespective of whether it occurred between
a Zoroastrian woman and Muslim man or vice versa.[33] Medieval Muslim
intellectuals, principally jurists, often took a parallel view by ruling such
unions invalid if the woman remained a Zoroastrian; the same was not true
in the case of a Christian or Jew.[34] Authorities of the Jewish gaonate, from
the middle of the seventh century A.D. onward, also sought to discourage
sexual contacts and weddings with Muslims by taking the position that such
interactions with persons "in a state of impurity" would lead to the Jews
involved becoming unclean too.[35] Christian Iranians also sought to discourage such sexual behavior by forbidding it and by assigning to unmarried
women the role of caring for orphans and waifs, despite Christian women
who entered Muslim households not having, in theory, to abjure their doctrines and rituals. The urgency attached by Christian men to the issue of their
women having sexual contacts with Muslims, and consequently adopting

Islam, is evidenced by the specific mention of this issue in the traditional account, possibly fictitious, of an agreement between the catholicos Isho'yahb II (d. A.D. 643) and the Prophet Muhammad (d. A.H. 11/A.D. 632).[36] But orthodox elites had little success in halting intercourse and matrimony between Iranians and Arabs, non-Muslims and Muslims, in the medieval period, especially as intermarriage among Zoroastrians, Jews, and Christians had occurred sporadically even prior to the Arab conquest.[37]

Another gender-specific reason for conversion to Islam lay in circumstances beyond women's control, namely their loss of social status once male relatives converted to Islam. Essentially, the legal standing of a Zoroastrian woman fell if a husband, brother, or father became a Muslim. Since Zoroastrians formed the largest confessional group from whose ranks Muslims arose in Iranian society, it is informative to consider the rulings of magi on this matter. A woman who found herself in such a situation could serve as the chagar wife of another Zoroastrian, not the chief one. She had only limited authority over any children she bore. She also became partially responsible for her own maintenance. Moreover, a Zoroastrian man usually had to function as her guardian in public settings. Surprisingly, the Zoroastrian community took no steps to rectify this situation or provide for the well-being of women and children placed in such plight. Concerns of abandonment by their men coupled with resulting decline in rank seem to have convinced many women to cast aside their Iranian religion in favor of the Arabian one, often taking their children with them.[38] Other groups did not follow the Zoroastrian model. Thus, a Christian woman's social and financial positions were not directly affected by the apostasy of other Christians. Indeed, Christian women often served as patrons, without oversight of male guardians, and disposed of their wealth as they saw fit.[39]

A third impetus for Iranian women turning to Islam also arose from conditions peculiar to the Zoroastrian community. Elaborate purity codes required Zoroastrian women to segregate themselves while menstruating and for forty days after childbirth, then undergo purification rituals before remingling with their families. Beyond the domain of arduous rites associated with this notion of impurity—such as isolation, donning special clothes, and using particular utensils while eating—these women also faced the psychological distress of periodically experiencing a physiological aspect that their religion regarded as an affliction of evil. Abandoning the confessional system that imposed such values and activities for one in which simply bathing rendered women ritually free from religious impurity appears to have met with favor.[40] To some extent the same could have been true for Jewish women too.

Aspects of Islamization

Converting to Islam, either actively or passively, brought about a series of repercussions that further cut ties between women who had recently become Muslims and members of their former community. Reactions by Iranian Jews, Christians, and Zoroastrians toward men and women who left their folds were not dissimilar. It is instructive, for instance, to consider the Zoroastrian community's position on apostates. In spiritual terms any Zoroastrian, male or female, who adopted Islam was branded a sinner whose soul allegedly could never reach paradise. With regard to temporal matters, he or she would be viewed as legally deceased and therefore bereft of rights and possessions. All property the individual possessed passed to family members remaining Zoroastrians or in their absence could be seized by the community. Only once Muslims began to outnumber Zoroastrians, after the fourth century A.H. or tenth century A.D., was it no longer possible for the latter to enforce this policy. A convert could now count on Muslim coreligionists among the local authorities to safeguard his or her valuables. Hence, Zoroastrians eventually had "no option but to act in the most prudent, least dangerous, fashion by permitting a convert [to Islam] to retain personal assets."[41] So loss of a group's members was compounded by loss of assets. Giving up on the apostates, other sects also sought to safeguard their finances. The gaonate, for instance, protected the Jewish community's finances by ruling that the inheritance of widows remained valid even if overseen by executors who became apostates or even when overseen by Islamic courts.[42]

Severing contact with the former group would have compelled converts to develop strong bonds to their newfound denomination. Through these latest ties much more than physical items were carried from one community to another. On a syncretistic note, most new Muslims received religious instruction orally—during which process attempts were seldom made to distinguish carefully Islamic doctrinal and ritual details from Christian, Jewish, or Zoroastrian ones. Since many Iranian female converts would have been functionally illiterate, there was no possibility of features specific to Islamic tradition being read or studied. As a result, Iranian praxis entered Muslim devotions. Some converts placed lamps before the *mihrab* (prayer niche) as a syncretic reconciliation of worshipping in a fire altar's presence with their newfound devotions toward Mecca. For former Christians, this niche replaced the cross. Others continued visiting Zoroastrian shrines, justifying their pilgrimages in the name of one or another Muslim saint.[43] A feminine

Muslim image, that of Fatima (d. A.H. 11/A.D. 633), daughter of the Prophet Muhammad, functioned as a religious model for Iranian women to emulate as chaste women, obedient wives, and devoted mothers. Indeed, Fatima would eventually be given the epithet *zahra/zohar* (radiant), an honorific previously held by the Zoroastrian female divinity Anahita (Anahid), whose own name refers to chastity.[44] Women must have been on the forefront of transmitting these and other innovations to their children using both the spoken Persian language and daily example.

Separation from former coreligionists together with pressure to conform to Islamic mores resulted in many Iranian women changing their names and dress to meet with approval from other Muslims. Conversely, those women remaining non-Muslim found their own public behavior increasingly regulated by the politically dominant Muslim community. Clothing, including styles and colors, became important visual markers of confessional allegiance and a means for isolating Zoroastrians, Jews, and Christians in public settings. The Umayyad caliph Umar II (r. A.H. 99–101/A.D. 717–20) and the Abbasid caliph Harun al-Rashid (r. A.H. 170–93/A.D. 786–809) both technically forbade Iranians from wearing Iranian-style jackets and silk garments. During the first two hundred years of Islamic rule, however, few attempts would be made to enforce these ordinances upon Iranians.[45] Around A.H. 235/A.D. 850, once Muslims had become the dominant urban polity, the caliph al-Mutawakkil (r. A.H. 232–47/A.D. 847–61) commanded that non-Muslim men "don yellow hats" and non-Muslim women "who ventured into public places should do so only when covered with a yellow shawl." Yellow had been assigned as the color for *dhimmi* (protected minority) communities because Muslims were forbidden from wearing garments tinted with saffron, source of the principal yellow dye in the Middle Ages. Yet the enforcement of Muslim social norms as a means of Islamization was at best haphazard, with medieval geographers and historians noting that non-Muslim Iranians—men and women—often ignored these stipulations unless forced to conform.[46] The situation would have been complicated further by Iranian women influencing the garb their Arab husbands and masters wore. Fabrics such as silk, styles such as the Iranian robe and pants, and even colors such as saffron yellow found favor among Muslim men, owing to the influence of their Iranian women.[47] Likewise, the choice of children's clothes fell within the domestic realm, with mothers playing a crucial role in determining whether their offspring eventually accepted or rejected dress codes established by Muslim administrators.

Another circumstance where women crossing religious boundaries had to reconcile old traditions with new ones related to diet. The most notable change must have related to the consumption of pork, acceptable to Zoro-astrians and many Christians but prohibited for Muslims and Jews. Again, these women opened new culinary avenues for men with whom they lived as wives, concubines, servants, and slaves. Meats other than pork, rice, and sugar became regular components of the diet of Muslims in Iran. Even the mode of dining changed when the use of bowls was gradually introduced.[48] Women remaining among their ancestral ecclesiastic groups would have faced the additional challenge of maintaining old dietary norms in situations where contact with Muslims became inevitable. To them largely fell the re-sponsibility of ensuring that food items prepared by Muslims met the codes of their own communities both in terms of the ingredients and the cooking utensils—for if either could be regarded as ritually unclean then the food supposedly would pollute a family that consumed it.[49] Of course, supervis-ing the cooking of food by Muslims—as advised by the magi and gaonim—brought Zoroastrian and Jewish women into even more frequent contact with the bearers of Islamic values.

In legal terms, the status of women did not experience any fundamental changes during the course of Islamization. As in Sasanian society, women (even Muslims if not freeborn) in the new Islamic society found themselves sold, purchased, exchanged, gifted, and inherited. Wealthy Umayyad and Abbasid men often acquired many women as a status symbol and kept large harems of wives and concubines just as Sasanian noblemen had once done. Transactions involving women as commodities may even have taken place across confessional lines—for instance, the caliph Ali b. Abi Talib (r. A.H. 35–40/A.D. 656–61) seems to have sold an Iranian princess named Izdundad to the Jewish exilarch Bostanai (d. ca. A.D. 660).[50] But many aspects of daily life continued as before for women. Glimpses of them as women of the court, merchants, mystics, artisans, midwives, vendors, bath attendants, and pros-titutes emerge in addition to the socially championed roles of mothers, wives, and daughters. Legal injunctions from the Muslim and dhimmi communi-ties reflected the reality of such day-to-day activities and discussed not just marriage, divorce, and children but also issues of commerce, property, lia-bility, testimony, crime, and punishment involving women.[51]

Change and Continuity

It is clear that women, although often ephemeral in the official record, par-ticipated actively in defining the culture and history of early Islamic Iran.

Through their lives vital information emerges on what responses were induced by military conquest, why individuals switched group affiliations, how communal identities came to be defined, and which adaptations facilitated reconciliation of the past with their present.[52] Simultaneously, certain situations remained fairly constant. Within the parameters stipulated by law, Muslim women of the dihqan class (landowning gentry) could exercise their economic might like their Zoroastrian forerunners once did. Low-rank Muslim and non-Muslim women entered Muslim households as concubines, maids, and slaves, just as social inferiors had once done in Sasanian society. Among Zoroastrians, women continued to experience inflexible purity laws. Christian Iranian women still felt the pressures of chastity and monasticism. Gender biases persisted in restricting roles for women within Judaism. Dhimmi women, therefore, went on converting to Islam to avoid the rigid rules of their religions. Others followed their menfolk who switched faiths. Yet others found the worship of Allah spiritually fulfilling.

Confessionally and socially, the centuries immediately following the Arab conquest proved, in sum, to be a transitional milieu when women and their children, one generation after the other, transmitted Sasanian cultural features into the nascent Islamic civilization of Iran. It was a time of both continuity and change, provoking divergent responses along communal lines. Reactions by non-Muslims and Muslims to the social variations of the seventh through tenth centuries A.D. are best summed up in two sets of comments—one pessimistic, the other optimistic: "The [final] age of alloyed iron entails evil rule by disheveled demons [descended] from the line of Hashim. . . . During that oppressive era disease, death, and poverty will blight the world." And, "We have come to claim what god promised us . . . your country, offspring, and blood."[53] As Iranian Zoroastrians, Christians, and Jews slipped into despondent resignation, emergent Muslim positions prevailed on most issues. Yet these often were mere reflections or modifications of earlier views. So once the tumult of political and religious reorientation had passed, the average woman of early Islamic Iran may well have found her life not very different in tone and structure from that of her female ancestors during Sasanian times—still constrained by men who suggested that domesticity and subservience were best.

NOTES

The Institute for Advanced Study (Princeton) and the National Endowment for the Humanities generously supported this research.

1. The boundaries established for Muslim women in Islamic society have been the subject of numerous studies. See Leila Ahmed, *Women and Gender in Islam* (New Haven: Yale University Press, 1992), 64–101; and the essays in Nikki Keddie and Beth Baron, eds., *Women in Middle Eastern History: Shifting Boundaries in Sex and Gender* (New Haven: Yale University Press, 1991), especially 23–73. On Zoroastrian women in Sasanian and Islamic societies, see Jamsheed K. Choksy, *Evil, Good, and Gender: Facets of the Feminine in Zoroastrian Religious History* (New York: Peter Lang, 2002), 84–103.

2. Richard N. Frye, *The History of Ancient Iran* (Munich: C. H. Beck, 1984), 337; and Robert Gobl, *Sasanian Numismatics* (Brunswick: Klinkhardt and Biermann, 1971), 54, plate 15.

3. *Chronica Minora*, pt. 1, Corpus Scriptorum Christianorum Orientalium, Scriptores Syri, vol. 1, ed. I. Guidi (Paris: Carolus Poussielgue, 1903; reprint, Louvain: Secretariat du Corpus SCO, 1960), text 17, trans. 16; Theodor Nöldeke, *Die von Guidi herausgegebene Syrische Chronik,* Sitzungsberichte der philosophisch-historischen Klasse der Kaiserlichen Akademie der Wissenschaften 128 (Vienna: Akademie der Wissenschaften, 1883), 28; Firdawsi (d. ca. A.H. 411/A.D. 1020), *Shah-nama,* trans. R. Levy (London: Routledge and Kegan Paul, 1967), 378–83, 395–96; among other sources such as the historian al-Tha'alibi (d. A.H. 429/A.D. 1038) and the poet Nizami (A.H. 605/A.D. 1209).

4. *Chronica Minora*, pt. 1, text 17, trans. 16; and the anonymous "Chronicle of A.D. 1234" in *The Seventh Century in the West-Syrian Chronicles,* ed. and trans. Andrew Palmer (Liverpool: Liverpool University Press, 1993), 117, for example.

5. The Old Testament book of Esther 1:10, 15, 2:2–4, 8–17, 4:4–6, 9–10, 7:1–10, probably set in Seleucid or Parthian times, circa 167–135 B.C., offers a glimpse into harem life in ancient Iran and its restrictions on access to the outside world. On this text, see also Shaul Shaked, "Two Judaeo-Iranian Contributions," in *Irano-Judaica,* vol. 1, ed. S. Shaked (Jerusalem: Ben-Zvi Institute, 1982), 292–303; and James R. Russell, "Zoroastrian Elements in the Book of Esther," in *Irano-Judaica,* vol. 2, ed. S. Shaked and A. Netzer (Jerusalem: Ben-Zvi Institute, 1990), 36–40.

6. Evidence for the veiling of monarchs comes from silver coins or *drahms* minted by each Sasanian king of kings where the folds of a fine gauze were etched on the cape and globe of the crown. See Gobl, *Sasanian Numismatics,* 7–8. This veil was lifted up, above the face, on the royal coin portraits but may have been lowered when the monarchs met with courtiers. Of course the tradition of Iranian monarchs staying out of public view is even attested by the story of *Esther* 5:1–2, which mentions the ruler seated alone enthroned, possibly behind a screen, in the inner court to which access was granted to others by his consent alone. Additional references to the seclusion of Sasanian rulers are found in Jamsheed K. Choksy, "Sacral Kingship in Sasanian Iran," *Bulletin of the Asia Institute,* n.s. 2 (1988): 42.

7. The Syriac records of Martha's execution and of Anahid's life and death at the hands of the Zoroastrian clergy are translated by Sebastian P. Brock and Susan A. Harvey, *Holy Women of the Syrian Orient* (Berkeley: University of California Press, 1987), 67–73, 82–99. On stylistic elements in those texts, such as the imitatio Christi, see Jes P. Asmussen, "Christians in Iran," in *Cambridge History of Iran,* vol. 3, pt. 2, ed. E. Yarshater (Cambridge: Cambridge University Press, 1983), 936–38.

8. Farrokhmard i Wahram, *Madayan i Hazar Dadestan*, pt. 1, ed. J. J. Modi (Bombay: Parsi Punchayet, 1901), pt. 2, ed. T. D. Anklesaria (Bombay: Fort Printing Press, 1913); *Syrische rechtsbucher*, vol. 3, ed. and trans. C. E. Sachau (Berlin: G. Reimer, 1914); *Babylonian Talmud*, ed. I. Epstein, trans. M. Simon, 30 vols. (London: Soncino Press, 1965–89). These compilations were intended as legal guidelines; they were not judgments rendered on specific cases.

9. Anahit Perikhanian, "Iranian Society and Law," in *Cambridge History of Iran*, vol. 3, pt. 2, 650–58, 665–79; and Judith Hauptman, "Images of Women in the Talmud," in *Religion and Sexism: Images of Woman in the Jewish and Christian Tradition*, ed. R. Ruether (New York: Simon and Schuster, 1974), 185–90, 193–96, provide detailed discussions of these issues, supported by numerous examples.

10. Compare Perikhanian, "Iranian Society and Law," 634–41.

11. Farrokhmard i Wahram, *Madayan i Hazar Dadestan*, pt. 1, 21–24, 36, 41, pt. 2, 4–5. All four types of marriage persisted after the Muslim conquest, as attested by Emed i Ashawahishtan (lived late ninth or early tenth century A.D.), *Rivayat*, ed. B. T. Anklesaria (Bombay: K. R. Cama Oriental Institute, 1962), 24–30, 161–62. On khwasray and ayoken, also consult Anahit Perikhanian, "On Some Pahlavi Legal Terms," in *W. B. Henning Memorial Volume*, ed. M. Boyce and I. Gershevitch (London: Lund Humphries, 1970), 349–53.

12. The most balanced assessment of this issue is by Richard N. Frye, "Zoroastrian Incest," in *Orientalia Iosephi Tucci Memoriae Dicata*, Serie Orientale Roma, vol. 56, pt. 1, ed. G. Gnoli and L. Lanciotti (Rome: Istituto Italiano per il Medio ed Estremo Oriente, 1985), 446–54. On Cambyses' action, see Herodotus, *History*, pt. 2, Loeb Classical Library, vol. 118, ed. and trans. A. D. Godley (London: William Heinemann, 1982), 3:31, 40–43. Contra Perikhanian, "Iranian Society and Law," 644, who unfortunately overstates the case by interpreting occurrences of khwedodah among ruling families and its mention in Magian juridical guidelines—that is, instances limited to a few elites and to hypothetical legal situations—as clear-cut evidence for supposed widespread practice. Ahmed, *Women and Gender in Islam*, 19, follows Perikhanian uncritically. The Egyptian data is gathered by K. Hopkins, "Brother-Sister Marriage in Roman Egypt," *Comparative Studies in Society and History* 22 (1980): 320–24.

13. Consult Jamsheed K. Choksy, *Purity and Pollution in Zoroastrianism: Triumph over Evil* (Austin: University of Texas Press, 1989), 94–102, for Middle Persian sources, stipulations, and rites.

14. *Herbedestan*, ed. and trans. F. M. Kotwal and P. G. Kreyenbroek (Louvain: E. Peeters, 1992), 38–41. This multiauthor priestly code, written during the ninth century A.D. and revised after the tenth century, was probably based on materials from the final centuries of Sasanian rule.

15. The basic source is *Acta Martyrum et Sanctorum*, ed. P. Bedjan, 7 vols. (Leipzig: Reprografischer Nachdruck, 1890–97; reprint, Hildesheim: Georg Olms, 1968). See also Susan A. Harvey, "Women in Early Syrian Christianity," in *Images of Women in Antiquity*, 2d ed., ed. A. Cameron and A. Kuhrt (Detroit: Wayne State University Press, 1993), 294–96.

16. Numerous references are found in the Babylonian Talmud. Also consult Hauptman, "Images of Women in the Talmud," 190–93.

17. See further Perikhanian, "Iranian Society and Law," 641–46. Two other articles providing overviews of certain aspects of women's lives in ancient Iranian cultures are by Jenny Rose, "Three Queens, Two Wives, and a Goddess: Roles and Images of Women in Sasanian Iran," and Richard N. Frye, "Women in Pre-Islamic Central Asia: The Khatun of Bukhara," both in *Women in the Medieval Islamic World*, ed. G. R. G. Hambly (New York: St. Martin's Press, 1998), 29–54 and 55–68, respectively.

18. Ahmad b. Yahya al-Baladhuri (d. A.H. 279/A.D. 892), *Kitab futuh al-buldan*, ed. M. J. de Goeje (Leiden: E. J. Brill, 1866), 266–67. Variations of this injunction are found in Abu Ja'far Muhammad b. Jarir al-Tabari (d. A.H. 311/A.D. 923), *Ta'rikh al-rusul wa l-muluk*, ed. M. J. de Goeje and others, 15 vols. (Leiden: E. J. Brill, 1879–1901), series 1, 2467.

19. Tabari, *Ta'rikh*, series 1, 2464.

20. Baladhuri, *Futuh al-buldan*, 389–90; Abu Zayd b. al-Balkhi (lived sixth century A.H./twelfth century A.D.), *Fars-nama*, ed. G. Le Strange and R. A. Nicholson (London: Luzac, 1921), 116; and Abu l-Hasan Ali b. al-Athir (d. A.H. 630/A.D. 1233), *Kitab al-kamil fi l-Ta'rikh*, ed. C. J. Tornberg, 14 vols. (Leiden: E. J. Brill, 1851–76), 2:420–21, 3:30–31, 77–78.

21. Abu Bakr Muhammad b. Ja'far al-Narshakhi (d. A.H. 348/A.D. 959), *Tarikh-i Bukhara*, ed. M. Razavi (Tehran: Bunyad-i farhang-i Iran, 1939), 61–62; and Baladhuri, *Futuh al-buldan*, 420.

22. Baha al-Din Muhammad b. Hasan b. Isfandiyar (lived seventh century A.H./ thirteenth century A.D.), *Tarikh-i Tabaristan*, ed. A. Iqbal (Tehran: Eastern Bookstore, 1942), 162–64.

23. For instance, consult Tabari, *Ta'rikh*, series 1, 2887, where two princesses are said to have been turned over to the Arab commander Abd Allah b. Amir b. Kurayz as his personal property.

24. Baladhuri, *Futuh al-buldan*, 413, mentions migration into Iran of Arab women seeking reunion with their husbands who had been part of the invading Muslim battalions.

25. Narshakhi, *Tarikh-i Bukhara*, 42–43, 52–53, provides the indigenous version of events, also preserved by Baladhuri, *Futuh al-buldan*, 410–11, 417–19. Tabari, *Ta'rikh*, series 2, 169–70, 1201–2, recorded succinct Arab renditions.

26. Yahya b. Adam (d. A.H. 203/A.D. 818), *Kitab al-kharaj*, trans. A. Ben Shemesh as *Taxation in Islam*, vol. 1 (Leiden: E. J. Brill, 1958), 52.

27. Members of the Iranian nobility who adopted Islam were denounced by Zoroastrian authors, as late as the eleventh century A.D., in *Bundahishn*, ed. T. D. Anklesaria (Bombay: British India Press, 1908), 1–2.

28. For example, Yahya b. Adam, *Kharaj*, 60.

29. Baladhuri, *Futuh al-buldan*, 318 (quotation); and Tabari, *Ta'rikh*, series 1, 2627, 2633, 2898, 2903.

30. The standard statistical study is Richard W. Bulliet, *Conversion to Islam in the Medieval Period: An Essay in Quantitative History* (Cambridge: Harvard University Press, 1979), 23, 43–44. Also see additional information in Jamsheed K. Choksy, *Conflict and Cooperation: Zoroastrians, Subalterns, and Muslim Elites in Medieval Iranian Society* (New York: Columbia University Press, 1997), 76–93; and "Conflict,

Coexistence, and Cooperation: Muslims and Zoroastrians in Eastern Iran during the Medieval Period," *Muslim World* 80 (1990): 228–29.

31. Baladhuri, *Futuh al-buldan,* 314; and Tabari, *Ta'rikh,* series 1, 2477, 2478, among other sources.

32. Celebration of Zoroastrian festivals at the caliphal court was recorded by Abu Uthman Amr b. Bahr al-Jahiz (d. ca. A.H. 255/A.D. 868), *Kitab al-hayawan,* ed. A. S. M. Harun, 7 vols. (Cairo: Mustafa l-Babi l-Halabi Press, 1938–45), 5:99–100; and Abu Abd Allah Muhammad b. Ahmad al-Muqaddasi (al-Maqdisi) (d. ca. A.H. 392/A.D. 1000), *Ahsan al-taqasim fi ma'rifat al-aqalim,* 2d ed., ed. M. J. de Goeje (Leiden: E. J. Brill, 1906; reprint, 1967), 194.

33. Jean de Menasce, "Problèmes des mazdéens dans l'Iran musulman," in *Festschrift für Wilhelm Eilers,* ed. G. Wiessner (Wiesbaden: Otto Harrassowitz, 1967), 229–30; and Jamsheed K. Choksy, "Zoroastrians in Muslim Iran," *Iranian Studies* 20 (1) (1987), 24. Both translate and discuss the main Zoroastrian source.

34. Malik b. Anas (d. A.H. 179/A.D. 795), *Al-Muwatta,* trans. A. A. Bewley as *The First Formulation of Islamic Law* (London: Kegan Paul, 1989), 216; Ya'qub b. Ibrahim al-Ansari Abu Yusuf (d. A.H. 182/A.D. 798), *Kitab al-kharaj,* trans. A. Ben Shemesh as *Taxation in Islam,* vol. 3 (Leiden: E. J. Brill, 1969), 66–67, 88–89; and Abu Hamid al-Ghazali (d. A.H. 505/A.D. 1111), *Kitab adab al-nikah* of *Ihya ulum al-din,* trans. M. Farah as *Marriage and Sexuality in Islam* (Salt Lake City: University of Utah Press, 1984), 81. See also Michael G. Morony, *Iraq after the Muslim Conquest* (Princeton: Princeton University Press, 1984), 238–39.

35. *Geonica,* 2d ed., ed. and trans. L. Ginzberg (New York: Hermon Press, 1968), 2:203–4. This geonic response specifically cites Jewish administrators' concern about the intermingling of religious communities in large cities such as Baghdad.

36. Morony, *Iraq,* 343, 364–67, 370–71, discusses the agreement and Nestorian codes intended to inhibit sex or marriage between Christians and Muslims, both intended to safeguard the Eastern Christian community's socioeconomic base. See Andrew Palmer, *Monk and Mason on the Tigris Frontier: The Early History of Tur 'Abdin* (Cambridge: Cambridge University Press, 1990), 92–93, on the community-related activities of celibate women.

37. Evidence for marriages across confessional boundaries during Sasanian times is garnered by Morony, *Iraq,* 309–10.

38. Emed i Ashawahishtan, *Rivayat,* 5; and *Pahlavi Rivayat of Adurfarrobay and Farrobaysrosh* (written A.D. 800 and 1008 respectively), vol. 1, ed. B. T. Anklesaria (Bombay: M. F. Cama Athornan Institute, 1969), 2–3. For more details, refer to Choksy, "Zoroastrians in Muslim Iran," 23.

39. For instance, as benefactors of religious orders. See Palmer, *Monk and Mason,* 167.

40. Direct reference to Muslim attempts at allaying such fears of isolation among potential female converts from Zoroastrianism is found in a hadith (tradition) attributed to A'isha bint Abi Bakr (d. A.H. 58/A.D. 678), the Prophet Muhammad's favorite wife, recorded by Hamza b. Yusuf al-Sahmi (lived fifth century A.H./eleventh century A.D.), *Ta'rikh Jurjan wa kitab ma'rifat ulama ahl Jurjan* (Hyderabad: Osmania Oriental Publications Bureau, 1967), 83. This tradition is cited in Richard W.

Bulliet, *Islam: The View from the Edge* (New York: Columbia University Press, 1994), 33–34.

41. Emed i Ashawahishtan, *Rivayat*, 11–12. On the legal status of converts, see further Menasce, "Problèmes des mazdéens," 223–26; and Choksy, "Zoroastrians in Muslim Iran," 23.

42. *Geonica*, 2:176. This geonic response even permitted the apostate in question to be a family member. Such an ex-Jewish executor continued to have legal standing within the community for purposes of fulfilling the deceased's will if it benefited other Jews.

43. On the conflation of devotional trends, see Biancamaria S. Amoretti, "Sects and Heresies," in *Cambridge History of Iran*, vol. 4, ed. R. N. Frye (Cambridge: Cambridge University Press, 1975), 510–11; Richard W. Bulliet, "Conversion Stories in Early Islam," in *Conversion and Continuity: Indigenous Christian Communities in Islamic Lands, Eighth to Eighteenth Centuries*, ed. M. Gervers and R. J. Bikhazi (Toronto: Pontifical Institute of Mediaeval Studies, 1990), 128–31; and Richard N. Frye, *The Golden Age of Persia: Arabs in the East* (London: Weidenfeld and Nicolson, 1975; reprint, 1988), 101, 140–41.

44. Consult the *tafsir* (commentary) on Qur'an sura 2:102 by al-Tabari, *Jami albayan an ta'wil ay al-Qur'an*, vol. 1, ed. and trans. J. Cooper, W. F. Madelung, and A. Jones (Oxford: Oxford University Press, 1987), 485. For a partial discussion on this issue, refer to Jacques Duchesne-Guillemin, "There Are More Things in Heaven and Earth," *Orientalia Iosephi Tucci Memoriae Dicata*, Serie Orientale Roma, vol. 56, pt. 1, ed. G. Gnoli and L. Lanciotti (Rome: Istituto Italiano per il Media ed Estremo Oriente, 1985), 258–59.

45. Abu Yusuf, *Kharaj*, 93. In general, see Arthur S. Tritton, *The Caliphs and Their Non-Muslim Subjects: A Critical Study of the Covenant of Umar* (London: Oxford University Press, 1930), 123.

46. Citation from Tabari, *Ta'rikh*, series 3, 1389–90. A detailed discussion of this passage is available in Norman A. Stillman, *The Jews of Arab Lands: A History and Source Book* (Philadelphia: Jewish Publication Society of America, 1979), 167–68. Boaz Shoshan, "On Costume and Social History in Medieval Islam," *Asian and African Studies* 22 (1–3) (1988): 41–47, describes the role of headgear in differentiating Jews and Christians from Muslims. Choksy, *Conflict and Cooperation*, 131–32, does the same for Zoroastrians.

47. Morony, *Iraq*, 259, provides more details.

48. Ibid., 209, 259.

49. In terms of the Jewish community, see *Geonica*, 2:24, 218, 259. For Zoroastrians, consult Choksy, *Purity and Pollution*, 103–4.

50. Morony, *Iraq*, 258–59, 320–21; Ahmed, *Women and Gender in Islam*, 83–84.

51. For brevity's sake only two examples, relating to female members of the numerically dominant groups (Muslims and Zoroastrians), will be cited: Malik b. Anas, *Muwatta*, 306 (debt); Emed i Ashawahishtan, *Rivayat*, 7–9 (ownership of property).

52. Compare the pertinent general observations by Joan W. Scott, *Gender and the Politics of History* (New York: Columbia University Press, 1988), 24–25, 27.

53. *Zand i Wahman Yasht*, ed. and trans. B. T. Anklesaria (Bombay: K. L. Bhargava, 1957), 4, 36–37; Tabari, *Ta'rikh*, series 1, 2254. The pessimistic, indeed apocalyptic, tone

of the anonymous Middle Persian *Zand i Wahman Yasht* (compiled ninth to thirteenth centuries A.D.) has parallels in many Jewish and Christian records of that time, including the *Apocalypse of Pseudo-Methodius* written in northern Mesopotamia (second half of seventh century A.D.). The latter text, composed in Syriac, then translated into Greek and Latin, laments: "The land of the Iranians was given to devastation . . . sending its inhabitants to captivity, slaughter, and devastation." Citation modified from Palmer, *West Syrian Chronicles*, 232.

3 Women and the Urban Religious Elite in the Pre-Mongol Period

RICHARD W. BULLIET

HISTORIANS OF early Islamic Iran and of medieval Islamic education agree that women sometimes gained reputations for learning, just as they sometimes did for Sufi activities. The preservation of female names in biographical dictionaries of the tenth and eleventh centuries proves this point. The rarity of female names in these compilations raises a question, however. Why so few? This chapter examines the entries on women in biographical dictionaries from Baghdad, Nishapur, and Gorgan in an attempt to understand how their names came to be included and what broader social meanings might be inferred from their inclusion.

Al-Khatib al-Baghdadi completed his *Ta'rikh Baghdad* in 1070.[1] Women account for 30 out of the total number of 7,831 biographies. Abd al-Ghafir al-Farisi (d. 1135) wrote his *al-Siyaq li Ta'rikh Naisabur* as a continuation of a much longer work by al-Hakim al-Naisaburi (d. 1015) entitled *Ta'rikh Naisabur.* Al-Hakim's compilation contained 2,698 biographies, only 3 of them of women. Al-Farisi included 22 women (1 of them also included by al-Hakim and al-Khatib) among his 1,699 biographies. As for Gorgan, 1,194 of its scholars have biographies in the *Ta'rikh Jurjan* of Hamza al-Sahmi (d. 1035). Among them are 12 women. A final work surveyed from the same period, Abu Nu'aim al-Isfahani's *Kitab dhikr akhbar Isbahan,* contains 1,881 biographies but none of women.

Altogether, a survey of 15,303 biographies from five works yielded only 67 biographies of women, a paltry four-tenths of a percent of the total sample. This representation may be taken as a fair indication of the insignificance of women in urban-based biographical dictionaries of the pre-Mongol period, as opposed, for example, to being peculiar to Iran. The *Ta'rikh Baghdad,* after all, reflects an Arab rather than an Iranian milieu. Only 4 of the women in it are identifiable as Iranian, and 3 of them are included in a single entry as sisters of a noted Sufi.

These five works are not representative of the biographical-dictionary genre as a whole, however. Dealing with earlier times, Ibn Sa'd's compilation on the companions of the Prophet Mohammad contains extensive reports about his wives and other women of the first generation. And in the Mamluk period, al-Sakhawi devotes an entire volume of his twelve-volume *Daw al-lami* to women, giving information on 1,075 individuals.[2] Ibn Sa'd's concern for women obviously derives from the prominence of the female members of the prophet's family, but the increase in information on women during the Mamluk period calls for an explanation.

Is it possible that women participated in society more in the fifteenth century than they did prior to the twelfth century? Were Muslim gender attitudes in general during the post-Mongol period subtly different from what they had been earlier? Or did the nature of biographical dictionaries change over the centuries, making it possible for more women to meet the compilers' criteria for inclusion?

To address the last possibility first, I would argue that the genre of the biographical dictionary did, indeed, change. The works surveyed here are all based on specific cities. In styling them "histories" and usually including a topographical and historical survey of the city as a preface or appendix, their compilers seem to have concentrated on the affinity represented by living in an urban center and to have had in mind a sort of intellectual history of the city's development as an Islamic community. Moreover, their core sources of information seem to have been books relating to the transmission of prophetic traditions (hadith), particularly books in which generations of students of tradition wrote down notes about their teachers. In the *Ta'rikh Jurjan,* for example, it is apparent that some names are mentioned solely because a person named al-Jurjani appeared in an *isnad,* the chain of oral transmitters going back to the prophet with which every hadith began. In these cases, al-Sahmi includes no information about the individual whatsoever. He simply cites the isnad and the accompanying *matn* or text of the hadith. His goal is to make sure than anyone from Gor-

gan who had anything to do with the pious activity of hadith transmission
is properly memorialized.

In some biographies, however, extensive anecdotes are related, most often when the subjects are members of the city's major families. Sometimes
these are known to the compiler through personal experience, sometimes
they are family lore passed down through generations, and sometimes the
specific context of the anecdote—what happened while so-and-so was traveling for purposes of studying hadith, for example—indicates that it was
retold in scholarly circles to enhance the individual's reputation.

Although these city-based biographical dictionaries were undoubtedly
used by hadith scholars to look up obscure names included in isnads, they
were clearly not intended for this purpose alone. Hundreds of entries contain no information relating to when the individual lived or died, a key desideratum for isnad checkers, and none of the compilations has any form of
indexing other than the alphabetical list of entries by their *ism* or given name.
An isnad referring to a person by some other part of his name, for example
as *Ibn* Hamdan, *Abu* Bakr, or simply al-Sijistani, could not be checked. Any
scholar familiar enough with such all-too-common shorthand references to
know the first name of the Ibn Hamdan, Abu Bakr, or al-Sijistani referred to
would have had little need to look up the person.

Even though the process of hadith study was intimately tied into the compilation of the works under examination, therefore, the rationale for including or excluding specific biographies is not a simple derivative from this process. Since it was possible for a compiler such as Abu Nu'aim al-Isfahani to
exclude women entirely, the other three Iranian authors, al-Farisi, al-Sahmi,
and al-Hakim, must have had some reason for including those few they did.
In exploring this reason, it is useful to include al-Khatib al-Baghdadi's *Ta'rikh
Baghdad* as a point of comparison.

All four authors, for example, occasionally mention male relatives other
than father and grandfather, whose names were normally a part of any person's genealogy. In half of the biographies of females, the woman is described
as a sister, wife, or mother of someone specific, and notable men among their
ancestors also find mention. Both al-Khatib al-Baghdadi and Hamza al-Sahmi segregate their entries on women and place them at the end of their works,
just as Ibn Sa'd and al-Sakhawi do.

Turning to the specific content of the biographies, Maleeha Rahmatallah's pioneering work, *The Women of Baghdad in the Ninth and Tenth Centuries as Revealed in the History of Baghdad of al-Hatib,* divides al-Khatib's
female subjects into four categories: royal family, saints, scholars, and tradi-

tionists (someone who transmits hadith).[3] This categorization is applicable to the entries in the Iranian compilations as well, especially if royal family is taken *mutatis mutandis* to mean distinguished women of the most aristocratic local families. The six women (four of them of Iranian origin) mentioned by al-Khatib in association with Sufi activities—only one actually being called a Sufi—are paralleled by one Sufi from Gorgan and one from Nishapur. Another from Nishapur was known for spending all of her wealth on Sufis.

Rahmatallah singles out two Baghdad women as scholars who were sufficiently educated in Islamic law to issue legal opinions (*fatawa*, sing. *fatwa*). No legal scholars are specified for Gorgan, but one woman was known for her preaching. In Nishapur, one woman was recognized for excellent Arabic and handwriting, another spent liberally in support of scholarship, and a third taught children; but none was a legist. As for traditionists, an important subcategory of religious scholarship, Rahmatallah cites three particularly noteworthy women in Baghdad. She could have cited many others, however, for al-Khatib makes specific reference to traditions reported by most of the women he includes.

In Gorgan, three quarters of the women included recited hadith. In Nishapur, all but three of al-Farisi's twenty-two women learned hadith, and at least thirteen transmitted hadith, one explicitly "from behind a screen." Many studied hadith with family members: father, mother, paternal uncle, grandfather, and grandmother are mentioned. Of those who heard hadith from non-family members, six studied with one teacher, four with two teachers,[4] two with three teachers, three with four teachers, and one with seven teachers.

The most notable tradition reciter was Karima bint Ahmad al-Marwaziya who is included in al-Farisi's compilation. Her biographical notice says little except that she studied the *Sahih* of al-Bukhari with al-Kushmaihani, an aged man from the Marv area who was famous for having a copy of the *Sahih* taken down in dictation from a copy made at al-Bukhari's own dictation. In other words, Karima al-Marwaziya's recitation of the *Sahih* was one step closer to al-Bukhari's original than almost anyone else's. For that reason, Abd al-Ghafir al-Farisi himself studied the work with her, and so did al-Khatib al-Baghdadi, although he did not include her in his biographical dictionary because she did not spend time in Baghdad.

On the whole, therefore, Rahmatallah's descriptive categories seem sound: a few noble names, a few women involved in mysticism, and a much larger number known for scholarship in hadith or, more rarely, other disciplines. But to return to the question asked at the outset. Why so few? Did those compilers who deigned to notice women at all decide to include, as a token gesture perhaps, a small subset of a larger number? Or was public recognition of women in urban religious society really as rare as the numbers indicate?

To answer this question, we must look more closely at the twenty-two women mentioned by Abd al-Ghafir al-Farisi. Fourteen belonged to one of four complex extended families that provided the main leadership of the Shafi'i religious, social, and political faction of Nishapur in the eleventh century.[5] The largest number of them, seven, were relatives of Abd al-Ghafir al-Farisi himself. These fall into two groups: on the one hand, his sister, his mother, and his grandmother; on the other, his daughter-in-law, her first cousin, her paternal aunt, and the aunt's daughter. Through their marriages, these women link together four parts of this extended family.

The model of female attainment and obvious inspiration for all her descendants was al-Farisi's grandmother Fatima. Described by her grandson as the most outstanding woman of her age, she was raised by her father, the famous Sufi Abu Ali al-Daqqaq, to be the son he never had. He saw that she received an extensive education from seven different teachers, including both Sufis and hadith specialists, and he also imparted to her his own Sufi teachings. He married her to the up-and-coming Sufi Abu al-Qasim al-Qushairi, who was then a comparative newcomer to Nishapur but who eventually became one of the most famous Sufis in Islamic history as well as a stalwart leader of the Shafi'i faction. Fatima and Abu al-Qasim had six children together. Various members of her family list her among their teachers, and she is mentioned several times as an important Sufi personage in a text from Darband, a city hundreds of miles from Nishapur on the western side of the Caspian sea.[6] That she also taught in a more public way is apparent from the life of a scholar from Qazvin who studied the first part of one particular book under one teacher, the middle part under another, and the final part under Fatima bint Abi Ali al-Daqqaq.[7]

Information as to which of al-Qushairi's total of eleven children were Fatima's offspring is not provided, but one daughter, possibly the only one, was Umm al-Rahim Karima. Al-Qushairi married this daughter to one of his students, the son of an outstanding Nishapuri scholar named Abu al-Husain Abd al-Ghafir al-Farisi, the grandfather and namesake of the Abd al-Ghafir al-Farisi who compiled the biographical dictionary. Karima studied with her father, her mother, her father-in-law, and at least three other teachers. Her daughter Durdana, the historian al-Farisi's sister, studied with her mother, Karima, her grandmother Fatima, her grandfather Abu al-Qasim al-Qushairi, and her father. It is also noted that as a child she studied under one other person.

Turning to Abd al-Ghafir al-Farisi's in-laws, he was a close friend of a man named Abu Nasr al-Shahhami who died young at the age of forty-two. Abd al-Ghafir led the prayers at his funeral. He includes a biography of Abu Nasr's daughter Fatima but does not note any special attainments for her. Abd al-Ghafir married his own daughter to the son of Abu Nasr's brother Zahir, a noted hadith reciter and composer of legal documents. He notes in his biography of Zahir's daughter Sa'ida (his own daughter's sister-in-law) that she studied under at least four teachers besides her grandfather. He also includes a biography of the sister of Abu Nasr and Zahir, who is named both Zumra and Zarifa. She studied with three teachers in addition to her father. The last woman he mentions in this family is Shari'a, the daughter of Zumra and her husband Abu Abd Allah al-Furawi. Al-Furawi was a Sufi in the tradition of Abu al-Qasim al-Qushairi, to whom his father had been particularly devoted. He also studied hadith and eventually became a paramount figure in Shafi'i scholarly circles in Nishapur.

Moving outside Abd al-Ghafir al-Farisi's immediate family circle, the one female member of the Shafi'i Bahiri family whom he mentions is A'isha (or Jum'a), the wife of Abu Sa'id Isma'il al-Bahiri. This Abu Sa'id was a close associate of Abd al-Ghafir's family. Indeed, he was a longtime student of his grandfather and namesake Abu al-Husain Abd al-Ghafir. A'isha was her husband's paternal first cousin—a rarely occurring pattern among the marriages recorded for eleventh-century Nishapur—her father being almost unique as both a member of Nishapur's scholarly elite and an active warrior in the sultan's army.

Turning to the al-Sabuni family, al-Farisi preserves biographies of three daughters and one niece of Abu Uthman al-Sabuni, the acknowledged leader of Nishapur's ulama in the generation of Abu al-Qasim al-Qushairi. He was a figure of great authority, particularly in Shafi'i circles, and was undoubtedly regarded as a mentor by everyone who shared al-Farisi's religious and legal affiliation. All of his daughters—Fatima, Khadija, and Mubaraka—learned hadith from the "masters of al-Asamm."[8] His niece Karima, the daughter of his Sufi brother Abu Ya'la, transmitted hadith from a different source.

The official head of the Shafi'i faction in Abu al-Qasim al-Qushairi's generation was Imam al-Muwaffaq al-Bastami. Their closeness was proven by political events. When an order came from the Seljuq vizir Amid al-Mulk al-Kunduri to silence the teaching of Ash'ari theological doctrines, Imam al-Muwaffaq's son and successor, Abu Sahl Muhammad al-Bastami, and Abu al-Qasim al-Qushairi were among the four leaders slated for arrest. Al-Qushairi was imprisoned, but Abu Sahl escaped to his estates where he raised a band of retainers and successfully attacked the city to free al-Qushairi from jail. The point of this story for present purposes is to emphasize that Imam al-Muwaffaq's two sisters, A'isha and Hurra, whose biographies are included by al-Farisi, were somewhat older contemporaries of al-Farisi's mother and undoubtedly knew her well, given the closeness of the al-Bastami and the al-Qushairi families.

The conclusion to be drawn from this long and intricate concatenation of names and relationships is that almost two-thirds of al-Farisi's entries on women pertain to women whom he knew personally and had kinship connections with or to women in the social circle of his mother. (Two other women, Umm al-Khair Fatima al-Baghdadi and Fatima al-Hamadhani, might possibly be added to this group since both of them were students of al-Farisi's paternal grandfather.) To be sure, all but one of these women had scholarly credentials, some of them impressive ones, but there would seem to be no question but that they were included primarily because of the family and social connections with the compiler.

If we set these biographies aside and look at the remainder of the women in the Nishapur compilations, Rahmatallah's categories afford plausible explanations. In the category of nobility, we find Jum'a bint Ahmad al-Mikali. The Mikalis were the most aristocratic Iranian family in Nishapur, tracing their descent from a line of petty kings.[9] The Mikalis were occasionally important in caliphal politics as military commanders or courtiers. Nothing specific is said of Jum'a except that her father made her study hadith.

Of similar notability was Umm al-Husain Jum'a al-Mahmiya al-Uthmaniya. She is the sole woman to appear in more than one of the biographical dictionaries surveyed. Al-Khatib al-Baghdadi, al-Hakim al-Naisaburi, and Abd al-Ghafir al-Farisi all mention her. Her lineage goes back to the son of the caliph Uthman who had a son, Mahmi, by a woman from a town southeast of Nishapur. That son married the daughter of a local dignitary, and their descendants made much of their caliphal ancestry. Jum'a was the daughter of a great-grandson who became a leading political figure in the region. She married a man with a lineage almost as grand, going back to the lieutenant of the first Arab conqueror of the Nishapur area. He was also the grandson of Abu Amr Ahmad al-Harashi, the founder and first leader of the Shafi'i law school in Khurasan, whose father had succeeded to the leadership upon Abu Amr's death.

Of the three biographers of Umm al-Husain Jum'a, al-Khatib alone gives details about her learning. He lists four men she studied with when she visited Baghdad, three other men from whom he himself received hadith transmitted on her authority, and yet another man whose name is included in an isnad as the person from whom she transmitted hadith. In short, while her illustrious Arab descent was doubtless an important aspect of her persona, she was notable as a traditionist as well, possibly on a par with Karima al-Marwaziya who was discussed above as a transmitter of al-Bukhari's *Sahih*.

Of the remaining five Nishapuri women included by al-Farisi and al-Hakim, one was the granddaughter of the most prestigious Shafi'i and dominant religious personage at the end of the ninth century, Muhammad b. Ishaq b. Khuzaima. Another was the daughter of one of the city's early chief judges. There is also a pair of sisters, both of whom transmitted hadith. The biography of one says that a group of people studied hadith with her "because of her name" (*bi-sababi ismiha*). Unfortunately, no details about these sisters' family connections are offered. The final woman is noted as a financial benefactor of the ulama both during her lifetime and through her bequests. She studied hadith with several people, but only one is named.

A similar detailed exploration of the dozen women from Gorgan would add little to the picture already drawn. Most urban biographical dictionaries had few or no entries for women, and the number drops still further when the personal connections of the compiler are removed from consideration. The reason for this can be inferred directly from the seven biographies of women belonging to al-Farisi's own family. The total number of biographies of family members is seventy-nine, thus the women account for 9 percent. Yet each of the seventy-two men had mothers, wives, sisters, and daughters, or some assortment thereof. This means that al-Farisi selected only seven women for inclusion among some two or three hundred women he knew of personally or through his female connections within his extended kin group. He excludes, for example, his own daughter, one of his sisters, all of his nieces, his paternal aunt, his paternal grandmother, and at least three maternal aunts.

Given the illustrious example of the pious and learned matriarch Fatima bint Abi Ali al-Daqqaq, Abu al-Qasim al-Qushairi's wife, there was probably as strong an incentive in this family for women to study hadith and involve themselves in religious scholarship as there was in any family in Nishapur. And al-Farisi's obvious favoritism toward his own kin makes it more than likely that he would have included other learned female relatives if there had been any. It seems reasonable to conclude, therefore, that even in the most learned and pious Nishapuri families, female involvement in learning and hadith study was rare. Consequently, it seems likely that the negligible representation of women in pre-Mongol urban biographical dictionaries truly represents their unimportance in the world of Islamic scholarship and is not simply the result of deliberate bias or an aberration arising from the technique of compilation.

Finally we can return to the question broached earlier. Was Muslim urban culture in the Mamluk period sufficiently different from pre-Mongol Iran to account for the increase in female visibility indicated by al-Sakhawi's 1,075 biographies of women? Obviously, fifteenth-century Egypt and Syria differed in many ways from eleventh-century Iran. For one thing, religious education was dominated in the Mamluk period by endowed madrasas (schools), some of them established by women. Yet religious acceptance of female scholars was still minimal. As Berkey says about women and education in medieval Cairo:

> The intellectual, as opposed to the purely administrative side of institutional education, however, presents an entirely different picture. Women played virtually no role, as either professor or student, in the formal education offered in schools of higher education and supported by their endowments. The chronicles and biographical dictionaries of the Mamluk period yield not a single instance of the appointment of a woman to a professorship or, indeed, to any post in an endowed institution of education, except that of controller. Nor did any women, so far as we know, formally enroll as a student in an institution providing endowed student fellowships.[10]

One important change associated with madrasa education, however, was a lessening of the preoccupation with isnads that contributed so strongly to the procedure for compiling urban biographical dictionaries earlier. With formalized madrasa training came a greater concentration on complete books as objects of study and the definitive elimination of thousands of hadith that were classified by specialists as weak but that had earlier been in circulation and sometimes specifically sought out as rarities. A fifteenth-century compiler of biographies would probably have been amused at the idea of including a person simply because he showed up in some isnad, somewhere, bearing the name al-Jurjani. In addition, the later compilations do not always reach as far into the past as al-Hakim al-Naisaburi and Abu Nu'aim al-Isfahani did in trying to portray the intellectual and religious development of their communities from the Arab conquest onward. Al-Sakhawi's twelve volumes concern only the fifteenth century, for much of which he could rely on living memory.

Some increase in the incidence of women can be accounted for by fewer entries devoted to otherwise unknown names in isnads and by a greater reliance on living memory. But beyond that I think it is necessary to assume that the passage of time brought with it an ever-greater intensification of the importance of religious scholarship and pious reputation as the touchstones of urban life. As a coherent social body—I hesitate to use the word class—the ulama took form gradually.[11] Religious knowledge and pious example were honored from the outset in Muslim communities; but the coalescence of these attributes in certain families, and of an unspoken public conferral of local leadership upon such families, was slow. In Iran, the tenth century culminates in the emergence of a strong, family-based, ulama social formation of the type often taken for granted in later Islamic history.

Within this milieu, as we have seen, education of women was not only possible but praised. Yet the behavioral limits prescribed for women limited their access to teachers and, at a later stage in life, students. From the limited data available, I would surmise that the importance and social embeddedness of the ulama intensified between the period surveyed here and that reflected by al-Sakhawi's work in the fifteenth century. As the religious and scholarly dimensions of life increased in social importance, the number of women in elite urban families who were drawn toward study or religious benefaction increased as well. The result was a somewhat more extensive participation of women in such activities and consequently a higher frequency of inclusion in biographical compilations. But the behavioral constraints on such women seem not to have lessened, nor does the overall position of women within the urban religious elite seem to have changed. The scant sprinkling of women mentioned in biographical dictionaries of the tenth and eleventh centuries had grown to a robust handful by the fifteenth century, but nothing, it seems, had fundamentally changed in the relationship of women to religious learning.

One further conclusion might be hazarded from the data and analysis presented above. Considering that when religious education was imparted to women, the teachers were most often male and female family members (a situation best illustrated by the case of the family of Abd al-Ghafir al-Farisi), and hence it is worth asking what kind of documentary trace such education might possibly have left.

Male children and young men, particularly in the pre-madrasa period prior to the twelfth century, could be expected to maintain, or have their male relatives maintain for them, some record of their education since this played a role in establishing their social status and might become professionally relevant if they became teachers or hadith reciters later in life. There is substantial evidence that compilers of biographical dictionaries used such personal educational memoranda in carrying out their projects. Can the same practice be assumed for girls and women receiving religious education? Probably not. As individuals whose social status was dependent on male kin, whose public roles were highly circumscribed, and whose prospects for teaching outside the family were scant, what reason would they have had for chronicling their educational experiences?

If Abd al-Ghafir al-Farisi, from knowledge of his own family and of the female associates of his mother and grandmother, was able to choose a dozen or so female names worth memorializing, this was indeed only a small proportion of the women he was related to or knew reasonably well. But if one were to assume a similar proportion of educated female kin in the families of other notable members of Nishapur's (male) ulama, the total number of educated women who are *not* mentioned in al-Farisi's compilation would be fairly substantial.

Thus, while the evidence at hand strongly indicates a limited degree of religious education for females in eleventh-century Nishapur, it can also be argued that the surviving sources substantially underrepresent those women who were learned. It can further be argued that this underrepresentation was in part a product of women having no reason to maintain records of their educational experiences, and in part a product of ulama possessing little knowledge of the lives of high-status women outside the circle of their own kin.

Since many, if not most, ulama record their father or grandfather among their teachers, it is possible that within the family young girls received some of the same lessons, or hadith recitations, as well. Such education within the home would have left little trace, but it should not be discounted in considering the lives of women in ulama families in this period.

NOTES

1. The biographical dictionaries referred to in this essay are: al-Khatib al-Baghdadi, *Ta'rikh Baghdad* (Beirut: Dar al-Kitab al-Arabi, n.d.); Richard N. Frye, ed., *The Histories of Nishapur* (Cambridge: Harvard University Press, 1965), containing manuscript facsimiles of Abd al-Ghafir al-Farisi's *al-Siyaq li Ta'rikh Naisabur* and al-Hakim al-Naisaburi's *Ta'rikh Naisabur;* Hamza al-Sahmi, *Ta'rikh Jurjan* (Hyderabad: Osmania Oriental Publications Bureau, 1950); Abu Nu'aim al-Isfahani, *Kitab dhikr akhbar Isbahan,* ed. S. Dedering (Leiden: E. J. Brill, 1931–34); and Shams al-Din Muhammad al-Sakhawi, *al-Daw al-lami li-ahl al-qarn al-tasi* (Beirut: n.p., n.d.).

2. Huda Lutfi, "Al-Sakhawi's *Kitab al-Nisa* as a Source for the Social and Economic History of Muslim Women during the Fifteenth Century A.D.," *The Muslim World* 71 (1981): 104–24.

3. Baghdad: Baghdad University, 1952.

4. There is ambiguity in three of these cases and in two others as well, because of

the notation of hadith being learned from *ashab al-Asamm,* the "masters (that is, special students) of al-Asamm." This is the most common teaching reference in al-Farisi's compilation; but even though the names of some of al-Asamm's direct students are known, it is never specified whether people who studied with several of them were considered to have studied with the "students of al-Asamm" in general or whether there was one specific class in which hadith transmitted from al-Asamm were recited by one or another of his students. Here, I am presuming the latter to be the case.

5. See Richard W. Bulliet, *The Patricians of Nishapur* (Cambridge: Harvard University Press, 1972), chapters 9–12 for detailed histories of all five families. The social and political significance of identification with the Shafi'i school of legal interpretation in eleventh-century Nishapur is discussed in chapter 3.

6. Personal communication from Dr. Alikber Alikberov, who has studied the text, the "Rayhan al-haqa'iq wa bustan al-daqa'iq" of Abu Bakr Muhammad al-Darbandi, in an unpublished dissertation from St. Petersburg University.

7. Abd al-Karim b. Muhammad al-Rafi'i al-Qazwini, *Al-Tadwin fi akhbar Qazwin* (Beirut: Dar al-Kutub al-Ilmiyya, 1987), 1:346.

8. See note 4.

9. Richard W. Bulliet, "Al-i Mikal," *Encyclopedia Iranica* (London: Routledge and Kegan Paul, 1985), 1:764.

10. Jonathan Berkey, *The Transmission of Knowledge in Medieval Cairo: A Social History of Islamic Education* (Princeton: Princeton University Press, 1992), 165–66.

11. For a more extended discussion of the process here described, see Richard W. Bulliet, *Islam: The View from the Edge* (New York: Columbia University Press, 1994).

4   Eleventh-Century Women:
Evidence from Bayhaqi's History

JULIE SCOTT MEISAMI

MODERN SCHOLARS often paint a gloomy picture of medieval Muslim wom-
en as victims of a male-dominated society, secluded, invisible, debarred from
public affairs, and treated negatively by male writers. This view—which arises
largely from a back-projection of contemporary agendas and is largely based
on an essentialist construction of a monolithic and static Islam considered
to be inherently and institutionally misogynistic—has often inhibited the
interpretation of medieval texts.[1] As Kandiyoti warns, "The question of wom-
en in Muslim societies has remained closely tied to a predominantly ahistor-
ical consideration of the main tenets of Islamic religion and their implications
for women."[2] In attempting to discern attitudes toward or gather evidence
about women in Muslim societies, we must avoid conflating ideology with
history and assuming that medieval texts reflect rigid Islamic views that inform every statement, every story, every historical account. This point is especially true in the case of historical texts, which are all too often viewed as
mere mines from which to extract facts without regard for the historian's
intent, method, or style. As Waldman states, "The criteria of validity for the
facts obtained from historical narratives are largely external; rarely are they
related to the internal dynamics of the work from which the facts have been
taken or to the interaction of the author's mind with the material he has
presented."[3] Facts are the historian's raw material only.

The Persian historian Abu al-Fazl Bayhaqi (d. 470/1077), whose *Tarikh-i Mas'udi* is discussed here, records many episodes in which women figure either prominently or as "bit players." Bayhaqi served in the Ghaznavid chancery (*divan-i risalat*) under successive rulers for most of his life.[4] The *Tarikh-i Mas'udi*, the sole surviving portion of his lengthy history of the Ghaznavids covering the period 366–451/977–1059, deals with the reign of Mas'ud I (r. 421–32/1030–41), the son and successor of Mahmud (r. 389–421/999–1030).[5] His narrative is based both on eyewitness testimony (his own and that of reliable informants) and on documents (letters, decrees, treaties), many of which he had composed and of which he kept copies. This fact, together with the abundance of circumstantial detail that characterizes his narrative, would appear to ensure its factuality; but as we shall see, other motives often condition Bayhaqi's selection and presentation of materials.

Like any historian, Bayhaqi selects and presents his facts in a way calculated to be meaningful in terms of his larger purpose. For him (as for other premodern historians), history is not merely factual but exemplary and ethical—that is to say, rhetorical.[6] On the level of fact, he includes what is relevant to his narrative; on the level of style, he employs both descriptive and factual statements embodying literal meaning, and rhetorical strategies signaling the significance of those statements and often aimed at persuasion or admonition. Rather than taking the historian's statements at face value, we must consider their function in the larger context of meaning.

Before turning to Bayhaqi's history, let us begin with a few historical facts. Royal Ghaznavid women were indeed secluded; they lived in separate and independent harem quarters with their own functionaries and provision for expenses (and often as not owned their own property), and when they traveled with the sultan's entourage they occupied special tents.[7] But had these once independent Turkish women "lost their former liberty" under the Ghaznavids?[8] The Ghaznavids, although ethnic Turks, were by Mahmud's time several generations removed from their steppe origins and had inherited the harem system, along with other aspects of Perso-Islamicate court culture, from their Samanid predecessors (204–395/819–1005).

Although women's and men's realms (their physical space) were largely separate, many women were at least the equals of men with respect to learning, which was accessible to all regardless of sex.[9] Learning was prized by the Ghaznavids; early on, Mahmud had set his heart on transforming Ghazna into a cultural center to rival Bukhara (or indeed Baghdad), and "whenever he found a man or a woman who was master of some art, he would send them there" (TB 263; see note 5). For women, learning was not confined to professionals or to women of the royal house; nor did it imply mere literacy or strictly religious learning.

That the sultans "took numerous wives" and that the motives for marriages were often material as well as political are also true.[10] The status of women was often precarious. "On the death of a Sultan, the new ruler often took over those of his predecessor's wives and concubines whom he desired. When Mahmud died, the Sultan's women were looked after by his sister, Hurra-yi Khuttali, and those who were no longer wanted were assigned estates on whose revenues they could live. When Muhammad was deposed . . . he had to make over his harem, together with other possessions, to Mas'ud."[11] But although the impression may arise that women were merely chattels, royal women were, through marriage, an important means of legitimizing rule. If women required protection, they were often astute enough to make their own arrangements, and when their opinions were ignored the results could be disastrous, as was the case at the end of Mas'ud's reign.

To conclude, however, that "women's place was in the harem; and how often would they be forgotten in those corners, for their entire lives. . . . Those women who played political roles are very few," is to assume that women simply could not have been otherwise.[12] As in other periods of Islamic history, women (including royal Ghaznavid ones) were politically important and active, although this activity often took place behind the scenes. In her study of women of ruling families in the Seljuq period, Lambton observes that women were often prominent in public affairs: "Many . . . were capable and vigorous. Some were ambitious, and sometimes unscrupulous and quarrelsome. Some were cultured women and remarkable for their charitable benefactions and their patronage of the religious classes."[13] While the visibility of Seljuq women was perhaps greater than that of Ghaznavid ones, there are points of similarity between them, and Lambton's study demonstrates the unwisdom of generalizing about medieval Muslim women. So, for that matter, does Bayhaqi's history.

Medieval writers are often accused of conforming to prevailing "Islamic social norms concerning women,"[14] and Bayhaqi is no exception. Bayani asserts that "in several places Bayhaqi, influenced by the beliefs of his day, points to the differences between women and men and to the inferiority of women."[15] Lambton observes that under the Seljuqs, "the general consensus was opposed to the participation of women in public affairs." She cites two texts: a document appointing a *muhtasib* (censor of public morality), which "instructs him . . . to prevent women from mixing with men in learned assemblies and listening to exhortations," and Nizam al-Mulk's chapter on "those who wear the veil" in his *Siyar al-muluk,* which, she says, represents the vizier's "uncompromising hostility to the intervention of women in political affairs, perhaps partly because of his unhappy experiences with Terken Khatun, Malik Shah's wife."[16] In interpreting such examples, we must consider their context and genre. A document appointing a muhtasib may be expected to be normative in terms of the shari'a (Islamic law) but does not necessarily reflect actual social practices.[17] Nizam al-Mulk's chapter appears in the second section of his *Siyar al-muluk;* the first section contains many accounts in which women play both positive and politically active roles.[18]

Genre has much to do with content, and this is indeed the case with the "negative opinion of women" voiced by Bayhaqi in a digression entitled "On the Meaning of This World," which follows his announcement of the death of the Ghaznavid sultan Farrukhzad and the succession of his brother Ibrahim in 451/1059. Among the sayings on kingship and government quoted in this passage—in which Bayhaqi, writing less as a historian than as an adviser to princes, sets himself to rebut an "ingrate"[19]—is the well-known hadith: "When Kisra Parviz died, news of this reached the prophet [Muhammad], who asked, 'Whom have they put in his place?' They replied, 'His daughter Puran.' He responded, 'A people who have entrusted their affairs to a woman will not prosper.' This is the greatest proof that rule requires a sagacious, effective, and powerful man; when he is not thus, a man and a woman are the same" (TB 485). There are, Bayhaqi says, kings who acquit themselves admirably and kings who make mistakes; "thus it has been since Adam's time." His central theme is the need for a strong and just ruler, embodied (so he asserts) in the newly enthroned Ibrahim. The genre is that of "advice to princes," which wavers between extolling women for their sagacity and piety and warning against their involvement in rule.

Another apparent negative comment on a woman ruler occurs early in the history. When in 421/1030 Mas'ud, preparing to march east from Isfahan to claim the Ghaznavid throne (see below), was appointing his deputies over the conquered city of Rayy, that city's notables came to him to declare their loyalty. Their spokesman, the *khatib* of Rayy, expressed their views:

> For nearly thirty years they were captives of the Daylamids, and the customs of Islam were obliterated; for rule had passed from the likes of Fakhr al-Dawla and the Sahib Isma'il [ibn] Abbad to a woman and an incompetent youth. They had raised their hands to God [in prayer], until He inspired the sovereign of Islam, Mahmud, who came here to their aid, freed them from the tyranny and corruption of Qarmatis and evildoers, uprooted those incom-

petents who could not protect us and cast them out of the land, and appointed over us a just, kind, and prudent lord [Mas'ud] after he himself returned
home in prosperity. (TB 23)

The Buyid Fakhr al-Dawla (d. 386/997) had been succeeded by his nine-
year-old son, Majd al-Dawla, whose regent was his mother, Sayyida Umm al-
Muluk. Unable to challenge Sayyida's power, Majd al-Dawla devoted himself to "the pursuit of knowledge and the pleasures of the harem." When
Sayyida died in 418/1028, Majd al-Dawla was unable to cope with the responsibilities of government. Threatened by civil disorder, he sought the assistance
of Sultan Mahmud, only to find himself taken prisoner and sent to India.[20]
The declaration of the people of Rayy is clearly meant to be conciliatory and
to confirm their anti-Buyid sentiments and their orthodoxy; the reference
to Sayyida is theirs, and Bayhaqi makes no comment upon it.

Elsewhere he tells us that after Samanid power had crumbled and Mah-
mud had taken Khurasan, he consulted with his vizier, Ahmad ibn Hasan
Maymandi, about launching a campaign against Rayy. Maymandi told him,
"That region is no threat; its ruler is a woman." Mahmud laughed and said,
"If that woman were a man, I would need to have a mighty army in Nisha-
pur," and while Sayyida remained alive, he did not attack Rayy (TB 344–45).
Although the point of this example is to contrast Mahmud's good sense with
Mas'ud's lack of same, Sayyida herself is presented as a ruler whose decisive
presence, in historically much-contested Rayy, made Mahmud cautious about
committing troops to a campaign against the region.

The context of this episode illustrates Bayhaqi's use of examples from the
past. Maymandi was in fact attempting to dissuade Mahmud from campaign-
ing against Rayy ("which is very far from us"), although initially he appears
to flatter the ruler by designating his opponent as a woman. Mas'ud rarely
heeded advice, whether direct or indirect. As Abu Nasr Mishkan, head of
Mas'ud's chancery, observed, "This king is the opposite of his father with respect to resolution and boldness"; for however stubborn Mahmud might be,
"when he would consider, he would return to the straight path. The nature
of this king is different: he acts arbitrarily and without reflection" (TB 514).[21]

Context is all-important for interpreting Bayhaqi's history, in which
"moral evaluation is . . . an integral part of the description of events."[22] But
if, as Humphreys argues, we must begin our evaluation of Bayhaqi's narrative "by identifying the moral framework within which [the historian's] data
was selected and shaped,"[23] we must do so not according to an assumed system of Islamic values that Bayhaqi blindly follows but by discerning those
criteria that were relevant for Bayhaqi himself.

Bayhaqi's history of Mas'ud's reign begins with his successful bid for the Ghaznavid throne. Around 406/1015–16, Mahmud had declared Mas'ud his successor (*vali ahd*), but shortly before his death he changed his mind and appointed instead Mas'ud's half brother Muhammad.[24] Mahmud died in the spring of 421/1030, following his return from the campaign in the west in which he had taken Rayy and Isfahan, and leaving Mas'ud in charge of the conquered territories. Muhammad was placed on the throne; he ruled a scant five months before he was deposed by a palace plot in favor of Mas'ud. Among the plotters (who included important officials of the court and the army) was Mahmud's sister Hurra-yi Khuttali, who was devoted to Mas'ud (cf. TB 146) and who immediately after Mahmud's death wrote Mas'ud the following letter urging him to return and claim the throne:[25]

Our ruler Sultan Mahmud died in the afternoon of Thursday 23 Rabi' I [421/ 30 April 1030]—may God have mercy on him!—and the fortune of [his] servants has come to an end. I and the women of the harem are all in the citadel of Ghaznin. The day after tomorrow we will make known his death. At night the king was buried in the Piruzi garden, while we still longed to see him, for we had not seen him for a week. Affairs are in the hands of Hajib Ali.[26] After the burial, swift horsemen went that night to Guzganan so that your brother Muhammad might come here quickly and ascend the throne.[27] Because of her great affection for the amir's [Mahmud's] son, this very night your aunt has written a [secret] letter in her own hand and commanded that [two trusted messengers] be appointed at once to bear it secretly from Ghaz-nin and take it to his camp as swiftly as possible. The amir knows that his brother is not equal to this great task; this house has many enemies, and we women [*awrat*] and the treasuries are in great peril. He must take charge of affairs quickly, for he is his father's vali ahd. He must not occupy himself with the region he has conquered or take any other; for what has happened so far has been chiefly due to his father's power, and once the news of his [Mah-mud's] death is revealed, matters will take on a different hue. The principal is Ghaznin, and then Khurasan; all else is secondary. Let him consider well about what I have written, and make ready to come with all speed, so that neither the throne nor ourselves will be lost [and let him] send the messen-gers back quickly, as your aunt is awaiting them anxiously. We will write to him of all that happens here. (TB 13–14)

Mas'ud prepared to march eastward (although he was not pleased, as his plans for further conquests in the west were now in ruins; TB 12). While he was appointing local governors and deputies, more letters arrived from court notables and the army and from Mas'ud's mother and aunt, who informed

him that Muhammad was occupied with pleasure and drink and who urged
him to return swiftly (TB 19).

The concealment of Mahmud's death, the secret burial, and the summon-
ing of Masʿud were clearly done with the cooperation, if not at the instigation, of the royal Ghaznavid women, who were keenly aware of their own
precarious position should civil war break out.[28] Bayhaqi makes no comment
on the propriety of Hurra-yi Khuttali's interference in politics. Indeed, we
sense that had the royal women not been so insistent, Masʿud would not have
returned with such alacrity. But we must ask how this account functions in
terms of Bayhaqi's larger purpose. On the one hand, it testifies to the extent
of support for Masʿud and the urgency with which his return was sought (in
the letter, words emphasizing speed occur no less than seven times), an urgency made all the more pressing by the desperate state of the royal women.
On the other hand, Masʿud is seen to vacillate, uncertain of his priorities; this
trait would lead to his eventual downfall and the Ghaznavids' loss of Khurasan, the importance of which the letter stresses. Moreover (as Bayhaqi's audience knew), Masʿud lost little time in turning against not only those who
had supported Muhammad but also those who had deposed him; his vendettas provide a major theme of the history's first chapters.

One victim of these vendettas was the Sipahsalar Asightigin Ghazi, Mahmud's military commander of Khurasan, who on Mahmud's death had declared for Masʿud and secured the support of Nishapur. Even though he was a
loyal servant of both sultans, his power and arrogance provoked the "old
guard," the Mahmudiyyan, to plot to bring him down by playing on Masʿud's
fears. Unwittingly involved in this plot was a widowed *hurra* (freeborn woman) of good family, who was "wise and experienced" and "had a fine hand and
wrote Persian exceedingly well." She was the adoptive mother of a slave woman (*kanizak*) who was in charge of Ghazi's harem and visited there regularly.
As Masʿud became increasingly mistrustful of Ghazi, the plotters "induced
some people, in such a way that no one would know, to deceive [the hurra] by
appearing to warn her" that Ghazi would soon be arrested (TB 299–300):

> [The hurra] went and told the kanizak, who told Ghazi, and made him greatly
> afraid, saying, "Deal with this matter, for you are in danger." Becoming anx-
> ious, Ghazi said to her, "Summon the hurra so that we may consider more
> carefully; I will repay her if this disaster is averted." The kanizak did so; [the
> hurra] replied that she could not come because she was afraid but would
> report all that happened through notes. "You know how to read," she told
> the kanizak; "you will tell the general." [The woman sent notes reporting

whatever she heard.] But the Mahmudiyyan were clever in this affair—and how could she know this?—so that Fate had its way. On the afternoon of 9 Rabiʿ II 422 [5 April 1031] they told her, "Tomorrow when Ghazi comes to court he will be arrested," and made it appear that this was so. The woman wrote a note at once reporting the matter; the kanizak told Ghazi, who was greatly alarmed, for others had also made him fearful. (TB 299–300)

Ghazi fled that night, along with the kanizak, several female slaves and *ghulam*s (slave soldiers, perhaps his guard), and all his moveable wealth; but the next day he was caught and brought back to Nishapur. Shortly after, he was sent to the citadel of Ghazna, where he later died.[29] No comment is made on this woman's interference in politics (and only sympathy for her becoming the tool of the Mahmudiyyan); the episode demonstrates the pervasive atmosphere of intrigue at Masʿud's court, which affected everyone, not merely the male actors on the political stage.[30] Bayhaqi's invocation of fate (which is not to be taken at face value), here as in many other instances, serves to heighten the sense of moral corruption and impending doom.

Accounts relating to marriage alliances figure importantly in Bayhaqi's history. In addition to their factual content, we may discern other motives behind their narration, signaled by the form they take, their context, and their manner of presentation. Lambton notes that, for the Seljuqs, "it was common tribal practice to exchange brides to mark the conclusion of hostilities between two different tribes or to consolidate an existing alliance or friendship" and that "marriages were perhaps sometimes made with the intention of controlling younger members of the family."[31] Both situations apply, with some variations, to the Ghaznavids, with whom such alliances represent far more than tribal practice.

Mahmud's sister, Hurra-yi Khuttali, had been married to the Maʾmunid Khwarazmshah Abu al-Hasan Ali (d. ca. 399/1005–9) and after his death to his brother and successor Abu al-Abbas Maʾmun.[32] Bayani suggests that the Maʾmunid princes, fearing that Mahmud intended to annex the fertile region of Khwarazm, sought these marriages in order to ensure their security.[33] If so, this hope seems to have been futile. When Mahmud obliged Abu al-Abbas to pronounce the *khutba* (portion of the Friday prayer in which the reigning sovereign is named and acclaimed) in his name, the Khwarazmian military commanders rebelled; and when in 407/1016 Abu al-Abbas was murdered, Mahmud seized his opportunity (TB 919–20).

Bayhaqi (drawing on Biruni's lost history of Khwarazm) describes Mahmud's eagerness as he consulted with his vizier, Maymandi: "There is no longer any excuse; Khwarazm is ours. We must seek vengeance for his blood, execute the murderer of our brother-in-law, and take his kingdom as our inheritance." Maymandi agreed, but counseled strategy, and suggested that an envoy be sent to frighten the Khwarazmians by threatening an invasion unless the murderers were sent to Mahmud's court and the khutba pronounced in his name. This strategy would encourage them to produce some men and accuse them of the murders; the envoy should first feign approval, then tell them to send the hurra back in proper fashion, lest Mahmud use her detainment as an excuse to invade: "Meanwhile we will make our preparations; when we have heard that the hurra has arrived safely in Amul, we will turn our wicks higher and say those things that we cannot say today because the hurra is there" (TB 920–22). The envoy was dispatched, Hurra-yi Khuttali was safely returned, and Mahmud marched on Khwarazm, where, after sacking its capital, Gurganj, and punishing the regicides, he installed his slave general Altuntash as Khwarazmshah.[34] Although the source may be Biruni, the style is Bayhaqi's: the vividness, use of dialogue, and exploration of motives are typical of his manner of presentation, as is the emphasis on the all-important matter of consultation. While Hurra-yi Khuttali is not an actor in this scene, she is a presence, and no action is taken until her safety is assured.

Mas'ud's two major marriage alliances—with the Qarakhanids of Transoxiana and with Bakalijar (Abu Kalijar) ibn Surkhab, the ruler of Gurgan and Tabaristan—were in effect continuations of his father's policies.[35] Bayhaqi describes the diplomatic exchanges and lavish celebrations taking place and focuses both on their material aspects—bride-prices and dowries, exchange of costly gifts, wedding ceremonies, and public festivities—and on their political and diplomatic ramifications. In neither case, however, was the desired political end achieved; and the detailed accounts of negotiations, expenditures, and ceremonies serve to point out the ultimate futility of these alliances.

The Qarakhanid prince of Kashghar, Bughra Khan, whose sister had been betrothed to Mas'ud and to whom Mahmud had promised his daughter Hurra-yi Zaynab, had been put off by that ruler, and the marriages were not concluded in Mahmud's lifetime.[36] In 422/1031, Mas'ud sent envoys to Bughra Khan to renew the agreement. The negotiations dragged on; in 425/1034 the envoys returned with Mas'ud's bride, Shah Khatun, and a daughter of Bughra Khan's brother, Arslan Khan, who was intended for Mas'ud's son Mawdud but who died on the way (TB 547–48). Ghazna was decked out with splendor that had not been seen since Mas'ud had come there to ascend the throne, "for this was the first bride who had been brought there from Turkestan, and the amir wanted the Turks to see something the likes of which they had never seen before" (TB 548). The festivities lasted for days, unprecedented largesse was distributed (which amazed the Turkish envoys), the nobles played games and organized drinking parties, and the populace rejoiced (TB 549–50).

Later Bayhaqi relates that at this time, Bughra Khan had sent his own envoy asking that Hurra-yi Zaynab be sent to him. Mas'ud was preparing to do so when word reached him that Bughra Khan "had said some unseemly things concerning [her] inheritance" (presumably that Zaynab, as Mas'ud's sister, should bring some territories with her). Angered, Mas'ud "sent Bughra Khan's envoy back with his mission unfulfilled" and wrote to Arslan Khan complaining of Bughra Khan's greed. Arslan Khan rebuked his brother; Bughra Khan became Mas'ud's bitter enemy and secretly supported the Seljuqs against him (TB 693–96).

As for the Ziyarid Bakalijar (a vassal of the Ghaznavids), it seems to have been his withholding of tribute that prompted the marriage.[37] In 424/1033, Mas'ud appointed Abd al-Jabbar ibn Ahmad ibn Abd al-Samad (whose father had been made vizier after Maymandi's death) to bring Bakalijar's overdue tribute and his daughter to Nishapur (TB 480, 494). He returned with tribute, a bride, and an oath of allegiance from Bakalijar. The festivities were impressive. The bride, accompanied by the noble Nishapuri women and her own female attendants, was installed in the Hasanaki palace complex, to which servants from the sultan's harem were appointed. The marriage celebration was lavish:

> No one saw the bride [*vadi'at*], who was in the bridal litter. At night the prince went from [the palace of] Shadyakh with many courtiers and three hundred special ghulams, all mounted, and three hundred on foot before him, and five palace *hajib*s [chamberlains] to the Hasanaki palace. He went to the harem with ten personal servants who were allowed to see the women. . . . The sun of the sultan's eyes fell upon the moon; the Gurganis' honor was increased by the brilliance of that sun, and things went well, as god had decreed. But those who are outside [*biruniyyan*] have nothing to do with such matters, neither in those times nor today; nor can my pen execute my thoughts. (TB 507–8)

Bayhaqi describes the elaborate throne, made of precious metal and gems, that formed part of the bride's dowry (TB 510). But further delay on Bakalijar's part in sending his annual tribute provoked Mas'ud into launching a punitive expedition against him in 426/1035–36, which ended in the sack of Amul and the extortion of great sums of money from its citizens (TB 573–619).[38]

A more puzzling marriage was arranged by Mas'ud between his thirteen-year-old son Mardanshah and the daughter of the influential and wealthy Hajib Biktughdi (Beghtoghdi). This somewhat testy general had suffered a crushing defeat by the Seljuqs at Nasa in 426/1035 (TB 625–36) but continued to occupy an important position at court. In 428/1037, following the escheat of the estates and belongings of the recently deceased Nushtigin-i Khassa, Mahmud's former cupbearer and the governor of Marv, Nushtigin's palace with many of its effects was given to Mardanshah and his governorship to Biktughdi, who was then commander of the palace ghulams (TB 690, 678–79). That same week, the marriage was arranged and the contract drawn up by Abu Nasr Mishkan. Biktughdi was heard to comment that he "had not the strength to bear such favor, and how could he? But [he] knew what he had to do and what the purpose [of this] was, and he set about making preparations at once." A year later the contract (*ahd-i nikah*) was celebrated ostentatiously; then Mardanshah was returned to his mother's care in the harem. Early in 430/1038–39, Biktughdi's daughter, who was also quite young, was brought to Mardanshah, and the wedding was celebrated with great magnificence (TB 690–92).

Bayani comments, "Mas'ud was in such a hurry over this arrangement that he could not wait until the boy and girl matured"[39]—although marriage arrangements between minors were not unusual. She sees in this behavior evidence of Mas'ud's greed (of which there can be no doubt). Biktughdi bestowed lavish stipends on the court servants in connection with the *aqd* (marriage contract); the bride's *jahaz* (bridewealth) amounted to "tens of thousands of dirhams," and Bayhaqi "was astonished that anyone could assemble so much" (TB 692). But the matter seems more complex, and various motives were probably involved, among them Mas'ud's wish to favor a much-loved younger son, and his desire to ensure the loyalty of his newly appointed governor and to confirm his own continued favor for Biktughdi, so as to forestall any dissension concerning his authority.

The retrospective account of a marriage arrangement involving the daughters of Mahmud's younger brother Amir Yusuf, which occurs within the larger narrative of Mas'ud's arrest and imprisonment of his uncle, is more significant in terms of Bayhaqi's ethical purpose. Yusuf had been brought up by Mahmud, had served him devotedly, and had supported his policies toward Muhammad "in order to retain Mahmud's affections" (TB 324). But despite the fact that Muhammad had appointed him military governor of Khurasan, Yusuf participated in the plot to depose him. Yusuf had two daughters, one of marriageable age, the other still immature. Mahmud arranged the marriage of the elder to Muhammad and betrothed the younger (as a sort of consolation prize) to Mas'ud. He ordered a lavish wedding to be held in Muhammad's palace and showered him with favors. He "bestowed kingly robes upon him and gave him many gifts. Then everyone left, leaving the palace to the bridegroom and the hurra. As fate would have it, the bride took a fever. At night they brought the bride in her litter; the river of Ghaznin was filled with the womenfolk of the nobles, and many candles and torches had been lit to escort the bride to the king's pavilion. That poor inexperienced girl, decked with gold, ornaments, and jewels, died as she sat there, and everything was ruined." Mahmud was distressed and ordered that the girl intended for Mas'ud be betrothed to Muhammad instead. "Amir Mas'ud was very upset but did not dare say anything." When Muhammad came to the throne, the girl, who was then fourteen, entered his harem in Ghazna; when he was deposed, she was sent to the fortress in which he was imprisoned. She remained there a short while before she returned, homesick, to Ghazna, where she was still living when Bayhaqi was writing his history. "And Mas'ud was angered at such insults from his brother, and conquering Fate lent a hand, so that Yusuf fell from high position into the pit" (TB 324–25).

This account, which precedes that of Mas'ud's revenge for the insult suffered at Yusuf's hands (actually at Mahmud's, but Yusuf provided a convenient scapegoat), bears all the hallmarks of Bayhaqi's rhetorical strategy: the invocation of fate and the statement that he presents this background "so that slanderers should not loose their tongues too quickly about this great king Mas'ud, but speak the truth; for the nature of kings, their circumstances and habits, are not like those of other men, and what they see no one else can" (TB 324). Such features are signals alerting us to Bayhaqi's purpose; their very ambiguity suggests that more is here than immediately meets the eye. Commenting on the emotional scene of the young bride's death, Bayani asks, "How could that poor girl, burning with the fever of sickness and near death, be adorned and hung with gold and ornaments and sent to her wedding?"[40] The pathos of the scene underlines Mahmud's irrationality in wishing to show favor to Muhammad, at all costs, over Mas'ud, as does his immediate reaction to the girl's death: his betrothal of Mas'ud's promised bride to his brother, about which Mas'ud dared say nothing but which influenced his later actions.

Mas'ud arrested Amir Yusuf in 422/1032, on the latter's return from Qusdar, where he had been sent on the pretext of quelling a revolt in Makran (TB 78). The charge was treason, based on the reports of spies, and in his betrayal, a woman, indirectly and unintentionally, played a part. During Mahmud's lifetime it had been the custom of the wife of the Qarakhanid Arslan Khan

Mansur ibn Ali (d. 415/1024) to send to him each year from Turkestan "an exceptional ghulam and a choice virgin kanizak as a gift; and the amir would send her kerchiefs of linen and fine muslin, pearls, and Rumi silks" (TB 329).[41] One of these ghulams, Tughril, pleased the sultan so much that he made him one his favorite cupbearers. One night at a drinking party, the inebriated Yusuf was smitten by Tughril. His conduct betrayed him; Mahmud, angered, rebuked him sharply, then pardoned him and gave Tughril to him. Yusuf cared for Tughril, made him his chamberlain (hajib), and "held him dearer than his own sons." When Tughril matured, Yusuf found him a wife from a reputable family and "celebrated his wedding with such excessive ostentation that some wise men disapproved" (TB 330–31). When Mas'ud sent Yusuf to Qusdar, Tughril was sent to spy upon his master. "And how could Yusuf know that his heart, his liver, his love, were spies over him?" (TB 326). Tughril reported his master's indiscreet remarks to Mas'ud ; Yusuf was seized and imprisoned and died the following year. Tughril obtained a position at court but was universally despised; he died young and disappointed. "And such is the fate of ingrates" (TB 325–29).

A dying bride, a child-bride hastily transferred from one brother to another, a gift with unforeseen and evil consequences, a treacherous beloved: all these are signs of the moral turpitude underlying the surface grandeur of the Ghaznavid court, of the perils lying in wait for all. "Put not your trust in princes" might be Bayhaqi's motto. Before discussing a final critical episode, we may consider a different blend of the factual and the rhetorical in Bayhaqi's retelling of an incident occurring during Mas'ud's youth, based on an account obtained from the *dabir* (official) Abu Sa'id Abd al-Ghaffar, who had been in Mas'ud's service since the age of fourteen.[42] In 401/1010, Mahmud left the princes Mas'ud and Muhammad, both fourteen, and their uncle Yusuf, who was seventeen, in Zamindavar, while he went on campaign against the Ghur. Abd al-Ghaffar's grandfather was summoned to serve the princes, as was his grandmother, who was "pious, respectable, and a reader of the Qur'an; she knew writing, Qur'anic *tafsir* [exegesis], and the interpretation of dreams and had memorized many accounts of the life of the prophet." A marvelous cook, she used to prepare delicacies for the young princes, who would send for her to converse with them and read them stories of the prophet (TB 133).

The governor of Zamindavar was Baytigin, who had been Mahmud's first ghulam. He had a learned and pious wife, whom Mas'ud respected greatly; when he came to the throne, he treated her as the equal of his own mother, and whenever he was in Ghazna he would converse with her about events in his father's reign. Baytigin owned some peacocks that were like household pets and of which Mas'ud was fond. Abd al-Ghaffar relates:

> One day he [Mas'ud] called to my grandmother from the roof and summoned her. When she came, he told her, "I dreamed that I was in the land of Ghur, and there was a fortress there, just like here, with many peacocks and roosters. I would take them and put them under my cloak, and they would fly and flap about underneath. You know everything; what does this mean?" The old woman said, "God willing, the amir will conquer the Ghurid princes and subjugate the Ghurids." "I have not taken over my father's rule," he said. "How should I conquer them?" The old woman answered, "When you grow up, if God so wills it, it will be so; for I remember the sultan your father when he was here in his youth and ruled this territory; now he has seized or is seizing most of the world. You will be like your father." The prince answered, "God willing!" And afterwards it was as he had dreamed, and Ghur was subjugated by him. (TB 135)

Mas'ud's conquest of Ghur took place in 411/1020, during his governorate of Herat. Afterward he told Abd al-Ghaffar, "Your grandmother prophesied well" (TB 137–44). Dreams predicting greatness are recurrent in historical writing, and Abd al-Ghaffar's grandmother evokes the paradigmatic figure of the "wise woman" who appears in many medieval accounts.[43] Is it felicitous coincidence that fact and topos come together here?

Waldman links Abd al-Ghaffar's mother with another wise woman: the mother of Mahmud's former vizier Hasanak who was executed by Mas'ud in 422/1031. The account of Hasanak's trial and execution is perhaps the rhetorical high point of Bayhaqi's history. Once *ra'is* (leader) of Nishapur, Hasanak (Abu Ali Hasan ibn Muhammad Mikali) was appointed vizier in 416/1025. A powerful but arrogant official (and a supporter of Muhammad's succession), he incurred the enmity of both Mas'ud and the latter's close adviser, Abu Sahl Zawzani.[44] Bayhaqi's description of the events leading up to Hasanak's execution on a trumped-up charge of heresy and of the indignities heaped upon him present the former vizier in the role of a martyr, an image reinforced by the historical digression that follows.

Hasanak was arrested, brought to trial, condemned, and imprisoned, and his property was confiscated. After some vacillation, Mas'ud finally gave in to Abu Sahl Zawzani's insistence that Hasanak be executed. Following his detailed description of the proceedings and of Hasanak's subjection to various abuses, Bayhaqi moves to Hasanak's mother, who was, he says, "a strong-minded woman." "I heard that this matter was hidden from her for two or three months. When she heard of it, she did not grieve as women do, but wept so in anguish that those present wept blood at her pain. Then she said, 'What a great man was this son of mine, to whom a king like Mahmud gave this world, and a king like Mas'ud the next.' She held a fine mourning ceremony for her son, and all wise men who hear of this will approve, and so they should" (TB 236).

"Such things have happened in the world," says Bayhaqi, and relates a long story about the anti-caliph Abd Allah ibn al-Zubayr (d. 73/692). When the latter was besieged in Mecca by the army of the Umayyad caliph Abd al-Malik ibn Marwan (led by the notorious general Hajjaj), he asked his mother, Asma bint Abi Bakr, whether he should surrender. She asked him, "Did you rebel against the Umayyads for the sake of the faith or of this world?" "By God, for the faith," he replied. "I have not taken so much as a dirham from this world." "Then," said Asma, "stand fast in the face of death, execution, and mutilation . . . for your father was al-Zubayr ibn al-Awwam and your maternal grandfather Abu Bakr." Abd Allah feared that he would be mutilated after death. Asma replied, "When they slaughter a sheep, he feels no pain when he is mutilated and skinned."

Abd Allah and his followers stood fast; the battle went against them, and all were killed. Hajjaj sent Abd Allah's head to Abd al-Malik and had his body exposed on a cross. They informed his mother of his death. "She did not grieve but said, 'We are God's, and to Him we return. Had my son not done as he did he would be neither the son of al-Zubayr nor the grandson of Abu Bakr.'" After some time, Hajjaj was told about her endurance and her utterance. He said, "Praise be to God Almighty! If A'isha and this sister of hers had been men, this caliphate would never have passed to the Umayyads! Such indeed is courage and endurance!" He arranged for some women to take Asma by a route where she would see her son. "When she saw the cross, she recognized her son; she turned to a noble woman and said, 'Isn't it time this rider was brought down from this horse?' She said no more, but went away; they reported this to Hajjaj, who marveled and then ordered that Abd Allah be taken down and buried" (TB 241).

Bayhaqi concludes, "Although this story is somewhat long, yet there is benefit in it. I have produced two other cases as well, so that it may be seen that Hasanak had companions in this world greater than he; if what happened to him happened to them, it should not be marveled at. Further, if his mother did not grieve, but uttered such words, let no slanderer say that this could not be so; for there are many differences between men and women, and your Lord creates as He wishes and chooses whom He will" (TB 241–42).[45] While the "two other cases" (those of the viziers Ja'far ibn Yahya al-Barmaki, executed by Harun al-Rashid, and Ibn Baqiyya, crucified for his insolence toward the Buyid Adud al-Dawla) are irrelevant here, they illustrate Bayhaqi's rhetorical and analogical method, his juxtaposition of historical narrative with stories from the past that serve as comment. Here Bayhaqi is in full rhetorical flow, presenting his factual materials in a manner serving his larger ethical purpose, blending present with past to call attention to the recurrent patterns of human history.

Bayani cites Bayhaqi's concluding statement as proof that he believes that women are inferior to men.[46] Waldman links Hasanak's mother with the "wise woman" topos: "In many folk traditions, old women are seen to possess the world's secrets; at the same time readers can be expected to dismiss old women's words as silly if they want to, since old women are absolved from having to make sense or to be taken seriously."[47] Under this topos she includes the story of Abd al-Ghaffar's grandmother and another concerning Abu Nasr Mishkan's mother, who died in 423/1031. Bayhaqi recalls that this wise woman (*zan-i aqila*) had told Hasanak, after he had been made vizier and had begun to encounter hostility from Mahmud, "My son, when a king appoints a man vizier, even though he loves him, he will be his enemy within a week; [for the vizier] will become his partner in rule, and rule cannot be exercised in partnership" (TB 434).

The topos is indeed recurrent. Innumerable instances could be cited in which women—usually older ones—rebuke, either directly or indirectly, a ruler or other important personage (not necessarily male) for improper or abusive conduct or utter words of warning. Such words are meant to be taken to heart, not least by the audience or reader. Hasanak's execution provides an object lesson: "Such was Hasanak and his fate . . . and his story is a great admonition. . . . How stupid is the man who fixes his heart on this world!" (TB 234). But this is only the obvious lesson. Hasanak is linked with the martyred Ibn al-Zubayr and with two viziers whose punishment was, if merited, excessively vindictive; all share the common feature of being victims of rulers jealous of their power. In this analogy, Mas'ud and Zawzani are implicitly linked with other vindictive tyrants, and Hasanak's mother with Asma bint Abi Bakr, one of the most respected women in Islamic history, and her sister A'isha. The digression as a whole is framed by the two references to Hasanak's mother, and Bayhaqi explicitly warns against "not taking seriously" his account by suggesting that only a "slanderer" might cast doubt upon it. Men and women are different, not just as members of classes but as individuals.

Other women play bit parts in Bayhaqi's history. Some are linked to court
intrigues, illicit liaisons, or jealousies in the harem. For example, the general
Abu al-Hasan Simjuri—whose father, Abu Ali Simjuri, had been defeated in
battle by the Ghaznavids in 385/995—fled to the Buyid Fakhr al-Dawla in
Rayy but returned to Nishapur "because of a woman" and was seized and
imprisoned (TB 262–63). Mas'ud's governor of India, Ahmad Yanaltigin, was
said to be "the spitting image [atsa] of Mahmud . . . and there was talk about
his mother and Mahmud. They were good friends, but only God knows the
truth." When Yanaltigin rebelled against Mas'ud in 424/1033, he claimed
publicly to be Mahmud's son (TB 515, 517). The dabir (official) Abu al-Qasim
Iraqi (d. 429/1037) was thought to have been poisoned by his wives, who were
angered because he had married a musician (TB 772). Mas'ud's favorite son,
Sa'id (d. 430/1038), was afflicted with an ailment that made him impotent;
his women, believing that he had been bewitched, employed an old woman
who gave him a remedy that paralyzed and sent him into a coma from which
he never recovered (TB 747–48).

Other women are briefly glimpsed in accounts of military campaigns,
battles, and raids. After the sack of Amul, a beer seller who supplied Mas'ud's
general Biktughdi attempted to molest a young girl but was prevented by her
father and brothers and was wounded in the ensuing fracas. Biktughdi went
to the girl's village with an elephant and some ghulams and did much looting and killing. When Mas'ud was informed of this, he punished Biktughdi
severely (TB 601–2). Not only does this episode highlight Biktughdi's rather
crude and intractable character; the presentation of Mas'ud as clement and
just in this instance is highly ironic in view of his recent ruthless sack of Amul,
about which Bayhaqi is outspokenly critical. When Mas'ud was defeated by
the Seljuqs in 431/1040, the Turks opened the borders of the Oxus. People
began to pour in, in the hope of plundering Khurasan. Bayhaqi read in a letter
that "in Amul an old woman was seen, with one hand, one eye, and one leg,
carrying an ax. She was asked, 'Why have you come here?' She replied, 'I've
heard they're digging up the treasures of Khurasan from under the ground;
I've come along to take some away'" (TB 790–91). This is the world upside-
down, in which order has vanished and chaos reigns.

With the closing events of Mas'ud's reign we again encounter the wom-
en of the Ghaznavid royal house. When Mas'ud, fleeing eastward in disar-
ray after his defeat by the Seljuqs at Dandanqan, reached the outskirts of
Ghazna, the kutval (castellan) of the citadel arrived with new royal regalia,
equipment, and clothing. Mas'ud's mother, his aunt Hurra-yi Khuttali, and
his other aunts and his sisters sent servants with much-needed items (as did

relatives of other nobles and troops), for the army had lost most of its baggage and equipment to the Seljuqs (TB 862–63). The extent of the catastrophe that had befallen the army and its demoralized state are highlighted by this detail; and the narrative has come full circle, as the royal women, again concerned for their safety, attempt to hearten Mas'ud and stiffen his resolve. But bad news from all quarters made Mas'ud despair of holding Ghazna, and he determined to make for India. He had Amir Muhammad and his four sons brought from the fortress in which they had been imprisoned, enrolled the sons in his own service (which was tantamount to making them hostages), and secured oaths of allegiance from them and their father. Then Mas'ud's daughter, Hurra-yi Gawhar, "was quickly betrothed to prince Ahmad [ibn Muhammad], until other [brides] could be found for other [princes], and the wedding was celebrated" (TB 893–94).[48]

> After that, as secretly as possible, he sent trusted servants to load up [on camels] all of the treasuries—gold, dirhams, robes, jewels, and other sorts of items, everything that was in Ghaznin—and they began preparations [to depart]. They sent messages to the *hurrat*, the aunts and sisters, the *valida* [Mas'ud's mother] and the daughters, saying, "Get ready to come with us to India; let nothing remain in Ghaznin that you might be anxious about." Whether they wished to or no, they began to prepare. Hurra-yi Khuttali and the valida were asked to give their opinion in this matter; they did so and were told in answer, "Let anyone who wishes to fall into the enemy's hands remain in Ghaznin." No one dared say any more. (TB 895)

Mas'ud would have done well to heed the opinions of his mother and aunt, as well as those of his advisers, for, as other historians inform (this part of Bayhaqi's history is lost): "Four days after the failure of the sultan's advisers to dissuade him from his plan, early in Rabi' I 432/November 1040, all the stores of precious metals, ornaments, and fine clothes . . . together with the members of the sultan's harem were loaded on camels and the whole assemblage departed for India. Also in the column were Muhammad's four sons and Muhammad himself." As the column was crossing the Indus, a section of the army and some of the palace ghulams mutinied, plundered the treasure, and set up Muhammad as sultan, apparently by force. Mas'ud himself was soon captured and imprisoned, with his wife Shah Khatun, in the fortress of Giri. Shortly after, he was killed, perhaps at the instigation of Ahmad ibn Muhammad.[49]

From the information provided by Bayhaqi's history, we can see that women did indeed "interfere" in politics in various ways, that they were of importance in marriage alliances, and that their intellectual company was often sought by rulers. But this information is often presented in larger contexts, by means of self-conscious narrative and rhetorical strategies that show that it is not just information but serves broader purposes. Abd al-Ghaffar's grandmother, Hasanak's mother, and Amir Yusuf's dying daughter provide cases in point. It may be unwise to generalize from such information. But as the moral drama of Mas'ud's reign unfolds, we see that from the very outset women play a variety of roles—major and minor, wittingly or unwittingly—in that drama. They (like men) act as advisers whose counsel is, often as not, disregarded; they (like men) may be pawns in larger political games whose outcome may be positive or negative; they (like men) may fall victim to court intrigues; they (like men) may function as exemplars whose words and deeds provide moral comment on the events in which they figure.[50] Bayhaqi's history (like premodern history in general) presents ethical example and moral truth, displays the tension between the ideals of kingship and government and the realities of politics, and particularizes the universal through the individual without losing sight of the fact that it is through the individual that the universal paradigms of human history are proven valid. Such preoccupations affect Bayhaqi's treatment of events and persons. We must read those preoccupations *out of* his history rather than reading *into it* attitudes determined by some illusionary construct of Islam.

NOTES

This chapter was originally written in 1993; I made minor changes in 2001 and 2002. Since 1993, far more books and articles have appeared dealing with medieval Muslim women than can be referred to here. The most recent study relevant to this chapter (but with totally different conclusions) is Soheila Amirsoleimani, "Women in Tarikh-i Bayhaqi," *Der Islam* 78 (2001): 229–48.

1. See, for example, Leila Ahmed's contention that "throughout Islamic history the constructs, institutions and modes of thought devised by early Muslim societies that form the core discourse of Islam have played a central role in defining women's place"; *Women and Gender in Islam: Historical Roots of a Modern Debate* (New Haven: Yale University Press, 1992), 1. On essentialist constructs of Islam, particularly as relevant to literature, see Julie S. Meisami, "An Anatomy of Misogyny?" *Edebiyat*, n.s. 6 (1995): 303–15.

2. Deniz Kandiyoti, "Islam and Patriarchy: A Comparative Perspective," in *Women in Middle Eastern History: Shifting Boundaries in Sex and Gender,* ed. Nikki Keddie and Beth Baron (New Haven: Yale University Press, 1991), 23.

3. Marilyn Waldman, *Toward a Theory of Historical Narrative: A Case Study in Perso-Islamicate Historiography* (Columbus: Ohio State University Press, 1980), 2.

4. On Bayhaqi's life and career, see G.-H. Yusofi, "Bayhaqi, Abu'l-Fazl," *Encyclopaedia Iranica* 3:889–94. On Bayhaqi's history, see Waldman, *Historical Narrative;* Julie S. Meisami, *Persian Historiography to the End of the Twelfth Century* (Edinburgh: Edinburgh University Press, 1999), 79–108.

5. All references are to *Tarikh-i Bayhaqi,* ed. Ali Akbar Fayyaz (Mashhad, Iran: n.p., 1995), abbreviated as TB. All translations are my own.

6. On ethical-rhetorical historiography, see Julie S. Meisami, "Dynastic History and Ideals of Kingship in Bayhaqi's *Tarikh-i Mas'udi,*" *Edebiyat,* n.s. 3 (1) (1989): 57–77; "The Past in Service of the Present: Attitudes towards History in Eleventh-Century Persia," *Poetics Today* 14 (1993): 247–75, and the references cited therein; and *Persian Historiography,* 10–12, 281–83.

7. See Shirin Bayani, "Zan dar Tarikh-i Bayhaqi" (Women in Bayhaqi's history), in *Yadnama-yi Abu al-Fazl Bayhaqi* (Bayhaqi memorial volume) (Mashhad, Iran: Danishgah, 1971), 89; C. E. Bosworth, *The Ghaznavids, Their Empire in Afghanistan and Eastern Iran, 994–1040.* 2d ed. (Beirut: Librairie du Liban, 1973), 135–39, 187.

8. Bayani, "Zan," 69.

9. See Richard Bulliet, *The Patricians of Nishapur: A Study in Medieval Islamic Social History* (Cambridge: Harvard University Press, 1972), 47–60.

10. Cf. Bayani, "Zan," 59.

11. Bosworth, *Ghaznavids,* 138–39.

12. See Bayani, "Zan," 90.

13. A. K. S. Lambton, *Continuity and Change in Medieval Persia: Aspects of Administrative, Economic, and Social History, Eleventh–Fourteenth Century* (London: I. B. Tauris, 1988), 77–78.

14. Denise Spellberg, "Political Action and Public Example: 'A'isha and the Battle of the Camel," in *Women in Middle Eastern History,* ed. Keddie and Baron, 49.

15. Bayani, "Zan," 70.

16. Lambton, *Medieval Persia,* 269.

17. See, for example, Huda Lutfi, "Manners and Customs of Fourteenth-Century Cairene Women: Female Anarchy versus Male Shari' Order in Muslim Prescriptive Treatises," in *Women in Middle Eastern History,* ed. Keddie and Baron, 99–121.

18. For a fuller discussion, see Meisami, *Persian Historiography,* 147, 158.

19. The passage begins, "Should someone say, 'How weighty and elevated is the business of government! If it falls into the hands of a powerful, experienced, and authoritative ruler, he will accomplish [rule] in such a way as to acquire both faith and this world; but if it falls into the hands of an incompetent, he will despair of himself, and the people of him.' God forbid that one who has enjoyed their favors should speak improperly of one of the kings of this house" (TB 484–85). This statement appears to reflect the uncertainties surrounding the Ghaznavid succession after Mas'ud's death. On Farrukhzad's reign and Ibrahim's succession, see C. E. Bosworth, *The Later Ghaznavids: Splendour and Decay* (New York: Columbia University Press, 1977), 45–51.

20. See Muhammad Nazim, *The Life and Times of Sultan Mahmud of Ghazna* (New Delhi: Munshiram Manoharlal, 1971), 80–83; Bosworth, *Ghaznavids,* 53–54, 85–86.

21. On the importance of the theme of consultation in Bayhaqi's history, see Waldman, *Historical Narrative,* 103–4; Meisami, "Dynastic History," 70.

22. R. S. Humphreys, *Islamic History: A Framework for Enquiry* (Princeton: Princeton University Press, 1991), 143.

23. Ibid.

24. The brothers had been rivals for many years, and Mahmud pitted them against each other, often showing excessive favor to Muhammad at Mas'ud's expense. See TB 158–61; Nazim, *Sultan Mahmud,* 168–70; Bosworth, *Ghaznavids,* 227–29. The issue of a divided succession is an important one for Bayhaqi, and a number of his digressions, which concern Harun al-Rashid's division of his succession between his sons al-Amin and al-Ma'mun, point to the unwisdom of such a policy.

25. It may be asked why Muhammad was placed on the throne at all. Historians explain that he was currently the designated successor and that civil disorder, which would have occurred without a ruler on the throne, was avoided. Compare Abd al-Hayy Gardizi, *Zayn al akhbar* (Ornament of histories), ed. M. Nazim (Berlin: Iranschahr, 1928), 93–94; TB 5–6. It is clear that from the outset plans were set in motion to bring back Mas'ud.

26. This was Ali ibn Il Arslan (Ali Qarib), Mahmud's chief hajib, who had some kinship (by marriage?) with him; he later fell victim to Mas'ud's vendetta against those who had supported Mahmud's policies. See TB 56–70; Gardizi, *Zayn,* 92–93; Bosworth, *Ghaznavids,* 231–33.

27. Muhammad was at the time governor of the province of Guzganan.

28. Cf. Bayani, "Zan," 83–85.

29. See TB 300–302; Bosworth, *Ghaznavids,* 110, 232–33.

30. Not only noble but more ordinary women played a part in these intrigues. Singers, old women, and female servants often served as unofficial spies because they had access to the harem and to private chambers (cf. TB 145–46; Bosworth, *Ghaznavids,* 96). One such woman was the *mutriba* (musician and/or singer) Sitti Zarrin, who "was very close to Sultan Mas'ud, so much so that she was a sort of female chamberlain [*hajiba*] at the lower palace, and the sultan would give her messages for its inhabitants on every subject" (TB 510). It was Sitti Zarrin who gave Bayhaqi details about the jahaz of Bakalijar's daughter (see above). She and another singer, Andalib, provided the account of Mas'ud's marriage with Shah Khatun.

31. Lambton, *Medieval Persia,* 260, 259.

32. Nazim, *Sultan Mahmud,* 57; Bosworth, *Ghaznavids,* 237. Bayani ("Zan," 78) states that "Hurra-yi Khalji" was the wife of Abu al-Abbas and that "the Khwarazmshah Abu al-Hasan Ali had also taken to wife another of Sultan Mahmud's sisters." They are in fact the same person.

33. Bayani, "Zan," 78.

34. Nizam, *Sultan Mahmud,* 56–60.

35. Mas'ud also attempted to gain influence over the Seljuqs by proposing marriage alliances: "a daughter of the *amid* of Khurasan, Suri, for Yabghu, a daughter of the Ghaznavid amir Abdus for Tughril, and another free-born wife for Chaghri. But only Yabghu accepted Mas'ud's presents and was inclined to accept the proffered alliance, for the Seljuqs had by now become suspicious of the Sultan's good faith" (Bosworth, *Ghaznavids,* 243). Bayhaqi does not mention this; Bosworth suggests that "it fell within the lacuna of our text" (ibid., 302n.6). The sons of the Qarakhanid ruler of Bukhara and Samarqand Alitigin (d. 426/1034; see TB 603; Bosworth, *Ghaznavids,*

236) also sought alliances with Mas'ud after their father's death. In 428/1036, they sent an envoy to him suggesting three means of cementing good relations: that they be honored by a bride from Mas'ud's side, that a bride from their side be betrothed to one of Mas'ud's sons, and that Mas'ud arrange a peace between them and the Qarakh-anid Arslan Khan. Mas'ud, advised that they would be valuable allies, agreed, and appropriate arrangements were made (see TB 666–68).

36. In 416/1025, Bughra Khan had gone to Balkh, intending to proceed to Ghazna to claim his bride and seek Mahmud's help against Alitigin. Mahmud asked him to return home, since he himself was on the way to Somnath, saying that "meanwhile he . . . would probably succeed in defeating his rivals in Turkestan, and then it would be possible to conquer Transoxiana with their united forces. The prince understood perfectly the true character of such an answer and left Balkh feeling that he had been insulted"; W. Barthold, *Turkestan Down to the Mongol Invasion*, 2d ed. (London: Luzac, 1958), 285; see TB 693.

37. Bakalijar was the uncle of the young Ziyarid prince Anushirvan, who succeed-ed his father, Manuchihr ibn Qabus, to whom Mahmud had given a daughter in marriage. When Anushirvan died (possibly poisoned), Bakalijar assumed power and asked Mas'ud to confirm his rule; Mas'ud did so and sent envoys asking for the stip-ulated tribute and Bakalijar's daughter in marriage (TB 433–34). Bayani ("Zan," 75–77) suggests that Mas'ud's motive was to establish a claim over Ziyarid territories and speculates that the daughter "may have been able, for a while, to preserve her fami-ly's interests and status with Mas'ud" and stave off Ghaznavid aggression.

38. See Meisami, *Persian Historiography*, 95–98.

39. Bayani, "Zan," 80.

40. Ibid., 79.

41. Bayani identifies this woman as the wife of Bughratigin (ibid., 75). For the cor-rect identification, see Bosworth, *Ghaznavids*, 101.

42. Bayhaqi first met Abu Sa'id Abd al-Ghaffar in 421/1030 in Balkh, where he was employed in the chancery. Under Mas'ud's successors, he held various ambassado-rial posts; when Bayhaqi was writing his history, Abd al-Ghaffar was ra'is of Bust, residing in Ghazna. Bayhaqi had long wished to include an account of Mas'ud's youth in his history but had been unable to do so until, in 450/1058–59, he was approached by Abd al-Ghaffar, who provided him with both an oral and a written account (TB 130–32).

43. See Waldman, *Historical Narrative*, 108n.77.

44. On Hasanak, see Nazim, *Sultan Mahmud*, 136–37; Bosworth, *Ghaznavids*, 182–84. On his execution, see also Waldman, *Historical Narrative*, 93–94, 166–73; Meisami, "Exemplary Lives, Exemplary Deaths: The Execution of Hasanak," *Actas XVI Con-greso UEAI* (Salamanca: AECI, 1995) and *Persian Historiography*, 88–91.

45. Quoting the Qur'an 28:69.

46. Bayani, "Zan," 70–71.

47. Waldman, *Historical Narrative*, 104. She associates this topos further with the findings of cultural anthropologists to the effect that "in some Iranian tribes . . . women past child-bearing age become free to say the most outrageous things, things that younger women could not get away with" (ibid., 108n.8). She also views "the use of wise women to say important things" as a form of *taqiyya*, the dissimulation of

one's true beliefs and opinions, which she considers an informing feature of Bayhaqi's history (ibid., 104; see also 10–11 and passim).

48. Bayani ("Zan," 77) speculates that Mas'ud feared a claim on the throne from
Muhammad's sons. Muhammad was placed on the throne briefly after Mas'ud's
murder, although his son Ahmad exercised actual power. Muhammad and all but one
of his sons appear to have been killed by Mas'ud's son and successor Mawdud after
being defeated by him in battle (see Bosworth, *Later Ghaznavids,* 15–25).

49. On these events, see Bosworth, *Later Ghaznavids,* 17–19; Gardizi, *Zayn,* 109–10.

50. This is not the place to discuss "wise men," but we may note the importance
of such figures (notably Abu Nasr Mishkan) as conveyors of both practical and time-
less wisdom.

5 Women in the Seljuq Period

CAROLE HILLENBRAND

A woman is basically flesh, and flesh must be preserved. If it is not preserved, it begins to smell and then there is no cure for it. So treat women
with respect and give them what they want—but lock your door of your
house and keep other men away.

—Yusuf Khass Hajib, *Wisdom of Royal Glory*

THE SUBJECT of medieval women is a daunting one. The sources on which
to base generalizations do exist, but they are by their very nature often opaque
or difficult to evaluate. It is easy to exaggerate or distort evidence from a wide
variety of literary genres, geographical locations, and historical periods. The
Seljuq sultanate (1030–1190) was a key moment in medieval Iranian and Islamic history because it witnessed the arrival in the eastern provinces of the
Muslim world of many Turkish nomads organized along tribal lines. Their
irruption into Iran and subsequent infiltration into Anatolia and parts of
Syria brought new ways of life to the Islamic world.[1] The Seljuq period saw
the encounter between the long-Islamicized eastern Iranian provinces with
their high level of culture and scholarly achievement and the nomadic lifestyle of the Seljuq Turks only recently converted to Islam. What would be the
impact of the Islamic world on the freer way of life of the nomadic Turkish
women who came with the conquerors? Would the greater independence of
nomadic women have any influence at all on the lives of urban and rural
Muslim women?

This chapter assesses some of the existing evidence on which to answer
these two questions and to highlight some facets of women's lives in the
Seljuq period. The evidence discussed derives from the Seljuq world generally because the Seljuq sphere of influence was not restricted to Iran itself but

also included parts of Syria and Anatolia where the Rum Seljuqs ruled until the Mongol conquest (1243) and beyond.

The evidence used in this chapter comes from a wide variety of sources— Seljuq legal and literary works, historical chronicles, biographical dictionaries, monumental inscriptions, and works of art. Inevitably, the picture emerging will remain impressionistic. Not all facets of every social class of women in the Seljuq period can be addressed here, because evidence on some aspects of women's lives, especially those not from court circles, is virtually nonexistent.[2]

Women's Position: The Theoretical View of the Fuqaha and the Intelligentsia

The general position of women as laid down in the shari'a is well known. Works of Islamic jurisprudence (*fiqh*) followed a rigid format established over several centuries. By the Seljuq period, they contained a complete *Book of Marriage*. Al-Ghazali's magnum opus, *Ihya ulum al-din* (Revivifying of the sciences of religion), and his so-called summary of it in Persian, *Kimiya-yi sa'adat* (Alchemy of happiness), both contain lengthy discussions of marriage.[3] He discusses the importance of physical beauty in relation to other attributes that he deems necessary and desirable in a model wife. His basic message is clear: chastity before beauty. Enumerating the eight qualities to be sought in a wife—piety, good character, beauty, light dowry, fertility, virginity, good lineage, and a not-too-close kinship with the would-be husband—al-Ghazali puts beauty only third after piety and good character, and he cites the Prophet Mohammad as saying that a wife should be sought for her religion, not her beauty. Nevertheless, beauty is a desideratum in a wife since it evokes love and affection in a man. The woman's role in marriage should be in accordance with the Qur'an and sunna. She should be well treated and taught her duties as a Muslim wife and mother. Al-Ghazali's tone is firm but not overtly hostile to women.[4]

Another legist of the Seljuq period, Ibn al-Jawzi, devotes a complete work (*Kitab ahkam al-nisa*, Book of rules for women) to a discussion of the statutes governing women's conduct within Islam.[5] Chapter 24, on the topic of women's Friday prayer, reveals the view common to many medieval *fuqaha* (religious lawyers) that women are distracting in the mosque. Although Ibn al-Jawzi is forced to concede that women are entitled to pray in the Friday assembly—there are, after all, irrefutable hadiths confirming this—he then adduces some arguments raising doubts about the validity of this practice. On the question of the rows of worshippers in the mosque, he states that any prayer performed by men who line up behind women is invalid. Since it can happen that men arrive late at the mosque and are therefore forced to place themselves behind rows of women (who have arrived on time), it would be easier to suggest that women should not go to the mosque. On the permissibility of women's presence in the mosque, Ibn al-Jawzi judges that if they are fearful of creating disorder in the minds of men, it is preferable for them to remain at home. Aware, however, of the hadith in which the prophet states that the mosque should not be forbidden to women, Ibn al-Jawzi concludes that the Friday prayer in the mosque is not a duty for women. The placing of his subsequent chapter, entitled "Why women must avoid going out," is revealing.[6]

An amplified picture of the ideal role to be played by Muslim women in the Seljuq period emerges from contemporary works of *adab* (secular literature). These are permeated with perennial Near Eastern attitudes to women. Certain familiar stereotypes and themes appear, such as the dangers of women stepping outside their traditional domestic role and meddling in affairs of state. Such attitudes are found especially in the Mirrors for Princes literature, a genre that gives advice to the ruler on how to rule, usually through a series of edifying anecdotes.[7] The *Siyasatnama* (Book of government) of the Seljuq *wazir*, Nizam al-Mulk, is typical. In the work's second half, the author analyzes what has gone wrong with Seljuq government and suggests some solutions. Chapter 42, "On the subject of those who wear the veil," is devoted to women. The tone is profoundly negative. The chapter begins with an outspoken pronouncement that combines Islamic legal ideas with what some might call more universal, deep-seated prejudices about women and with the author's own practical experience of dealing firsthand with women at the Seljuq court: "The king's underlings must not be allowed to assume power, for this causes the utmost harm and destroys the king's splendour and majesty. This particularly applies to women for they are wearers of the veil and do not have complete intelligence."[8] Nizam al-Mulk goes on to stress that women's role is to procreate and to adopt a chaste and abstemious bearing. "But when the wives of the king begin to play the role of rulers, they base their orders on what interested parties tell them because they are not able to see things with their own eyes."[9] The whole fabric of the state is thus undermined, and he concludes with the harsh statement, "In all ages nothing but disgrace, infamy, discord and corruption have resulted when kings have been dominated by their wives."[10]

Although the edifying anecdotes that then follow are set in the dim and distant past—involving, as they traditionally did in the Mirrors genre, pre-Islamic Iranian figures such as Khusraw and Kayka'us as well as Adam and Eve and Alexander the Great—the chapter is given an Islamic coating with the Qur'anic quotation (4:34), "Men are in charge of women," and the hadith, "Consult women but whatever they say do the opposite and that will be right." Nizam al-Mulk comments sagely, "If women had been able to control themselves, God would not have set men over their heads."[11]

Another Persian Mirror for Princes (dating from the mid-twelfth century) is the anonymous *Bahr al-fava'id* (Sea of precious virtues). Book 7 in chapter 1 deals with the subject of children's education. Its author states that children (male) should be preserved from seven evils, the third of which is "association with women." He argues that constant contact with women makes young men effete. Such contamination can begin in early infancy. Indeed, even the suckling woman must be devout, for she can influence the baby at this stage through her nourishment.[12]

In chapter 11, book 16, the author exhorts men to teach their wives necessary religious knowledge—the rules of prayer, purification, and menstruation. Men must also treat their wives equally if they possess more than one. In sexual matters, the man should think not only of his own pleasure but should also seek to satisfy the woman since not to do so is weakness in a man.[13]

A third Mirror for Princes, existing in both Persian and Arabic versions, is *Nasihat al-muluk* (Counsel for kings), usually attributed to al-Ghazali.[14] This Mirror clearly springs from a Seljuq milieu and has pungent words to say on the topic of women, encapsulating no doubt much folk wisdom and familiar stereotypes. Some comments take the form of jokes, such as the following: "A sage wished his short wife were tall. People asked him, 'Why did you not marry a wife of full stature?' He answered, 'A woman is an evil thing and the less there is of an evil thing the better.'"[15]

Alternatively, women are likened to ten species of creatures; these include the pig and the ape: "The woman who resembles the pig in character knows full well how to eat, break crockery, and cram her stomach. . . . She always wears filthy clothes and an unpleasant smell emanates from her." As for the ape, "the woman who has the character and peculiarities of the ape concerns herself with clothes of many colors—green, red and yellow, with trinkets and jewels—pearls or rubies, and with gold and silver." The climax of the argument concerns the virtuous woman who "has the peculiarities of the sheep . . . in which everything is useful."[16]

Women's Roles: Evidence in Medieval Historical Sources

Descending from the ideal to reality, what did women in the Seljuq period actually do, as opposed to what Islamic law and the men of the turban prescribed that they should do? Certain aspects of women's lives may be taken for granted in this context: be they urban or rural Persians or nomadic Turks, their principal roles were those of wife and mother. Urban Persian women in the Seljuq period passed their time carrying out domestic responsibilities in the house and in spinning, weaving, and needlework. Some of them worked as craftswomen, servants, nurses, midwives, singing-girls, dancers, and prostitutes. Rural women (in areas such as Gilan and Tabaristan) performed similar duties in addition to undertaking considerable physical labor on the land.[17]

Nomadic Turkish women also worked hard looking after their husbands, children, and extended families; cooking; preparing furs and other garments; loading baggage carts; and tending animals. They were by all accounts toughened by the rigors of their difficult existence. The writings of travelers, both Muslim and European, though later than the Seljuq period, give a general picture of Turkish and Mongol nomadic life and suggest, as is well known, that women in this milieu enjoyed a greater degree of independence than their urban counterparts.[18] Ibn Battuta, a careful and well-informed observer who visited Turks in the Caucasus and Crimea, comments, "A remarkable thing which I saw in this country was the respect shown to women by the Turks."[19] In a mosque in Shiraz in Iran, Ibn Battuta was surprised at the impressive number of women who (despite the reluctance of the fuqaha already discussed) were there at the Friday prayer.[20]

Medieval Islamic painting provides artistic impressions of the physical appearance of Turkish women, both high-class and lowly, urban and nomadic.[21] These women are, however, seldom described in historical sources. A rare exception is the Nestorian theologian and physician of Baghdad Ibn Butlan (d. 1066), who wrote a treatise on how to buy slaves and how to detect bodily defects in them. Describing different kinds of slave-girls, he extols the physical qualities of Turkish women in particular: "Fair skinned, the Turkish women are full of grace and animation. Their eyes are small but enticing. They are thick-set and are inclined to be of short stature. There are very few tall women among them. They are prolific in breeding and their offspring are but rarely ugly. They are never bad riders. They are generous; they are

clean in their habits; they cook well; but they are unreliable."²² Thus speaks
the shrewd observer who combines medical knowledge with some commonly
held beliefs and prejudices. It would appear that women of the Seljuq Turkmans remained unveiled in accordance with the traditions of their nomadic
heritage. The evidence of Islamic painting indicates that women at the court
also were not always veiled.²³

The historical chronicles most frequently mention women in the context
of marriage alliances (and women are alluded to only rarely). Here women
were used in a complex network of political ties and family relationships. The
same emphasis emerges from a collection of biographies of women of the
ruling elite, by the Baghdad historian Ibn al-Saʿi.²⁴ This work includes elev-
en biographies from the Seljuq period, all dealing with the wives or concubines of caliphs or sultans. Within the rigid limitations of its genre it sheds
light on some aspects of the lives of royal women. The Seljuq sultans contracted marriages with high-ranking women of their family, usually cousins.
They also married women of the ruling families of neighboring Turkish
dynasties such as the Karakhanids and Artuqids.

From the beginning of Seljuq rule, women were used to cement alliances
for high political stakes, especially in the fragile relationship between caliph
and sultan. The most notorious example was the marriage of Sultan Tughril and the daughter of the caliph al-Qaʾim in 455/1063. The betrothal had
taken place two years earlier, although the caliph had erected all kinds of
obstacles to the match and had employed delaying tactics to what he perceived as a highly distasteful and politically dangerous marriage. On the personal level, al-Qaʾim's daughter, whose age is not mentioned, was probably
not enthusiastic at the prospect of enforced proximity to Tughril, a seventy-
year-old Turkish nomad, even if he was "sultan of the East and West." She
clearly considered him to be beneath her and did not rise for him when he
paid her ceremonial visits in the period preceding the wedding. The marriage proved short-lived; she was reprieved from her ordeal by Tughril's
death soon afterward.²⁵

Sometimes women were married off several times by their male relatives
in the course of a short period. One Seljuq princess, for example, the daughter
of Ridwan, married in succession three Turkman amirs of the Artuqid fami-
ly.²⁶ Once married, the woman usually stayed with her husband's family, even
after his death. If the widow was no longer remarriageable, she would still remain with her husband's clan. Occasionally it was possible for a high-ranking
woman to return to her own family after her husband's death or even before,
if she could put enough pressure on those empowered to permit her to do so.

Arslan Khatun, Sultan Tughril's niece, for example, left Baghdad with her uncle, having complained that her husband, the caliph, had repudiated her.[27]

In the case of a royal marriage, the bride's entry into the groom's city was a grand event. She was often carried on a bridal litter. Ibn Bibi, historian of the Seljuqs in Anatolia, describes how the bride of Ala al-Din Qayqubad I (r. 616–34/1219–37) was brought from Syria to her future husband: "The amirs and army commanders of Syria set up as a bridal litter seven pavilions of gold and silver; they decorated it with different jewels and attached it to the back of mules."[28]

A caliph's betrothal was also an opportunity for munificence. The Baghdad historian Ibn al-Jawzi describes how the caliph al-Muqtafi distributed jewels, camphor, and amber on the occasion of the drawing up of his marriage contract with Fatima Khatun, daughter of the Seljuq sultan Muhammad, in 531/1136.[29] A royal bride often received lavish gifts at the time of the wedding. When the caliph al-Mustazhir married Sayyida Khatun, daughter of the Seljuq sultan Malikshah, he gave his bride clothes, money, jewels, slave-girls, servants, and riding animals.[30]

Marriage consummation is a subject barely alluded to in the sources. It is noteworthy to mention in this context the delightfully overblown tone of the account of the wedding of the Seljuq sultan of Rum, Izz al-Din Kayka'us I (r. 607–16/1210–19) to an unnamed royal woman from Syria. The ceremony's climax is recorded in unusual detail and even with relish by Ibn Bibi:

> The wives of the amirs who were present went out of the city to receive the bridal litter. . . . Noblewomen stood on both sides to attend the illustrious bridal litter. They went to the royal bedchamber and lowered the princess onto the bridal throne of mercy and good fortune. The illustrious king then went into the bridal chamber. The noblewoman with cheeks like Venus went behind the curtain of the chamber. The Sun of Sultans placed his foot on the bed with the Moon of Noblewomen. Kneeling down, the servants of the princess loosened the footwear from their mistress' feet. The sultan lifted the cap of royal dignity from his head and loosened the fastener from the royal belt. And in pursuance of the authority given by the shari'a he removed the delectable seal from that illustrious letter.[31]

Sometimes powerful emotions of love and grief emerge from the stereotyped, laconic historical chronicles and biographical dictionaries to suggest close and harmonious bonds between caliphs or sultans and their wives or concubines. The devotion of the caliph al-Nasir to his wife, Saljuqa (or Saljuqi) Khatun, especially impressed the chroniclers and biographers. According to Ibn al-Sa'i, "Al-Nasir felt such sadness and grief at her death that he was prevented from eating and drinking for days. Her house, with all the clothes and household effects, was left exactly as it was for a number of years; it was not opened up and nothing was taken out of it." Devotion to his wife's memory then prompted al-Nasir to endow next to her funerary *turba* a splendid *ribat* with a spacious courtyard and a beautiful garden overlooking the Tigris, which watered it.[32]

Nor were daughters always the curse that popular tradition made them. Although the eleventh-century writer Yusuf Khass Hajib expresses the commonly held view about daughters, that "the best is that they are not born at all, or else that they do not survive,"[33] they were clearly cherished by the ruling families of the time. The second Artuqid ruler of Mardin, Timurtash, for example, is described by his chronicler, Ibn al-Azraq, as "grieving at the death" in childbirth of his daughter Nura Khatun in 546/1151.[34]

How much freedom of movement did Seljuq women enjoy outside the home? What were the accepted norms? These questions are difficult to answer on the basis of the sources. According to the evidence of Islamic painting, urban women were seen occasionally in the presence of the *qadi* (judge) in the shari'a court or in specially segregated sections of the mosque. Elite women were seen at court, where there were also female entertainers.[35] High-ranking women, such as the wives of amirs and notables, were expected to leave the city walls, albeit at night sometimes, to receive an incoming bride of a similar status to their own.[36] Such women are also mentioned as leaving cities to undertake peace negotiations after sieges. A fine example was the redoubtable battle-ax, the mother of the Mirdasid ruler of Aleppo, who made a truce with the Seljuq sultan Alp Arslan.[37]

Less acceptable was conduct unbecoming to Muslim women, conduct deviating from the norms laid down by Islamic law and social conventions. Historical sources occasionally mention instances of such conduct and sometimes hint at possible improprieties. One such instance occurred in 543/1149 in the Jazira when a certain royal woman, the *khatun*, daughter of Erzurum's ruler and wife of Akhlat's ruler, passed through the town of Hisn Kayfa on her way to perform the *hajj* (pilgrimage to Mecca). Shortly afterwards certain notables arrived, and the ruler of Hisn Kayfa contacted the amir of nearby Mardin. The result of their deliberations was that "they stopped the Khatun from going to the Hijaz, which is what the Shah-i Arman [her husband] had asked them to do."[38] The woman was then questioned and sent back home. Her subsequent fate is not mentioned.

Ibn Jubayr, a Muslim Spanish traveler who traversed the Islamic world in 579/1183, mentions a similar episode. It concerns three royal Turkish women, khatuns, who had actually been successful in reaching Mecca to perform the pilgrimage. He concentrates especially on one of these, Saljuqa bint Mas'ud, who has already been mentioned. She was the daughter of the Seljuq sultan of Konya. Having dwelt on her high status, Ibn Jubayr takes time to mention that this princess "went with her personal servants and retinue to Mecca on the Friday night. She returned at nightfall on Saturday, and the arrows of conjecture flew at random concerning the cause of the departure of this much indulged princess."[39] A whiff of impropriety still hovered about independent action, therefore, even during the hajj.

The major nondomestic activities of elite women involved pious works and more especially the patronage of architecture. Such occupations, although probably relatively rare, are mentioned in historical sources and were clearly regarded as laudable in the eyes of Muslim men. The involvement of certain royal and other high-ranking women, usually wives of amirs, in architectural patronage is also recorded in monumental inscriptions throughout the Seljuq domains in Anatolia, Syria, Iran, and Central Asia. It would be erroneous, however, to place too great an emphasis on women's role in this sphere, because statistically the number of monumental inscriptions that name women is still small. Of the thousand-odd Arabic inscriptions from the entire Islamic world that survive from the years of Seljuq power, fewer than one hundred relate to women, and of those only seven come from the Seljuq world.[40] Of course, the evidence of inscriptions is patchy and incomplete. It is dangerous to generalize on the basis of chance survivals, especially since in the case of the Seljuq realms the buildings suffered from the onslaught of successive waves of Mongol destruction.

Nevertheless, it is interesting to examine in closer detail those Seljuq inscriptions naming women. It is important to stress that these are found not only on humble tombstones but also on grander buildings such as mausolea, madrasas (religious schools), caravanserais, and on one occasion a mosque. Among these inscriptions is one dated 512/1118 in the name of the daughter of the Seljuq sultan Mahmud, Zumurrud Khatun, on the mausoleum of Ali al-Rida at Mashhad. It was this Seljuq princess who undertook the monument's renovation.[41] A curiosity is the inscription dated 519/1125 on a tomb in Mecca that housed the earthly remains of a woman named al-Jamaliyya Baltun bint Abdallah, who was singled out "for having suckled the imam al-Mustazhir," the Abbasid caliph.[42] In the same area, in the environs of Mecca at Mina, an inscription in the name of al-Mustazhir's wife records the fact that she had endowed that place as a *waqf* (pious bequest) for Sufi women.[43]

Perhaps the most grandiose of the Seljuq monuments bearing an inscription naming a woman is to be found on the caravanserai known as Ribat-i Sharaf in Khurasan. The inscription dated 549/1154–55 mentions that the monument was erected (more accurately, repaired and refurbished) through the care of the khatun, the queen of women, "the glory of the family of Afrasiyab." She is then named "Qutlugh Balka Sayyida Turkan, daughter of the khaqan [emperor or king]."[44] This was the wife of Sultan Sanjar himself. Another Seljuq royal woman from Rum, Mahperi Khatun, erected five madrasas and a mosque at Kayseri.[45]

In the sphere of architectural patronage, the extant epigraphic evidence is corroborated fully in historical sources, both dynastic chronicles and biographical dictionaries. A few notable examples of textual evidence will suffice here. Isma Khatun bint Malikshah, wife of the caliph al-Mustazhir, was buried in a madrasa in Isfahan that she had endowed in favor of the Hanafi *madhhab* (school of law).[46] An even more active patron of architecture was Banafsha bint Abdallah al-Rumiyya, a specially favored concubine of the caliph al-Mustadi. She endowed a waqf on her house for it to be used as a madrasa and also built two bridges and a mosque in Baghdad.[47]

This prominent role of Seljuq royal women, proved both from epigraphic and textual evidence, in the sphere of architectural patronage raises some important issues.[48] Monumental inscriptions are highly public in nature, designed to record for posterity the names of those mentioned in them. There was thus clearly no ignominy attached to the public display of the names of prominent Seljuq women. Moreover, the vast majority of monuments founded by such women are Islamic foundations, that is, religious buildings. Public welfare, in this case the safety of travelers (often regarded as a royal responsibility), is the function of the caravanserai known as Ribat-i Sharaf, a grandiose structure, founded by a Seljuq royal woman whose name is writ large, literally and metaphorically, on it. Nor are these inscriptions mentioning women tucked away in remote corners of the Islamic world. A woman's name was engraved on the holy mausoleum of Ali al-Rida at Mashhad. Ibn Jubayr, describing the Seljuq princess of Rum, Saljuqa Khatun, comments, "She has provided many good works upon the pilgrim road, among them being public water works." He also points out that about a hundred camels were needed to transport her clothing and provisions for her journey to Mecca.[49] As seen above, women's names are also found in the heart of the religious center of Islam, Mecca, for successive generations of pilgrims to view when they arrived to perform the ceremonies of the hajj.[50]

Coupled with the costs of architectural patronage was largesse dispensed in acts of piety. The sources stress the virtue, piety, and charity of Seljuq women.[51] An especially noteworthy example appears to have been Shahan, the freedwoman of the caliph al-Mustansir. According to her biography as recorded by Ibn al-Sa'i, she enjoyed the use of large sums of money because of her highly favored status with the caliph. Quoting a verbal report from one of her household staff, Ibn al-Sa'i mentions that the monthly bill for work carried out for her by tinsmiths, cloth merchants, coppersmiths, jewelers, and other craftsmen exceeded one hundred thousand dinars. Shahan was well known for her generosity to the poor, widows, and orphans. Even after al-Mustansir's death she continued to receive generous grants of money from the new caliph, al-Musta'sim, who established her comfortably in Banafsha's house. Her retinue seems to have included numerous slave-girls, servants, and retainers.[52] This information, as well as other references in historical sources to the independent financial status of Seljuq royal women, goes far to explain how they were able to expend wealth of their own on buildings and pious deeds.

In the area of women's intellectual life, the sources yield less evidence. For example, Ibn Khallikan's biographical dictionary, *Wafayat al-a'yan,* a vast collection of biographies of prominent persons in the Islamic world until his own time, includes only seven biographies devoted to women, of which only three date from the Seljuq period.[53] Two of them were religious scholars. The first, Zaynab bint al-Shari (d. 615/1218–19), came from Nishapur. Ibn Khallikan names the teacher under whom she studied Islamic law, and he mentions that she obtained certificates authorizing her to teach. He describes her as a "woman of great instruction."[54] The second, Shuhda al-Katiba, Fakhr al-Nisa (pride of women), was the wife of al-Anbari, a prominent notable at the court of the Abbasid caliph al-Muqtafi. She is accorded high praise by Ibn Khallikan: "By her learning, she acquired an extensive reputation and ranked among the first scholars of the age; she wrote a beautiful hand and instructed great numbers in the Traditions, which she had received from the highest authorities."[55]

The third biography of a Seljuq woman included by Ibn Khallikan is that of a poet, Takiya bint Ghayth. Although she lived in Ayyubid Damascus, she is worth mentioning because Ibn Khallikan portrays her as a formidable old woman with the characteristics of wisdom and wit found in the stereotypes of women in Arabic and Persian adab (secular) literature. Indeed, she is shown to have had the last word, even with princes. The Ayyubid prince of Damascus, on reading a poem of hers in which she describes a party with wine drinking, said, "The old lady knows all those things from her youth." Takiya, on hearing his comment, decided to teach him a lesson. She composed another ode, this time about war, which she described perfectly. She then sent it to the prince saying, "My acquaintance with that [wine] is like my acquaintance with this [war]."

These three female biographies concern women of intellectual achievement. They were not from the milieu of the palace but presumably from the middle class. Occasionally a Seljuq royal woman is also mentioned as having intellectual merit. For example, according to Ibn al-Jawzi, the wife of the caliph al-Muqtafi, Fatima Khatun, daughter of the Seljuq sultan Muhammad, could read and write.[56]

What of the historically recorded, rather than alleged, political role of women in the Seljuq period? How justified were the antagonism and suspicion of Muslim writers of Mirrors for Princes toward women meddling in politics? The relationship between the Seljuq wazir Nizam al-Mulk and the wives of Alp Arslan and Malikshah may well have influenced the views on women expressed in his *Siyasatnama*. Certainly, it is likely that his attempts to discipline and restrict Malikshah's redoubtable wife, Terken Khatun, caused her to machinate against him and plot his downfall. The fact that Seljuq royal women had their own financial resources, granted to them by their husbands or sons, allowed them to enjoy some political influence; they could draw on the support of their own slaves or suborn the military. After the murder of Nizam al-Mulk in 1092, allegedly at the hand of the Assassins, Terken Khatun tried unsuccessfully to install her young son Mahmud on the throne. The evidence of the Seljuq historian al-Husayni is telling: "Terken Khatun had an immense influence over affairs during the days of Malikshah. [The first reason for this was that] she used to treat the soldiers kindly. . . . The second reason was that she belonged to the family of Turkish kings of Afrasiyab. The third reason was that the money was in her hands."[57] In his biography of Terken Khatun, Ibn al-Sa'i writes, Sultan Mahmud "took power after him [Malikshah], under the administration of his mother. She had with her around 10,000 Turkish mamluks. She ran the kingdom and led the armies until she died in Ramadan 487. When she died, the position of her son Mahmud collapsed."[58]

Royal women such as Terken Khatun played a dangerous game and often suffered a violent death. Later in the Seljuq period Inanch Khatun proposed marriage to Sultan Tughril II and lured him by mentioning her financial assets: "Now that God has made you ruler of your father's territories, I am one of your servants. I have a large amount of treasures and tremendous riches."[59] Tughril took the bait and duly married her. Then he had her killed.

The Seljuq period is punctuated with similar episodes demonstrating the

political involvement of royal women and, above all, the ruler's wife or concubine. The death of a sultan or amir was often concealed until the accession of the woman's son was safely assured by winning the support of the
military and gaining possession of the citadel and the treasury. One such
instance involved the khatun, daughter of Tughtegin of Damascus and wife
of Il-Ghazi, the Artuqid ruler of Mayyafariqin. Her husband died outside the
city in 1122. She and her son Sulayman brought the body as far as the gate of
Mayyafariqin, whereupon they placed Il-Ghazi upright on his horse and
maneuvered access into the city. Il-Ghazi's death was announced publicly
only when they had taken firm control of the citadel and the khatun's son
had been declared the new ruler.[60] The aim of such a subterfuge was not just
to secure the succession for her son but, more important, to ensure that she
herself would enjoy the power and privilege of being the ruler's mother. A
mother's involvement in state affairs, however, was often far from maternal.
The Seljuq prince Duqaq, for example, was allegedly poisoned by his own
mother with a bunch of grapes.[61]

Royal women influenced the actual running of state affairs. A telling example is that of the mother of the Seljuq sultan Arslan (d. 1175). According
to Rawandi, this woman even saw to the needs of the army and participated
in military campaigns.[62]

Rivalry, often intense, between wives and concubines contributed to the
general male perspective of lawyers and administrators that women's influence in the political sphere was pernicious. Of the eleven biographies of
Seljuq women included by Ibn al-Sa'i in his book, six cover the concubines
of caliphs and sultans. As well as sharing the virtuous attributes of piety and
good works, such women were known to work vigorously and unscrupulous-
ly to further the aspirations of their sons and their own share of political
power. In the later Seljuq period, for example, Inanch Khatun, wife of Pah-
lawan, complained bitterly to her husband that his two sons by a Turkish slave
mother had been given preferential treatment. "How can it please you that
the son of a slave-woman should be higher in status than my two sons?"[63]

Another example of women's involvement in politics concerns the fifth
Artuqid ruler of Hisn Kayfa (d. 581/1185). In accordance with traditional practice, he had married Saljuqa Khatun, daughter of Kilij Arslan II, but he fell
in love with a singing-girl whom he also took to wife. Soon she controlled
his kingdom and his purse. Saladin later made this uxorious vassal of his send
the singing-girl away.[64]

Although royal women in the Seljuq period were sometimes unscrupulous and ambitious, they were also sometimes praised for their qualities of

good leadership, determination, and high intelligence. Shahan, the freed-woman of al-Mustansir, presided over a *mazalim* court (which handled the redress of grievances) in her own right and had the status and prestige to see that her judgments were implemented.[65]

Conclusion

Inevitably, women in the Seljuq period led the same lives and shared the same fate as other women during the Islamic Middle Ages. Their domain was the home, their responsibilities were domestic and familial, and their lifestyle was circumscribed by Islamic social norms. Muslim men hedged them about with restrictions of movement and firm rules of behavior. Urban women fared worse than their rural counterparts, for urban women were valued possessions to be guarded. As al-Jahiz had observed in the Abbasid period, "The only purpose of high walls, stout doors, thick curtains, eunuchs, handmaids, and servants is to protect them [women] and to safeguard the pleasure they give."[66]

Yet it would appear that women learned strategies to loosen the constraints of their male-dominated society. The epigraphic, artistic, and textual evidence for the Seljuq period suggests that the evidence of the ulama's writings should be treated with caution: they speak about what should be rather than what is. It seems irrefutable that women of rank in the Seljuq period were not sim-ply underlings; especially after they had borne male children they were able to wield considerable political power and influence. Moreover, the stereotype is fleshed out in anecdotes from actual Seljuq historical chronicles. Young women are cited only as beloved daughters or as names in marriage contracts. But once liberated from her role as a sex object, a high-standing Seljuq wom-an was free to develop other aspects of her life.

Was there any perceptible shift in women's roles with the advent of Sel-juq nomads into the eastern Islamic world? It would certainly be misleading and dangerous to generalize here. The evidence discussed in this chapter, although restricted chronologically to the Seljuq period, is not hermetically sealed within that period. Earlier information from Buyid times and later data from Mongol sources reveal a much more nuanced chronology.[67] Evidence from Ibn al-Sa'i, for example, indicates persuasively that the court women of the early and middle Abbasid period are depicted as witty, cultivated, and skilled in poetry and music. The shift toward piety and good works, so prev-alent among elite Seljuq women, may well have occurred, or begun to occur, more than a century before the coming of the Seljuqs.[68]

The evidence adduced in this chapter strongly corroborates the view expressed by Ibn Jubayr, who came to the Seljuq domains from the extreme west of the Muslim world. He is struck by what to him anyway is a novelty—Turkish women of high rank, in whom, as he himself describes it, "there is this most strange combination of pious works and regal pride."[69]

Seljuq women often plotted, bribed, and murdered. They are portrayed as machinating and conniving, vigorous and effective. In any case, they were not to be ignored. They possessed, moreover, the social position and financial means necessary to exercise political power, to perform public acts of charity, to enhance the prestige of their menfolk and families, and to display the impeccable religious credentials associated with these latest converts to Islam.

NOTES

An earlier version of this chapter appeared as "Seljuq Women," in *The Balance of Truth: Essays in Honour of Professor Geoffrey Lewis,* ed. Cigdem Balim-Harding and Colin Imber (Istanbul: Isis Press, 2000), 145–63.

1. For an overview of the Seljuqs in Iran, see *Cambridge History of Iran* (Cambridge: Cambridge University Press, 1968), vol. 5, chaps. 1, 2.

2. The evidence cited in this chapter has been deliberately chosen to supplement data given by A. K. S. Lambton in her discussion on Seljuq and Mongol women. See Lambton, *Continuity and Change in Medieval Persia* (Albany: State University of New York Press, 1988), 258–96.

3. Al-Ghazali, *Ihya ulum al-din* (Revivifying of the sciences of religion) (Cairo: Matba'a al-istiqama, 1967), 2:27–77; al-Ghazali, *Kimiya-yi sa'adat* (Alchemy of happiness), ed. H. Khedivjam (Tehran: Ilmi va farhangi, 1976), 1:301–23.

4. Ibid.

5. Beirut: Manshurat al-maktaba al-asriyya, 1981.

6. See F. Mernissi, *Sultanes oubliées* (Paris: Albin Michel, 1990), 113.

7. See C. E. Bosworth, "Administrative Literature," in *Cambridge History of Arabic Literature, Religion, Learning, and Science in the Abbasid Period* (Cambridge: Cambridge University Press, 1990), 165–67.

8. Nizam al-Mulk, *Book of Government or Rules for Kings,* trans. H. Darke (London: Routledge and Kegan Paul, 1978), 179ff.

9. Ibid., 179.

10. Ibid., 179–80.

11. Ibid., 186.

12. See *The Sea of Precious Virtues (Bahr al-fava'id),* trans. J. S. Meisami (Salt Lake City: University of Utah Press, 1991), 80.

13. Ibid., 163.

14. Al-Ghazali, *Ghazali's Book of Counsel for Kings,* trans. F. R. C. Bagley (London: Oxford University Press, 1971).

15. Ibid., 163.

16. Ibid., 165–66.

17. See F. B. Spuler, *Iran in früh-islamischer Zeit* (Wiesbaden: Franz Steiner Verlag, 1952), 281–82.

18. It is perhaps unwise to generalize about the lives of nomadic women across several centuries and in different geographical areas. Nevertheless, the lifestyles of many Central Asian nomadic pastoralists—be they Turk or Mongol (and the sources often do not distinguish between them)—are unlikely to have changed greatly from the eleventh to the fourteenth centuries. The evidence of fourteenth-century European merchants and envoys who visited the Mongol court, for example, gives a general picture of the nomadic life they encountered en route. They note that nomadic women even participated in military campaigns. A vivid evocation of such women is to be found in the enigmatic, undated, and unprovenanced paintings associated with the name Siyah Qalam. See M. S. Ipsiroğlu, *Vollständige Faksimile Ausgabe der Blätter des Meisters Siyah Qalem* (Graz: Akademische Druck und Verlagsanstalt, 1976), plates 18, 24.

19. Ibn Battuta, *The Travels of Ibn Battuta*, trans. H. A. R. Gibb (London: Routledge, 1929), 1:146.

20. Ibid.

21. See A. S. Melikian-Chirvani, *Arts Asiatiques: Numéro spécial, Le roman de Varqe et Golshah* (1970); R. Ettinghausen, *Arab Painting* (Cleveland: World Publishing Company, 1962), 91.

22. Ibn Butlan, *Risala fi shira al-raqiq wa taghlib al-abid*, quoted in part in A. Mez, *The Renaissance of Islam*, trans. S. K. Bakhsh and D. S. Margoliouth (Patna: Jubilee Printing and Publishing House, 1937), 162.

23. See B. Faris, *Signes musulmanes et vision chrétienne* (Cairo: Mémoires de l'institut d'Egypte, 1961), plate 2.

24. *Jihat al-a'imma al-khulafa, min al-dara'ir wa'l-ima*, ed. M. Jawad (Cairo: n.p., 1960).

25. Ibn Khallikan, *Wafayat al-a'yan*, trans. Baron W. M. de Slane (Beirut: Librairie du Liban, 1970), 1843–71, 3:227–28; al-Husayni, *Akhbar al-dawlat al-saljuqiyya*, ed. M. Iqbal (Lahore: Panjab University Oriental Publications, 1933), 80; Ibn al-Athir, *Al-Kamil fi'l tarikh*, ed. C. J. Tornberg (Leiden: Brill, 1851–76), 10:16. See also G. Makdisi, "The Marriage of Tughril Beg," *International Journal of Middle Eastern Studies* 1 (1970): 259–75.

26. Their names were Balak, Sulayman, and Timurtash. See C. Hillenbrand, *A Muslim Principality in Crusader Times* (Leiden: Nederlands Historisch-Archaeologisch Instituut te Istanbul, 1990), 82, 145.

27. Ibn al-Athir, *Al-Kamil fi'l tarikh*, 10:16.

28. K. Erdmann, *Ibn Bibi als kunsthhistorische Quelle* (Istanbul: Istanbul Nederlands Historisch-Archaeologisch Instituut in Het Nabije Oosten, 1962), 23.

29. Ibn al-Jawzi, *Al-Muntazam fi tarikh al-muluk wa'l umam* (Hyderabad: Matba'a da'irat al-ma'arif al-uthmaniyya, 1940), 10:67; also Ibn al-Athir, *Al-Kamil fi'l tarikh*, 11:31.

30. Al-Husayni, *Akhbar al-dawlat*, 81.

31. Erdmann, *Ibn Bibi*, 23.

32. Ibid., 115–19.

33. Ibid., 187.

34. Two daughters had now predeceased him. See Hillenbrand, *Muslim Principality*, 141.

35. See *The Genius of Arab Civilisation,* ed. J. R. Hayes (Oxford: Phaidon, 1978), 51.

36. See Ibn al-Athir, *Al-Kamil fi'l tarikh,* 9:424.

37. See Ibn al-Adim, *Bughyat al-talab fi tarikh Halab,* partial edition by A. Sevim (Ankara: Türk Tarih Kurumu Basimevi, 1982), 16–39.

38. Hillenbrand, *Muslim Principality,* 121.

39. Ibn Jubayr, *The Travels of Ibn Jubayr,* trans. R. J. C. Broadhurst (London: Jonathan Cape, 1952), 189.

40. See *Répertoire chronologique d'épigraphie arabe,* vols. 7–9 (Cairo: Imprimerie de l'Institut français d'archéologie orientale, 1936–37). Most inscriptions mentioning women are found on tombstones.

41. Ibid., inscription no. 2978.

42. Ibid., inscription no. 3017.

43. Ibid., inscription no. 2977.

44. See A. Godard, "Khurasan Robat Sharaf," *Athar-i Iran* 4 (1) (1949): 13.

45. See Ülkü Bates, "Women as Patrons of Architecture in Turkey," in *Women in the Muslim World,* ed. L. Beck and N. Keddie (Cambridge: Harvard University Press, 1978), 245.

46. Ibn al-Sa'i, *Jihat al-a'imma,* 109.

47. Ibid., 111–15.

48. See Bates, "Women as Patrons," 245ff.

49. Ibid., 190.

50. Perhaps the relationship between the women mentioned in the inscriptions and specific Abbasid caliphs was a factor in their being "permitted" in Mecca. The prestige of their architectural patronage no doubt redounded on the caliphs themselves.

51. See H. Kilpatrick, "Some Late Abbasid and Mamluk Books about Women," unpublished paper, 1993.

52. Ibid.

53. De Slane's English translation (Ibn Khallikan, *Wafayat al-a'yan*) is more than 2,600 pages in length. For women in other biographical dictionaries, see Bulliet's chapter in this volume.

54. Ibn Khallikan, *Wafayat,* 1:551.

55. Ibid., 1:625.

56. Ibid., 1:276.

57. See al-Husayni, *Akhbar al-dawlat,* 74.

58. Ibid., 131–32.

59. Ibid., 184.

60. Hillenbrand, *Muslim Principality,* 44–45.

61. Ibn Khallikan, *Wafayat,* 1:274.

62. Rawandi, *Rahat al-sudur,* ed. M. Iqbal (London: Luzac, 1921), 290–93.

63. Al-Husayni, *Akhbar al-dawlat,* 175.

64. Ibn al-Athir, *Al-Kamil fi'l tarikh,* 11:307–8; Sibt b. al-Jawzi, *Mir'at al-zaman* (Hyderabad: Da'irat al-ma'arif al-uthmaniyya, 1951), vol. 8, part 1, 360.

65. Ibn al-Sa'i, *Jihat al-a'imma*, 122.

66. See C. Pellat, *The Life and Works of Jahiz* (London: Routledge and Kegan Paul, 1969), 257.

67. See B. Spuler, *Die Mongolen in Iran* (Berlin: Akademie-Verlag, 1955), 395–98.

68. Kilpatrick, "Some Late Abbasid and Mamluk Books."

69. Ibn Jubayr, *Travels*, 190.

6   Women in Timurid Dynastic Politics

BEATRICE FORBES MANZ

STUDIES ON DYNASTIC WOMEN in the Middle East show wide variations in their positions. Scholars often attribute such differences to the existence of competing ideologies: an Islamic ideology mandating seclusion set against Turkic and Mongol customs allowing women a relatively high and public position. Divergent traditions, however, do not explain the differences we see among dynasties of similar backgrounds. We need to consider more seriously the practical functions women filled in various Islamic societies to understand what determined their status.[1] In examining the history of women within the Timurid dynasty (771–913/1370–1507), which followed the Mongols in Iran and Central Asia, I move away from issues of tradition and approach the analysis of women's roles from a political standpoint in order to judge how women were affected by the structures of dynastic power. I examine two major issues: the function women filled in political life and whether or not contemporaries viewed their activity as legitimate.

What is immediately noticeable about Timurid women is the importance of their public role. Women were integral members of the group around the ruler, conspicuous in dynastic receptions, festivals, and weddings, and were major patrons of architecture. One can attribute their prominence partially to the Turco-Mongol heritage of the Timurids, but I would suggest that the primary explanation lies in the centrality of family relationships in the politics and legitimation of the Timurid dynasty. Like other rulers, Timurid sovereigns faced a crucial challenge: the need to maintain the collective prestige and charisma of the ruling family while retaining power over its individual members. Timurid rulers tried to attach and control their blood relatives and their followers by structuring them into an extended ruling family of which the sovereign was the patriarch. In this they resembled many other dynasties. What was somewhat less common was their practice of enhancing dynastic legitimacy through marriage with the house of Chinggis Khan. Women played a crucial part in both of these endeavors.

The Timurids as an In-Law Dynasty

When Temur came to the throne in Transoxiana in 771/1370, he had not inherited power but seized it, and from the beginning of his reign he used marriage as a way to gain legitimacy. In the Mongol world to which he belonged, only the descendants of Chinggis Khan could rightfully wield sovereign power. Since Temur was not of Chinggisid descent, he ruled through a puppet khan and strengthened his connection to the house of Chinggis Khan by marrying into it. He took one Chinggisid wife when he came to power and another later in his life. As his sons and grandsons matured, he found Chinggisid wives for many of them, giving them the right to the title of *guregen* (royal son-in-law), which Temur and some of his descendants displayed prominently on coins and in documents.[2] Temur's son and successor, Shahrukh (r. 811–50/1409–47), also took a Chinggisid wife but chose not to use the title; Shahrukh's son Ulugh Beg married two descendants of Chinggis Khan and featured the title prominently.[3] Ulugh Beg's Chinggisid marriages were arranged by Temur during his lifetime, and Shahrukh sought Chinggisid brides for a younger son, Muhammad Juki. In 812/1409–10, Shahrukh requested a bride from the khan of the Golden Horde but was sent instead the daughter of a powerful *amir* (tribal leader). In 821–22/1418–19, he applied to the Moghul or eastern Chaghadayid khan and received the daughter of the former khan, Sham'-i Jahan.[4] Abu Sa'id, who between 855/1451 and 862/1458 wrested power from the line of Shahrukh, likewise took a Chinggisid wife and the title guregen.[5]

The Timurids celebrated royal weddings with great pomp, and Chinggisid wives elicited particular ceremony. When in 800/1397 Temur married Tokel Khanim, the daughter of the Chinggisid Khidr Khwaja Oghlan, he sent dynastic women and amirs on a fifteen-day journey to meet her, and at every stage on their return they organized a feast. A new palace was named for her.[6] The wedding Shahrukh organized for Muhammad Juki's Chinggisid bride was an equally grand occasion. The bride, Mihr Nigar Khanim, arrived with a large suite, and Shahrukh's wife Gawharshad prepared a magnificent celebration and pitched a great tent in the Bagh-i Zaghan of Herat with a pavilion for each woman and prince.[7]

Chinggisid descent was an important asset for a dynastic woman. The prestige it could bestow is illustrated by the position of Temur's chief wife Saray Malik Khanim, daughter of the Chinggisid Qazan Khan who ruled Transoxiana in the 740s/1340s. She is mentioned frequently in the histories of Temur's reign and often accompanied him on campaigns. The Spanish ambassador Clavijo identified Saray Malik as Temur's senior wife; she had the largest tent enclosure among his wives and presided with Temur at his reception of foreign ambassadors, and she sat in front of the other royal women, accompanied by a magnificent suite.[8] Another prestigious Chinggisid princess was Khanzada, descended through her mother from Uzbek Khan of the Golden Horde. She was married first to Temur's senior son, Jahangir, and after Jahangir's death to Temur's third son, Amiranshah.[9] Although she quarreled with Amiranshah and after 801/1399 no longer lived with him, she retained a position of respect, now within the suite of Temur himself, where she is mentioned among the princesses. Her status was noted by Clavijo whom she entertained at Temur's court in 807/1404.[10]

Within the dynasty, marriage helped to legitimize the seizure of power by new branches of the family. Each of the major Timurid rulers—Shahrukh (r. 811–50/1409–47), Abu Sa'id (r. 855–73/1451–69), and Sultan Husayn Bayqara (r. 873–911/1470–1506)—displaced previously established lines of the dynasty. Shahrukh, Temur's youngest son, took the place of Pir Muhammad b. Jahangir, whom Temur had designated as heir on his deathbed. Abu Sa'id, descended from Temur's third son, Amiranshah, pushed out Shahrukh's descendants. Sultan Husayn, descended from Temur's eldest son, Umar Shaykh, took Khorasan from the line of Abu Sa'id. There is evidence that the transfer of power from one dynastic line to another was not accepted as a matter of course and required justification.[11] Shahrukh married numerous children and grandchildren to the descendants of Jahangir, especially those of Temur's original heir apparent, Muhammad Sultan, whose mother was a Chinggisid. Abu Sa'id married two descendants of Shahrukh: the daughter of Shahrukh's son Ulugh Beg and the daughter of Shahrukh's grandson Ala al-Dawla. Many children of these last marriages were named after their mothers' ancestors and took names such as Shahrukh, Baysunghur, and

Gawharshad.[12] Sultan Husayn strengthened his position by marrying a
daughter of Abu Sa'id, and after a few months when he found he could not
get along with her, he took her sister in her place.[13]

Since dynastic women connected the Timurid rulers both to the charisma of the Chinggisid house and to other lines of the dynasty, it is not surprising that they should have held a conspicuous ceremonial position. Several had their own garden palaces.[14] Their position is vividly described by
Clavijo, who was entertained separately by Temur's chief wife Saray Malik
Khanim and by his daughter-in-law Khanzada. The feasts these women arranged resembled those of Temur and other members of the Timurid dynasty.
They were held in the princesses' tents and featured much drinking and eating by both sexes.[15] For the later period we have no detailed descriptions, but
it is evident that women continued to play an important ceremonial role.
Their involvement in public occasions emerges from the reports about Shahrukh's powerful and visible wife, Gawharshad. Her part in celebrating the
marriage of Muhammad Juki was mentioned above. She also prepared a feast
on the first *id* (Islamic festival) after the death of her son Baysunghur in 837/
1433; Shahrukh organized a great celebration, and Gawharshad supervised
preparations and for several days arranged public meals.[16] When in 820/1417
ambassadors from the emperor of China arrived at Shahrukh's court, they
brought presents to princes and royal women by name.[17]

The Ruling Family

While women were important as links to various centers of power and charisma, they were even more crucial as agents of cohesion within the dynastic family. When Temur became sovereign he removed himself and his family and followers from the tribal society to which they belonged and placed
them as a special group above the rest. His personal followers were bound
to the dynasty through their appointments as guardians (or watchdogs) over
youthful princes and by marriage into Temur's family.[18] Like most medieval
kings, Timurid rulers were at once heads of state and patriarchs of an extended family that they managed with care. Both the idea and the reality of family were of central importance. The dynasty ruled by virtue of its descent from
Temur, whose image as conqueror and dynastic founder provided much of
its legitimacy.[19]

It was not easy to hold the royal lineage together. Too many people wanted the same prize, and there were too many sources of tension. Even strong

rulers suffered from insubordination or rebellion among their relatives, and their deaths unleashed destructive succession struggles. Each new Timurid ruler thus had to reconstitute around himself a group of family and followers, bound to him by ties of blood and personal loyalty and tying him to other branches of the dynasty and to members of the military class. Marriage among members of the dynasty began under Temur and continued to be important.[20]

Both Temur and his descendants married extensively into the families of their followers.[21] Although clearly inferior to members of the dynasty, senior amirs held great prestige, and their daughters could hold high positions as royal wives. Temur's wife Tumen Agha, daughter of the powerful amir Musa Taychi'ut, seems to have been only slightly less prominent than Saray Malik Khanim. Her position remained an issue even after Temur's death. She was persistently demanded as a wife by the dynasty's follower Shaykh Nur al-Din and was eventually handed over to him, although this marriage was considered disgracefully below her. When Nur al-Din rebelled and was defeated, Shahrukh rescued her, ceremoniously received her at the capital, and established her on her personal estates.[22] Shahrukh's wife Gawharshad, the daughter of a close follower of Temur, apparently held a higher position than even Shahrukh's Chinggisid wife Malikat Agha.

Having created an extended family group around himself, each Timurid ruler had to control it, which required considerable effort. Rulers took charge of forming and managing the relationships of those around them, arranging not only marriages but also birth and child rearing. Subordinate princes under the supervision of their appointed guardians began to lead armies and serve as provincial governors in their early teens, yet even as adults they exercised little control over their family life. The court historian Hafiz-i Abru reports that when Temur heard that a woman within the dynasty was pregnant, he assigned a guardian for the child, took charge of preparations for the birth, and gave directions on education.[23] Princely marriage and child rearing remained the sovereign's concern also under Shahrukh, who in most other ways allowed his princely governors to act with some autonomy. We can cite as an example Shahrukh's actions on hearing of the pregnancy of Aka Biki, wife of his son Ulugh Beg and daughter of Temur's first appointed heir, Muhammad Sultan b. Jahangir. Shahrukh sent for her to come to Herat, and she was met outside the city by royal women who escorted her to Bagh-i Zaghan where they had prepared for her a feast of several days with games and entertainments. When her daughter Khanzada was born, Shahrukh distributed presents and appointed nurses for the infant.[24]

Timurid rulers strengthened their hold on their family by removing children from their parents' care. Royal children, both boys and girls, were almost always entrusted as infants to people other than their mothers; these were often wives of the ruler or high-ranking amirs and their wives.[25] When Temur's grandson Ibrahim b. Shahrukh was born in 796/1394, for instance, Temur heard the news from Saray Malik and charged another wife, Tumen Agha, with the infant while appointing as guardian his close follower Uthman Abbas, whose wife Sadiqin Agha was a relative of Temur's and was to be Ibrahim's nurse. Ibrahim spent his childhood among Temur's wives, together with many of Temur's other grandchildren.[26]

Shahrukh's wife Gawharshad had charge of the education of Ulugh Beg's son Abd al-Latif, his daughter Hasiba Sultan Khanzada, and Baysunghur's son Ala al-Dawla.[27] Many of the ruler's grandchildren thus spent their childhood at the central court, and the ruler arranged and celebrated their circumcisions and marriages.[28] This practice was probably designed to avoid the formation of sub-dynasties in provinces governed by Timurid princes and to prevent dynastic women from promoting their own children at the expense of others. It contrasts with the Ottoman solution to the problem of family factions, which centered on control over sexual activity and reproduction.[29]

Women were important actors within the circle surrounding the ruler. In accounts of delegations sent to meet dynastic members, travels to and from cities, deaths of rulers, and removal of corpses to the capital city, we find princes, amirs, and dynastic women mentioned together.[30] For instance, in 830/1427 after a failed assassination attempt on his life, Shahrukh gave thanks for his recovery and scattered favors to the populace as did princes, in-laws, great amirs, and royal women.[31] Shahrukh's wife Gawharshad was prominent on many dynastic occasions. In 820/1417, she is mentioned in the suite of women, princes, and amirs who left the capital to welcome the prince Ulugh Beg on his arrival from Samarqand. In 831/1427, at the birth of Aba Bakr b. Muhammad Juki, she and her son Baysunghur went together to offer congratulations.[32]

Membership in the circle around the ruler bound together the ruler's wives and high-ranking amirs as people who knew the sovereign and guarded his interests or his memory. In the days following Temur's death, royal women consulted with the great amirs about the best way to implement his final instructions and handle his corpse.[33] Somewhat later, when Temur's close follower Shahmalik went to negotiate with Shaykh Nur al-Din, another and now rebellious follower, he took time to visit Temur's widow Tumen Agha. He rode to the moat near the building where she lived to greet her; she returned the greeting, and together they remembered Temur and wept.[34] Shah-malik was also close to Shahrukh and after Temur's death counted among his amirs. According to dynastic histories, in 808/1405–6 he received a forged letter ordering him to leave his post in Transoxiana. Other trusted amirs of Shahrukh's turned him back, and he consulted Shahrukh's wife Gawharshad, who assured him that Shahrukh would write no such letter and when un-able to convince him sent a messenger to Shahrukh.[35] At Shahrukh's death, since few important amirs were present in camp, it was Gawharshad who sent the news to absent princes and decided many of the first actions to be taken to prevent disorder.[36] We find Gawharshad later actively involved along with major amirs in trying to make peace among the princes struggling for pow-er after Shahrukh's death.[37]

The active relationship between dynastic women and major amirs is rem-iniscent of the political dynamics of the contemporary Mamluk sultanate and of the Ottomans at a slightly later date. The sultans used marriage to cement ties with high-ranking officers and created around themselves an extended family group.[38] Under the Mamluks, women's participation in state affairs may have been maintained from behind veils or curtains; for the Timurid dynasty this issue is unclear. Historians from within the dynasty write about communication between amirs and dynastic women without specifying what form it took. The French Dominican Jean of Sultaniyya writes that when Timurid women rode out they left only their eyes and noses visible. Anoth-er outside observer, the Spanish ambassador Clavijo, gives mixed evidence. He states that in Tabriz women went about fully veiled. When he writes about the dress of Saray Malik Khanim at the Timurid court, he mentions that her face was covered by a light veil, yet he describes her makeup and the com-plexion of other Timurid royal women, and it is clear that he spoke directly with them.[39]

Relationships within the Ruling Circle

People within the ruling group during the Timurid period were connected by a multiplicity of different ties, many of them managed by the ruler. When the system functioned well, it gave the ruler considerable control over the dynasty and its followers, but it also allowed a certain freedom to his subor-dinates because each had bonds of loyalty to many different people. For women in particular, ties might pull in different directions, and the sphere of influence and duty went well beyond the immediate household.

I want to examine two relationships crucial for women—marriage and maternity—to determine how they were used and how they shaped loyalties within the dynasty. Timurid rulers had numerous consorts, of which one or two held superior status. It is hard to tell to what extent the Timurids adhered to the formal Islamic limit of four legal wives at one time. Temur himself clearly did not; we know that he had at least five wives at the end of his life. For other Timurid rulers we cannot be certain. Although most have many women listed under them in the dynastic genealogy, wives and concubines are often not distinguished, nor are dates of marriage and death usually found either here or in other sources.[40]

Timurid princes took over the wives of their deceased brothers, particularly in the case of Chinggisid women.[41] We also find the practice of replacing a wife at her death or divorce with a woman related to her who was put formally in her place.[42] For this reason dynastic women were often married to more than one prince and might have children in both marriages, which could result in conflicting loyalties. For instance, Shahrukh's Chinggisid wife Malikat Agha found herself in a difficult position. She had earlier been married to Temur's oldest son, Umar Shaykh, by whom she had four sons: Pir Muhammad, Iskandar, Ahmad, and Bayqara.[43] Except for Pir Muhammad who died fairly early in the succession struggle, these men first gave allegiance to Shahrukh but then became insubordinate and were deposed by force. They were in fact Shahrukh's major rivals for power during his early rule.[44] By Shahrukh, Malikat Agha had one son, Soyurghatmish, who lived to young adulthood and received the relatively isolated governorship of Kabul. It may have been partly the activities of her older sons that gave to Malikat Agha and her son Soyurghatmish the clearly subordinate position they held in relationship to Gawharshad and her progeny.

Since many women were married to more than one member of the dynasty, it is not surprising that they maintained an identity as members of their own families and a certain level of independence from their husbands. In this regard, it is instructive to study the pattern of dynastic mausolea. Although it was common to place men and women within one complex, we rarely find women buried with their husbands. Quite a few were interred in buildings they had commissioned themselves or in shrines, apart from other members of the dynasty. Malikat Agha, for instance, died before Shahrukh and was buried in her own madrasa (religious school) in Balkh, away from the capital. Amiranshah's widow Khanzada was buried in Mashhad, while Amiranshah's corpse was brought to the mausoleum of Muhammad Sultan and Temur in Samarqand.[45]

Women were not infrequently buried with their parents or children and occasionally with their brothers and sisters. Thus, when Ulugh Beg's wife Aka Biki died in 822/1419, she was placed in the mausoleum of her father, Muhammad Sultan. The daughter and granddaughter of Shahrukh and Gawharshad, dying in 844/1440 and 845/1442, were both buried in the mausoleum constructed by Gawharshad in Herat, although they had married into other branches of the dynasty. Gawharshad's madrasa and mausoleum complex seems at first to have been closely connected with her own family, since her brother and grandnephew were buried there. Later it became the major mausoleum for the line of Shahrukh, who was placed there himself for a short time but later removed by Ulugh Beg and buried with Temur in Samarqand.[46]

Women of distinguished origin might have extensive property and large followings and could enjoy considerable independence from their husbands.[47] Such women might even defy their husbands, and when such independent behavior was used for the good of the dynasty it was considered praiseworthy. I will mention two examples.

Amiranshah's wife Khanzada had earlier been married to Jahangir by whom she bore Muhammad Sultan, Temur's first choice as heir apparent. In 799–800/1396–98, shortly after Muhammad Sultan's designation as heir, Amiranshah rebelled, probably because as Temur's eldest surviving son he wanted to succeed Temur himself.[48] One of his misdeeds was his treatment of Khanzada, whom he accused of unspecified misbehavior. She became furious, instituted an investigation to discover who had spoken against her, executed several people whom Amiranshah named as her accusers, and left for Samarqand, where she complained to Temur of Amiranshah's behavior and suggested that it would turn to open rebellion if left unchecked. Temur lost no time in acting on her information.[49] After this she remained in Temur's suite where she held an honorable position. When Khanzada joined Temur and warned him about Amiranshah's incipient rebellion, she was espousing the interests of her elder son over those of her second husband. Later, according to Clavijo, Khanzada worked unsuccessfully to improve Amiranshah's position although she remained with Temur. At the same time, she promoted the interests of her son by Amiranshah, Khalil Sultan. After Temur's death, Khalil Sultan succeeded in taking power briefly in Samarqand. To bolster his legitimacy, he named as figurehead khan Muhammad Sultan's son Muhammad Jahangir, his first cousin once removed on his father's side and his nephew on his mother's. Thus, for a brief span Khanzada had both a son as ruler and a grandson as figurehead.[50]

The second example of independent action is that of Aqa Biki (also called

Rajab Sultan), daughter of Amiranshah and wife of the prince Sa'd-i Waqqas
b. Muhammad Sultan who governed Qum. In 818/1415, Sa'd-i Waqqas, having
offended Shahrukh, deserted to Shahrukh's enemy, the Turkman Qaraqoyunlu
ruler Qara Yusuf. He then sent amirs to fetch his following and family from
Qum. Aqa Biki was a woman of high character, whose father had died at the
hands of the Qaraqoyunlu, and she refused to go. Instead, she seized the envoys, executed several amirs who had encouraged Sa'd-i Waqqas, and sent a
messenger to Shahrukh, who praised her actions.[51] It is clear that marriage did
not override all other ties; a woman's family of origin influenced her status and
might continue to claim a share of her loyalty and identity after marriage.

   Another relationship is that of maternity. How did a woman's genealogy affect her children's status, and how did male progeny enhance her prestige? Just as lineage was a factor in the relative positions of women, descent
through the female line could influence the status of Timurid princes. The
most striking illustration is Temur's choice of successor. Throughout his life
Temur limited succession to the line of his son Jahangir, the only son born
of a free wife. Jahangir is consistently named as the senior son in contemporary sources, although he was probably the second in actual age. After Jahangir's early death, Temur's first choice of successor was Muhammad Sultan,
Jahangir's son by his Chinggisid wife Khanzada. After Muhammad Sultan
died, Temur persisted in his course even though Jahangir's other son, Pir
Muhammad, whom Temur designated as successor on his deathbed, was an
unsuitable candidate who never managed to take the throne.[52]

   After Temur's death, it is not clear that maternal lineage affected the choice
of successor. Chinggisid descent on the mother's side did continue to be
significant for women. We see this clearly in the case of Khanzada, whose
Chinggisid descent came through her mother and whose descendants held a
prestigious position up to the dynasty's end. Ulugh Beg's wife Aka Biki, daughter of Muhammad Sultan and his Chinggisid wife, bore him a daughter who
once more bore the prestigious name Khanzada. When Aka Biki died, Ulugh
Beg put in her place a daughter of Khalil Sultan; these two women were only
distantly related on their paternal side but both descended from Khanzada.[53]

   Did women gain status and power by bearing sons to the ruler? What
evidence we have suggests that producing a son did not markedly enhance
the position of a low-status woman. It was high-born chief wives, not mothers
of important princes, who held power and prestige, a fact well illustrated in
Temur's period.[54] The wives who figure most prominently in the histories—
Saray Malik, Tumen, and Tokel—apparently produced no surviving children
but were of distinguished birth and thus of high rank among his wives.[55] The

concubine mothers of Temur's surviving sons, Umar Shaykh, Amiranshah, and Shahrukh, remain in the shadows, known only by name. Under later rulers and Timurid princes the situation appears to be similar. In some cases, women of high birth bore several sons, which may well have contributed to their position; Shahrukh's wife Gawharshad and Amiranshah's wife Khanzada provide examples. Concubines and low-born wives still remain in the background, and in several cases we cannot identify the mothers of powerful princes such as Shahrukh's sons Ibrahim and Ulugh Beg's son Abd al-Aziz. Maternity was not in itself a path to power.

The Use and Abuse of Power

How acceptable was women's use of power to those around them, and how was it reported in the contemporary histories? The role that women played in dynastic relations gave them independence of action and influence within the ruling group. If such powers were misused, women could seriously threaten the unity of this class, and this danger was recognized. Since most Timurid histories were written for the dynasty, their tone toward its members is usually flattering, at least on the surface. Nonetheless, while they applied the mandatory praises to Timurid princes, historians had ways to indicate disapproval. Probably the most common was to attribute an action to the instigation of bad advisers or simply "troublemakers." Historians sometimes assigned blame by noting the ruler's disapproval of an action or by using words with negative connotations.[56] In cases of misbehavior they considered extreme, historians criticized the ruler himself by relating the curses of the victims of persecution or even sometimes openly and directly. We are therefore not without guidance in judging contemporary reactions to women's behavior.

Two women were credited with exceptional influence in dynastic politics. How were they treated, and how did the period's histories judge them? Near the end of Temur's life, his grandson Khalil Sultan fell in love with Shad Malik, the concubine of an amir, and married her secretly. Shad Malik was apparently a person of undistinguished birth, and when Timurid historians admit her existence, they discuss her with open hostility. Her entry into dynastic politics is chronicled by the historian Sharaf al-Din Ali Yazdi, who makes it clear that her marriage to Khalil Sultan was considered unsuitable. Yazdi presents the marriage as an affront to Khalil Sultan's wife Jahan Sultan, who was Temur's grandniece.[57] She discovered it and reported to Temur, who ordered Shad Malik found and killed. When members of the dynasty interceded, partly on the grounds that Shad Malik was pregnant by Khalil Sultan, Temur relented sufficiently to decree that she be entrusted to his wife Tumen Agha until the child's birth; then she was to be humiliated by being handed over to a black slave.[58] When Temur died and Khalil Sultan achieved power, he took back Shad Malik, and she enjoyed great influence over him. If accounts are to be believed, she used her power to upset the rules of rank and hierarchy upholding the position of the ruling class, including dynastic women. Historians blame her for many of the excesses that Khalil Sultan committed during his four years in power, particularly his dissipation of the dynasty's wealth, which was handed out without regard to rank or service.[59] Shad Malik quarreled with Khalil Sultan's amirs, and, according to some historians, her excessive influence caused several to desert him. What was worst of all was that she pushed Khalil Sultan to dishonor the widows of Temur and Muhammad Sultan by marrying them off to his soldiers and followers, most of them men of distinctly lower class.[60]

It is not clear what happened to Shad Malik. One account states that her ears and nose were cut off and another that she poisoned Khalil Sultan and killed herself.[61] Shad Malik was a woman without the legitimate sources of power provided by birth and inclusion in the network of marriage and child rearing that bound together the dynasty and its closest followers. The power she possessed—of separate, exclusive influence—and the way she used it were a threat to that order. It is not surprising that she should have been unacceptable to Khalil Sultan's amirs and that Timurid historians should paint her in uniformly dark colors.

The other woman to discuss is Shahrukh's wife Gawharshad, a woman of high birth and recognized status, as much an insider as Shad Malik was an outsider. Gawharshad's father, Ghiyath al-Din Tarkhan, was a close follower of Temur and held the hereditary honorific *tarkhan,* a title bestowed by Chinggis Khan that conferred high status on its holders. Three of his daughters married into the dynasty.[62] Gawharshad was conspicuous in public dynastic occasions and as a patron of architecture. She was an integral part of Shahrukh's closest circle and seems to have had direct ties to his major amirs. In all these instances, her actions are reported without suggestion of disapproval. Nonetheless, in 861/1457 the ruler Abu Sa'id executed her, and we must determine how to interpret this action.

Despite the respect with which historians usually mention Gawharshad, all accuse her of one major fault—her active preference for one grandson, Ala al-Dawla b. Baysunghur, over all other descendants of Shahrukh. This favoritism threatened the family cohesion in which women played such an important role, and it is represented throughout the histories as a cause of dissension and of enmity toward Gawharshad. In 845/1441–42, Ulugh Beg's son Abd al-Latif, who, like Ala al-Dawla, had been raised by Gawharshad, left Shahrukh's court for Samarqand in anger at Gawharshad's favoritism. Shahrukh scolded Gawharshad, who likewise left, also for Samarqand where her son Ulugh Beg received her well. Gawharshad nonetheless continued her promotion of Ala al-Dawla's interests. The histories recount with disapproval that when Shahrukh was ill in 848/1444–45 she extracted an oath of loyalty to Ala al-Dawla from Shahrukh's powerful amir Firuzshah.[63] Some sources state that she discouraged Shahrukh from giving land or responsibility to his son Muhammad Juki or Baysunghur's other sons Sultan Muhammad and Abu'l Qasim Babur and that on Sultan Muhammad's rebellion in 850/1446 she pushed Shahrukh to go against him despite his reluctance to act. According to some, she was further responsible for Shahrukh's harshness against the Persian ulama who had encouraged Sultan Muhammad to rebel, and many of them were executed.[64] It seems doubtful that Gawharshad seriously wronged Sultan Muhammad, because during the disturbances after Shahrukh's death she and her followers found refuge with him.[65]

On Shahrukh's death in 850/1447, Gawharshad acted with care by immediately dispatching Ulugh Beg's son Abd al-Latif to bring order to the army's baggage train and to inform his father, although at the same time she sent the news to Ala al-Dawla in Herat.[66] Shahrukh's death initiated a protracted struggle among his descendants. Gawharshad remained an important political actor, and her preference for Ala al-Dawla made her an opponent to the other princes vying for power. What intensified the threat Gawharshad posed was the strength of her family, the descendants of Ghiyath al-Din Tarkhan. It is hard to judge what their position had been during Shahrukh's life. Several members held high posts, but it is not clear that they pursued a common policy. After Shahrukh's death, Gawharshad's relatives are frequently mentioned as a group, gathered around Gawharshad and Ala al-Dawla and referred to collectively as the Tarkhan amirs.[67]

Gawharshad and her relatives challenged other princes and powerful amirs. Within a few days of Shahrukh's death, Ulugh Beg's son Abd al-Latif was persuaded by "troublemakers" to believe that Gawharshad and her circle were plotting treachery in favor of Ala al-Dawla. Accordingly, he set out to forestall her, plundered her following, and took her and her relatives prisoner.[68] In 861/1457, Shahrukh's great-grandson Shah Mahmud b. Abu'l Qasim Babur became master of Herat, himself controlled by his powerful amirs, while outside the city Ala al-Dawla's son Ibrahim threatened to invade. Several amirs, including some Tarkhans and Amir Shir Hajji (the preeminent power behind the throne), cooperated with Gawharshad to propose mediation among the princes, hoping to end the cycle of conquest and reconquest ravaging Khorasan. This initiative threatened to increase the standing of the Tarkhan amirs at the expense of others closer to Shah Mahmud. Encouraged by "troublemakers," Amir Shir Hajji now decided to secure his primacy by murdering the leading Tarkhans; a few escaped but many were killed. In the event, Ibrahim b. Ala al-Dawla took Herat while Gawharshad in conjunction with the city's *qadi* (judge) arranged the defense of the fortress and the protection of the population.[69]

Shortly after these events, Abu Sa'id, the rising Timurid ruler from the line of Temur's third son, Amiranshah, arrived in Herat. Although Abu Sa'id at first received Gawharshad with respect, she was an obstacle to him. He was informed that she was still in touch with her great-grandson Ibrahim b. Ala al-Dawla and was giving him information about affairs within the city. Furthermore, Abu Sa'id needed support from the powerful amirs of Khorasan, and Amir Shir Hajji, understandably afraid of Gawharshad and the remaining Tarkhans, refused to come into Abu Sa'id's service while she was alive. Abu Sa'id had her executed in 861/1457.[70]

Did Gawharshad's execution indicate that the level of power she wielded was unacceptable or that as a woman outside her proper sphere she could be attacked with impunity? I think this is the wrong interpretation. Gawharshad was in no way exceptional in dying at the hands of her relatives, for she shared this fate with almost every male member of Shahrukh's line. Moreover, acts against her were considered reprehensible. Dynastic histories consistently ascribe actions taken against her to the influence of troublemakers.[71] Abd al-Latif's attack on her at Shahrukh's death did not go unpunished; when Ala al-Dawla captured him shortly thereafter, he had him brought before the court in the dress of a penitent and made him publicly repent of his treatment of his "mother" Gawharshad.[72] Ala al-Dawla was not an uninterested party in this affair, but the publicity of the punishment suggests consensus on the breach of morals involved. Gawharshad's execution was taken seriously enough to be used by the Aqqoyunlu Turkmans as a way to legalize the killing of Abu Sa'id in 873/1469. He was handed over to Gawharshad's great-grandson Yadgar Muhammad and executed in vengeance for her.[73] Both the *Matla al-sa'dayn* and the *Habib al-siyar* mention Abu Sa'id's execution of Gawharshad with explicit disapproval, as a blot on his reign.[74]

What historians did consider reprehensible was Gawharshad's single-minded promotion of Ala al-Dawla over Shahrukh's other descendants. This is reported to have angered Shahrukh and to have caused dissension within the family, and it is constantly mentioned as the reason why Timurid princes listened to those who incited them against Gawharshad. It was not Gawharshad's power but her misuse of that power to favor one member of the dynasty that was considered wrong and contributed to her downfall.[75]

Conclusion

The importance of women in Timurid politics did not lie primarily in their role as wives and mothers, influencing the men closest to them, or in their activities within a sequestered female world. Women were not a class apart but active members of a ruling group made up of both the dynasty and its followers, which was held together by ties of marriage and child rearing. Dynastic women owed loyalty to their family of origin, to their husbands and sons, and to the ruler who controlled much of the family life of his relatives. Marriage neither overrode a woman's ties to her own family nor limited her circle to the household of her husband. She might also become part of the ruler's suite, connected with the whole ruling group. Since the dynasty's followers and top military commanders belonged to this group, dynastic women had ties among them and could apparently deal directly with them. Within the ruling circle women played a public role on ceremonial occasions and as part of the group surrounding and advising the ruler.

All members of the ruling group could pose a threat to the sovereign's power, and if they did so they were punished. Princes attempted to achieve independence or sovereignty; amirs might desert or try armed rebellion. To women these paths were not open, but they did threaten the cohesion of the ruling class if they misused their influence to disrupt the relationships holding this group together. It was behavior of this sort, not the open practice of political power, that brought disapproval and punishment to royal women.

NOTES

1. Studying women within the Ottoman political system, Leslie Peirce shows how fundamentally their role in dynastic politics could change even within a single dynasty and tradition; *The Imperial Harem: Women and Sovereignty in the Ottoman Empire* (New York, 1993).

2. John E. Woods, "Timur's Genealogy," in *Intellectual Studies on Islam, Essays Written in Honor of Martin B. Dickson,* ed. M. M. Mazzaoui and V. B. Moreen (Salt

Lake City, 1990), 102; K. Jahn, "Timur und die Frauen," *Anzeiger der österreichischen Akademie der Wissenschaften,* Phil.-Hist. Klasse, 3, no. 24 (1974), 520.

3. Gottfried Herrmann, "Zur Intitulatio timuridischer Urkunden," *Zeitschrift der deutschen morgenländischen Gesellschaft,* Supplement 2, *XVIII deutscher Orientalistentag 1972, vom 1 bis 5 Oktober, 1972 in Lübeck* (Wiesbaden, 1974), 504–5, 517–19; Woods, "Genealogy," 116.

4. Ahmad b. Jalal al-Din Fasih Khwafi, *Mujmal-i Fasihi,* ed. Muhammad Farrukh (Mashhad, 1339/1960–61), 3:196, 236.

5. *Mu'izz al-ansab fi shajarat al-ansab,* MS Paris, Bibliothèque Nationale 67 (hereafter *Mu'izz*), fol. 151b. The last Timurid ruler of Khorasan, Sultan Husayn-i Bayqara, did not use this legitimation, but Abu Sa'id's sons, who continued to rule in Transoxiana, were also provided with Chinggisid wives; Zahir al-Din Muhammad Babur, *The Babur-Nama in English (Memoirs of Babur),* trans. A. S. Beveridge (1922; reprint, London, 1969), 21, 36, 47.

6. Sharaf al-Din Ali Yazdi, *Zafarnama,* ed. Muhammad Abbasi (Tehran, 1336/1957) (hereafter ZNY), 2:16.

7. Hafiz-i Abru, *Zubdat al-tawarikh,* ed. Sayyid Kamal Hajj Sayyid Jawadi (Tehran, 1372/1992) (hereafter *Zubdat*), 2:699–703.

8. ZNY, 1:406, 414, 416, 444–45, 487, 494; Ruy González de Clavijo, trans. G. Le Strange, *Narrative of the Spanish Embassy to the Court of Timur at Samarkand in the Years 1403–6* (London: Broadway Travellers' Series, 1928), 213, 258–61. Temur's other Chinggisid wife, Tokel Khanim, was second in rank to Saray Malik but is less frequently mentioned in the sources. See Ahmad Ibn Arabshah, *Tamerlane or Timur, the Great Amir,* trans. J. H. Sanders (London, 1936), 310.

9. *Mu'izz,* fols. 112b, 121b; ZNY, 1:180.

10. ZNY, 2:267, 360; Clavijo, *Narrative of the Spanish Embassy,* 244.

11. The importance of Temur's testament appointing Pir Muhammad b. Jahangir as heir is shown in several of the Timurid histories. See, for example, ZNY, 2:505; Taj al-Salmani, *Šams al-Husn, eine Chronik vom Tode Timurs bis zum Jahre 1409 von Tağ al-Salmani,* ed. and trans. H. R. Roemer (Wiesbaden, 1956) (Akademie der Wissenschaften und der Literatur, Veröffentlichungen der orientalischen Kommission, VIII; hereafter, *Shams*), 34–35, 39 (ff. 46a–47a, 53a). After Shahrukh's death, the Aqqoyunlu backed a pretender from his line in their contest with Abu Sa'id. See R. M. Savory, "The Struggle for Supremacy in Persia after the Death of Timur," *Der Islam* 40 (1964): 51–52.

12. *Mu'izz,* fols. 116a–117a, 121a, 151b, 153a–b; Abd al-Razzaq Samarqandi, *Matla al-sa'dayn wa majma al-bahrayn,* ed. Muhammad Shafi, vol. 2, pts. 2–3 (Lahore, 1949), no. 2, 878; *Mujmal,* 3:212.

13. *Mu'izz,* fol. 156b; Ghiyath al-Din b. Humam al-Din Khwandamir, *Habib al-siyar,* ed. Jalal al-Din Huma'i (Tehran, 1333/1954), 4:136.

14. Jahn, "Timur und die Frauen," 526–27.

15. Clavijo, *Narrative of the Spanish Embassy,* 244–48, 268.

16. *Matla,* 2, no. 2, 669. For other examples of Gawharshad's public role, see *Matla,* 2, no. 1, 319; 2, no. 2, 703; *Mujmal,* 3:207.

17. *Zubdat,* 2:665.

18. Beatrice F. Manz, *The Rise and Rule of Tamerlane* (Cambridge, 1989), 78.

19. Hafiz-i Abru, *Majma al-tawarikh*, MS Istanbul Fatih no. 4371/1 (hereafter *Majma*), fols. 1b–11a.

20. ZNY, 2:9–13, 459; Nizam al-Din Shami, *Histoire des conquêtes de Tamerlan intitulée Zafarnama, par Niẓāmuddīn Šāmī*, ed. F. Tauer (Prague, vol. 1, 1937, vol. 2, 1956). Volume 2 contains additions made by Hafiz-i Abru 2:136; *Matla*, 2, no. 2, 667, 878, no. 3, 899, 904; *Mujmal*, 3:212, 283; *Muʿizz*, fols. 116a–17a, 151b, 156b; *Babur-nama*, 36–37.

21. Manz, *Rise and Rule*, 78, 186n.31; *Muʿizz*, fols. 111b, 130a, 141b; John E. Woods, *The Timurid Dynasty*, Papers on Inner Asia, no. 14 (Bloomington, Indiana, 1990), 23–26, 34, 36, 44–46.

22. ZNY, 1:406, 444, 487, 494, 523, 2:285, 360; *Zubdat*, 1:435–36; *Mujmal*, 3:207; *Shams*, 98, 111–12, fols. 137a, 154a–155a.

23. *Majma*, fol. 8b.

24. *Zubdat*, 1:470–73.

25. *Muʿizz*, fols. 99b, 100a, 120b, 122b, 123a, 125a, 126b, 137 bis, 143a, 147b, 149b.

26. ZNY, 1:505–15, 2:140, 270, 285, 361, 434.

27. *Muʿizz*, fols. 140b, 144b; *Matla*, 2, no. 2, 717. The name Hasiba Sultan Khanzada is problematical. According to the *Muʿizz*, Ulugh Beg and Aka Biki had two separate daughters, Hasiba Sultan and Khanzada Begim, but both *Matla al-saʿdayn* and *Mujmal-i Fasihi* refer to a Hasiba Sultan Khanzada. The Khanzada here could be simply a title showing that Hasiba Sultan had Chinggisid blood. See *Muʿizz*, fol. 139b, also another manuscript of the same work, British Museum Or. 467, fol. 134b; *Mujmal*, 3:283; and *Matla al-saʿdayn*, manuscript, University Library of the Punjab, Pe II 4 6385, fol. 168a.

28. ZNY, 1:277–78, 2:287, 434; *Matla*, 2, no. 2, 650, 694.

29. Peirce, *Imperial Harem*, 39–45.

30. *Mujmal*, 3:245, 292; Dawlatshah Samarqandi, *The Tadhkiratuʾ sh-shuʿara (Memoirs of the poets)*, ed. E. G. Browne (London, 1901), 406; *Matla*, 2, no. 2, 879–81.

31. *Zubdat*, 2:921.

32. *Zubdat*, 2:664; *Matla*, 2, no. 1, 319.

33. ZNY, 2:489–90, 499–50.

34. *Zubdat*, 1:426.

35. *Shams*, 74–76, fols. 100b–101b.

36. *Matla*, 2, no. 2, 879; *Habib*, 3:636–38.

37. *Habib*, 4:64.

38. Abd al-Raziq, *La femme au temps des Mamlouks en Egypte* (Cairo, 1973), 28–29, 126–29; Peirce, *Imperial Harem*, 66–71.

39. Jean of Sultaniyya, "Mémoire sur Tamerlan et sa cour par un Dominicain, en 1403," ed. H. Moranvillé, *Bibliothèque de l'École des Chartes*, vol. 55 (Paris, 1894), 452; Clavijo, *Narrative of the Spanish Embassy*, 153, 258.

40. Woods, *Timurid Dynasty*, 17–18; *Muʿizz*, fols. 151b–52a. One suspects that Abu Saʿid, for whom nine wives are listed, apparently separate from concubines, probably also exceeded the shariʿa limit.

41. See the cases of Khanzada and Malikat Agha discussed below, and for further examples, see Woods, *Timurid Dynasty*, 20, 21, 29, 30; *Muʿizz*, fol. 129a.

42. *Muʿizz*, fols. 137bis b, 156b.

43. *Muʿizz*, fol. 101b.

44. Ismail Aka, "Timur'un ölümünden sonra güney-Iran'da hâkimiyet mücadele-leri," *Atsiz Armagani* (Istanbul, 1976), 3–15; *Majma*, fols. 501b–502a, 520b–21a, 531b–32a.

45. *Matla*, 2, no. 2, 751; *Mujmal*, 3:207; Lisa Golombek and Donald Wilber, *The Timurid Architecture of Iran and Turan* (Princeton, 1988), 1:261–62. Two other wives of Temur appear to have been buried in their own separate mausolea, although this cannot be fully verified; these are Saray Malik and Tumen Agha. See Golombek, *Timurid Architecture*, 1:254, 325; Bernard O'Kane, *Timurid Architecture in Khurasan* (Costa Mesa, Calif., 1987), 197–98; but also Roya Marefat, "Beyond the Architecture of Death: The Shrine of the Shah-i Zinda in Samarqand" (Ph.D. diss., Harvard University, 1991), 135–36. The female relatives of Sultan Husayn also commissioned mausolea for themselves. See Golombek, *Timurid Architecture*, 1:62; O'Kane, *Timurid Architecture*, 83, 96n.46.

46. *Zubdat*, 2:704; *Matla*, 2, no. 2, 659, 748, 760, 959; Golombek, *Timurid Architecture*, 1:304–7; *Habib*, 3:634, 4:20, 46, 78, 101.

47. According to Hafiz-i Abru, Temur investigated the landholdings of the dynasty and followers, including women, and renewed them (*Majma*, fol. 8a).

48. John E. Woods, "Turco-Iranica II: Notes on a Timurid Decree of 1396/798," *Journal of Near Eastern Studies* 43 (4) (1984): 331–37.

49. ZNY, 2:150–51.

50. Clavijo, *Narrative of the Spanish Embassy*, 316; ZNY, 2:505.

51. *Zubdat*, 1:588–91.

52. Woods, "Genealogy," 112; Manz, *Rise and Rule*, 128–47, 166.

53. *Mu'izz*, fols. 116a, 137bis b.

54. We can see this also reflected in the patronage of architecture and the arts, practiced largely by women of high birth. See Golombek, *Timurid Architecture*, 1:62, 302–7, 328; Marefat, "Shrine of the Shah-i Zinda," 74–78, 135–36.

55. Woods, *Timurid Dynasty*, 17–18; ZNY, 1:276–78, 444–48, 518, 2:142, 254; Clavijo, *Narrative of the Spanish Embassy*, 260–61.

56. One can cite as examples the words *mubalagha* and *ikrah kardan* (to insist, push, force) used when undue influence was exerted.

57. In the dynastic genealogy, the *Mu'izz al-ansab*, these are the only two wives mentioned; *Mu'izz*, fol. 126b.

58. ZNY, 2:454.

59. *Shams*, 121, fols. 166a–b. In attempting to assess the career of Shad Malik and the reactions it elicited, we are handicapped by the fact that the more sober dynastic historians largely ignored her while those enjoying gossip and defamation emphasized her role.

60. *Shams*, 117, 121, fols. 162b, 166a–b; Ibn Arabshah, *Tamerlane or Timur*, 283. It is possible that Shad Malik is given responsibility for these deeds in order to spare the reputation of Khalil Sultan, in the way that the peccadilloes of other princes were often blamed on the influence of wily Persian advisers.

61. Both come from authors with a fondness for scandal. See Dawlatshah, *Tadhkiratu' sh-shu'ara*, 354; Ibn Arabshah, *Tamerlane or Timur*, 293–94.

62. Manz, *Rise and Rule*, 186, n. 31.

63. *Matla*, 2, no. 2, 759–60, 838.

64. *Habib*, 3:634–35; Dawlatshah, *Tadhkiratu' sh-shu'ara*, 405; *Matla*, 2, no. 2, 851–52. It is possible that this was an interpretation encouraged by Sultan Muhammad as a way to downplay the friction between himself and his grandfather. See Dawlatshah, *Tadhkiratu' sh-shu'ara*, 339; O'Kane, *Timurid Architecture*, 83.

65. *Habib*, 4:26–27; Dawlatshah, *Tadhkiratu' sh-shu'ara*, 407; *Matla*, 2, no. 3, 940, 969.

66. *Habib*, 3:636–38; *Matla*, 2, no. 2, 879–80, 887.

67. *Matla*, 2, no. 2, 881, 886–88; *Habib*, 3:637, 4:64.

68. *Matla*, 2, no. 2, 881–86.

69. *Habib*, 4:64–65; *Matla*, 2, no. 3, 1127–30.

70. *Habib*, 4:67–68; *Matla*, 2, no. 3, 1143–44.

71. *Matla*, 2, no. 2, 881; *Habib*, 4:64, 68. The exception is Dawlatshah Samarqandi, who is consistently hostile to Gawharshad and blames her for Shahrukh's expedition against Sultan Muhammad, the execution of shaykhs and ulama who promoted his power, and the blinding of Shahrukh's nephew, Iskandar b. Umar Shaykh. See Dawlatshah, *Tadhkiratu' sh-shu'ara*, 339, 370, 405.

72. *Matla*, 2, no. 3, 888–91; *Habib*, 3:638–39.

73. H. R. Roemer, "The Successors of Timur," in *Cambridge History of Iran*, vol. 6 (Cambridge, 1986), 117.

74. *Matla*, 2, no. 3, 1143–44; *Habib*, 4:68.

75. For the exercise of open and legitimate power by women in the Safavid dynasty, see Maria Szuppe, "La participation des femmes de la famille royale à l'exercice du pouvoir en Iran safavide au XVIᵉ siècle," *Studia Iranica* 23 (2) (1994): 211–58; and 24 (1) (1995): 61–122; and her chapter in this volume.

7   Status, Knowledge, and Politics: Women in Sixteenth-Century Safavid Iran

MARIA SZUPPE

> After more than half of the urdu has gone by, the Shah's maidens pass on fine horses; and they ride like men and dress like men, except that on their heads they do not wear caps but white kerchiefs. . . . And I have seen that there were about 14–15 of those maidens, and they were beautiful, though their faces could not be fully seen. But what could be seen was beautiful and very fair.
>
> —Michele Membrè, a Venetian envoy to Shah Tahmasp's court, 1540

CERTAIN DIFFICULTIES face the historian writing about women not only of the sixteenth century but also during the whole Safavid period (1501–1722). These difficulties are due to the scarcity of information in the historical chronicles and collections of biographies (*tadhkira*) and in existing archival documents. Generally speaking, a tradition of Muslim historiography to record mainly political events, see history as that of the ruling dynasty, and avoid mentioning women is reflected in the writings of the Safavid period. Authors sometimes ignored this tradition when the female historical figure was of sufficient importance. For the Safavids, systematic archival documents and legal acts are lacking. Marriage contracts, wills, trade documents, charity-foundation acts, and other sources are important for the study of the social and legal aspects of any period's history.

    The information we have at our disposal concerns nearly exclusively predefined social groups, the upper levels of society moving within elite circles of power. It deals with certain spheres of activity but not with some others. And it deals mostly with royal women, who form a separate social group, as well as with—to a lesser extent—women of the military and administrative elite.

Importance of the Turkic Cultural and Political Tradition

A peculiarity of early Safavid society is the coexistence of Turkophone military elites and urban Iranophone administrative and religious ones. The military and logistic support of tribal leaders (*amirs*), mostly of eastern Anatolian, Azerbaijani Turkman, and Kurd origin, enabled the Safavid Sufi order, headed by twelve-year-old Shaykh Isma'il, to engage in political struggle in Azerbaijan at the end of the fifteenth century. Seizing power in Tabriz in 1501, Isma'il became the first shah of the Safavid dynasty and imposed Twelver Shi'i Islam as the official religion of Iran. His Turkman supporters, known as Qizilbash, pushed their military conquests in all directions. By 1510, the Safavid state extended (temporarily) from Baghdad to the Oxus river. In addition to being granted important positions at the court and in the provinces, Qizilbash amirs were settling in their new tribal territories in central and eastern Iran. Arriving from Anatolia and Azerbaijan with their people, horses, and livestock, they brought with them their own customs and ways of life, still remarkably close to their nomadic and not-so-distant Central Asian origin.

Turko-Mongol nomadic cultural tradition, as compared with Irano-Islamic customs of settled people, gave a much larger place to women's social and political activities and to family blood ties on both paternal and maternal sides. Among the Mongols and Ilkhans (thirteenth to fourteenth centuries), female members of ruling families enjoyed a privileged position.[1] They were entitled to a share of booty and had the right to participate in the *quriltay,* the all-Mongol assembly. Not only did they become regents of their minor sons, but also under certain circumstances they could themselves lay claim to the throne. Even after Islamization progressed among the Turko-Mongol tribes, women retained much of their social position. In 1404, the Castilian envoy at the court of Timur in Samarkand, Ruy González de Clavijo, was entertained at a feast, together with the amirs, by a Timurid princess. She and the women of her court sat with male and female guests. They took part in conversation, had wine served to their visitors, and ate and drank with them.[2]

In eastern Iran, during the Golden Age of the Timurid period in Herat (fifteenth century), the court lived in gardens outside the city. The Timurid harem was not a circumscribed place surrounded by high walls but was composed of tents and pavilions, moved from one garden to another in the same way the Timurid sultans and amirs did, and was not guarded by special walls.[3] In Herat, the princess Gawhar-Shad Begum (d. 1457), wife of the ruling Timurid sultan Shah Rukh (1405–47), not only was the largest patron of art and charities, but she also dominated the political scene during the first half of the fifteenth century.[4] Toward the century's end in Tabriz in western Iran, Saljuq-Shah Begum (d. 1490), mother of the reigning sovereign of the Aq Quyunlu Turkman confederation state, Sultan Ya'qub b. Uzun Hasan (1478–90), was participating in state affairs.[5]

The Safavids are thus direct heirs of both the Aq Quyunlu tribal state and the Timurid empire. Both of their predecessor states were a mixture of Iranian, Turkic, and Islamic cultural traditions, administrative practices, and political systems.

They Were Beautiful though Their Faces Could Not Be Fully Seen

This chapter deals primarily with the first century of Safavid rule, a period when the aspirations of the Qizilbash amirs to maintain the state in its loosely federal form strongly opposed the centralizing efforts of the court administration. These were the days when women of the Safavid elites were the most visible and more socially active than in the later period when they exercised their political power from behind harem walls. Traces of the Turko-Mongol (Timurid) pattern of an unhermetically closed harem can still be detected at the Safavid court in Qazvin in the mid-sixteenth century. Although women lived in their own quarter, its walls were less tightly closed in the sixteenth century than in the following one. Women were seen going in and out of the harem with escorts composed sometimes only of their maids.

Michele Membrè, a Venetian envoy to Iran in 1540, not only saw Qizilbash women in the streets of Tabriz but also met them while staying as a house guest of the Qizilbash amirs: The wives of the Qizilbash amirs are "very beautiful and wear beautiful, big, round pearls at their necks. These ladies are very agreeable and keep all their husbands' money. When the husband wants something he has to ask his wife for the money. So the said Qizilbash love their wives a great deal. The ladies ride through the town like men and go with maids instead of grooms; and they go with the face covered with a white kerchief, so only the eyes are seen."[6] They "dress like men, except that on their heads they do not wear caps but white kerchiefs. . . . And I have seen that there were about 14–15 of those maidens, and they were beautiful, though their faces could not be fully seen. But what could be seen was beautiful and very fair."[7]

In 1572, another traveler, Vincenzo d'Alessandri, thus described a wife of Shah Tahmasp whom he had seen during his visit in Qazvin, the second Safavid capital: "The women at times have permission from the King to come out of the palace; those, indeed, who have children, under the pretext of seeing them when they are ill. And I saw the mother of the Sultan Mustafa Mirisce, who was slightly indisposed, come out with her face covered with a black veil, riding like a man, accompanied by four slaves and six men on foot."[8] Some royal women possessed their own houses, in which they lived, outside the harem walls, as was the case of several princesses of the Safavid royal family in Qazvin in the second half of the sixteenth century.[9]

While women from the upper level of society went out, or rode out, with their faces more or less veiled, others, most probably from the lower-class milieus, could be seen in the streets of Safavid towns. European travelers' reports describe their clothing and appearance. Among them, Francesco Romano, who sojourned in Tabriz during Shah Isma'il I's period, expressed his not-always-flattering opinion on the subject of its female inhabitants and witnessed a variant of the early-sixteenth-century chadur (veil-wrap), which resembled the Central Asian *paranja:* "The women are short in proportion to the men and as white as snow. Their dress is the same as always has been—the Persian costume—wearing it open at the breast, showing their bosoms and even their bodies, the whiteness of which resembles ivory. All the Persian women—and particularly in Tauris—are wanton, and wear men's robes, and put them on over their heads, covering them altogether. These robes are of silk, some of crimson cloth, woolen cloth, velvet, and cloth of gold, according to the condition of the wearer."[10] D'Alessandri commented on the women of Qazvin in 1572: "The women are mostly ugly, though of fine features and noble dispositions, their customs not being refined as those of Turkish ladies. They wear robes of silk, veils on their heads, and show their faces openly. They have pearls and other jewels on their heads, and on this account pearls are in great demand in these regions, as it is not very long since they came into use."[11] Clearly both Romano and d'Alessandri are talking here about a social group distinct from the one that Membrè describes in court circles. Pearls as head ornaments are mentioned throughout the Safavid period by many other European travelers. Adam Olearius, a German visitor to Iran in 1637, especially mentions pearls but clearly says that the women he could observe were the beautiful courtesans of Qazvin.[12]

In the seventeenth century, the emergence of the fortified and centralized state of Shah Abbas I and the dismantling of Qizilbash tribes would contribute to the reduction of the amirs' power and the influence of their cultural background. Safavid society would turn more and more toward Irano-Islamic traditions, which would modify the position of royal and elite women. The royal harem as an internal power structure under the growing power of eunuchs would then ponder and often direct state affairs from behind closed doors. But in the sixteenth century it was still necessary for the Safavids to send royal princesses to provincial courts of their dignitary husbands in the hope and expectation that they could stay active in order to defend Safavid state interests. At the royal court, individual women still enjoyed the opportunity to participate and even to form and lead important political groups.

Dynastic Policy and Kinship Networks

One of the most widely used means to consolidate dynastic power is the creation of kinship networks by the ruling house with other politically or socially important social and power groups. The Safavids were no exception. When they attained power, they intermarried with military and civil dignitaries of Turkic and Iranian origin and with hereditary petty rulers of local states, either newly incorporated into the Safavid state or left temporarily semi-independent. This pattern was repeated in every generation. Cousin marriage, frequently practiced in Muslim communities, although present, was not the rule. Following this pattern, the circle of the royal sons-in-law (*damad*) enlarged to incorporate new allies. Kinship ties in the upper level of society became more tight and intricate as the different elite groups also intermarried among themselves.[13]

Safavid sources bring forward many examples of the engagement and marriage of a royal princess (sister, daughter, niece, or cousin of the shah) to a state dignitary or local ruler. Many women of the royal house were married more than once inside as well as outside the extended family. Some Safavid princesses stayed unmarried, and it is often they who later appear on the political scene. This is the case with some Safavid female politicians of the sixteenth century such as the princess Mahin Banu (1519–62), known as Shahzada Sultanum, the beloved youngest full sister of Shah Tahmasp. This is again the case with Pari-Khan Khanum II (1548–78) and Zaynab Begum (d. 1641/42), both daughters of Shah Tahmasp.

The analysis of the evolution of dynastic marriage strategy reveals several points. For every period of Safavid history, it reflects the priorities of domestic and foreign politics. It makes clear the existence or rather reveals the intricacy and subtlety of multiple kinship ties and obligations linking the Safavids to Qizilbash and civil dignitaries. And it stresses the social importance of matrilineal kinship as reflected in the status of women and their descendants as well as in that of royal in-laws.[14]

The mother and paternal grandmother of the future shah Isma'il I were Aq Quyunlu Turkman princesses, respectively a daughter and a sister of Uzun Hasan.[15] This is why Shah Isma'il I could appear to some as a lawful candidate for the throne of Tabriz even if it is not clear from the sources that the shah had effectively put forward such a claim. The Safavids also had family connections with dignitaries and notables of the region and the town of Ardabil, homeland and headquarters of the Safavid shaykhs. In the second part of the fifteenth century, a paternal aunt of Isma'il I, Shah-Pasha Khatun, was married to a dignitary of the Ardabil region. This alliance was used by the Safavids during the last phase of their struggle for power.[16]

Later the sisters of Shah Isma'il I became wives of important Turkman amirs whose support was essential for military conquest. The shah himself had Turkman wives. One of them was Shah-Beg(i) Khanum (d. 1540), who became famous under her title of Tajlu Khanum (crowned lady). She was an important counselor to her husband and later a power behind the throne of her son Shah Tahmasp. The latter, too, had a Turkman as chief wife.

Alliances with some Qizilbash families continued for more than one generation, such as that of Abdi Beg Shamlu and Qara Khan Ustajalu, each of whom married a sister of Shah Isma'il I. Two sons of Abdi Beg Shamlu and his Safavid wife achieved prominence and important posts under Shah Isma'il I and Shah Tahmasp. Durmish Khan (d. 1526) and Husayn Khan (d. 1534) were in turn governors of Herat and all of Khurasan as well as tutors of Sam Mirza, brother of Shah Tahmasp. A daughter of Husayn Khan was given in marriage to Sam Mirza. The office of governor of Herat became in practice hereditary in this Shamlu family line from the second part of the sixteenth century. In 1577, it was given to the grandson of Durmish Khan, Ali-Quli Khan Shamlu, and then to his descendants; some of the latter were to marry again into the Safavid family in the late sixteenth century.[17]

The son of the other Safavid princess and Qara Khan Ustajalu, Abdullah Khan Ustajalu, became one of the most important dignitaries of the state, holding successively the posts of *amir al-umara* and *divanbegi* before becoming governor of Shirvan from 1549 to 1566 or perhaps even to 1577, the year of his death.[18] Abdullah Khan contracted a union with his first cousin, Pari-Khan Khanum I, daughter of Shah Isma'il I. Their grandson, Salman Khan Ustajalu b. Shah-Quli Mirza (d. 1623–24), became one of the highest and richest dignitaries of the state. He married twice into the Safavid house: once to Shahr-Banu Khanum (d. 1583/84), daughter of Shah Tahmasp, and after her early death to another Safavid princess. When he died childless, his great fortune was returned to the state treasury.[19]

Matrimonial alliances with tribal groups were predominant throughout the sixteenth century. Tribal alliances were the means to enforce the loyalty of amirs to the Safavids and, at least in theory, to help the shah control provincial affairs. For the amirs they were the means to gain more political and social weight and to enrich themselves.

In the early sixteenth century, the Safavids needed to reinforce their position on the northern frontiers. Marriage alliances with rulers of Shirvan and Gilan are among the earliest. In the early 1520s, the Shirvanshah Sultan Ibrahim (Shaykh Shah), a local ruler of Shirvan, obtained the hand of a daughter of Shah Isma'il I, while the latter married a sister of the Shirvanshah. About the same time, the ruler of Rasht, Amira Dubbaj (Muzaffar Sultan), married Khanish Khanum I (d. 1564), another daughter of Shah Isma'il I. In 1567 or 1568, their grandson, Jamshid Khan b. Sultan-Mahmud Khan, married his own Safavid cousin, princess Khadija Begum (d. after 1627), daughter of Shah Tahmasp. The first wife of the eldest son of Shah Tahmasp, Sultan-Muhammad Mirza (the future shah Muhammad Khudabanda), was a daughter of Mir Abd al-Azim Gilani. In 1577, Khan-Ahmad Khan of Gilan, descending from a line of hereditary local rulers of Lahijan, became another royal son-in-law by marrying Maryam Begum (d. 1608/9), daughter of Shah Tahmasp.[20]

The vital problem for the Safavids was permanent control not only of Gilan but also of Mazandaran. In the second part of the century, they were actively engaged in local politics supporting one or another of the many petty rulers of Mazandaran. In 1565–66, two rival and closely related Mazandarani ruling families of Mar'ashi sayyid origin entered the Safavid house through marriage: Mir Sultan-Murad Khan, ruler of Sari, married a royal niece, Mah-Parvar Khanum;[21] and Khayr al-Nisa Begum (or Fakhr al-Nisa Begum), daughter of Mir Abdullah Khan II (the previous ruler of Sari, whom Mir Sultan-Murad Khan eliminated), married the eldest son of Shah Tahmasp. Khayr al-Nisa Begum, later given the royal title of *mahd-i uliya* (elevated cradle), not only gave birth to the future shah Abbas I (b. 1571) but was a powerful political person.[22]

Apart from the Shirvani and Mazandarani women, many Georgian and Circassian women also entered the Safavid harem. Some of them became mothers of royal children, and their influence and that of their relatives grew.

Sultan-Aqa Khanum, a Circassian from an important family and a wife of Shah Tahmasp, was the mother of the princess Pari-Khan Khanum II, a major political figure after Shah Tahmasp's death. The brother of Sultan-Aqa Khanum, known by his title of Shamkhal Sultan, held several high offices, and his daughter later became a wife of Shah Isma'il II. He also participated in his niece's political designs and acted for a time as her spokesman among the amirs.[23]

Finally, alliances with urban religious elites in the provinces also counted. The Safavid shahs concluded marriage alliances with members of spiritual and religious milieus of local origin and with those having connections with other respected families of the local elite. A typical example is that of the Ni'matullahi Yazdi family who were descendants of the celebrated Sufi shaykh of the fifteenth century, Shah Ni'matullah Vali Kirmani. In the sixteenth century, Shah Ni'matullah b. Amir Nizam al-Din Abd al-Baqi (d. 1564), an important religious personality of his period, became the brother-in-law of Shah Tahmasp by marrying Khanish Khanum I (widow of Amira Dubbaj of Rasht). In 1554 or 1555, their daughter, Safiya-Sultan Khanum, married her first cousin Isma'il Mirza (Shah Isma'il II). In a later generation, two grandsons of Shah Ni'matullah by his son Mir-Miran-i Yazdi married again into the Safavid house. Marriage alliances with members of religious circles continued throughout the Safavid period, and they intensified under the later Safavids proportionally to the loss of influence and prestige of the Qizilbash amirs. Already several daughters of Shah Abbas I were married to religious dignitaries.[24]

Being a royal in-law conferred on a person much prestige. It also gave him the effective means of social ascension through nominations to high central or provincial offices. The sources reveal that royal in-laws sometimes nurtured ambitious designs for their offspring. Mirza Salman, the Iranian vizier of Shah Muhammad Khudabanda, having married his daughter to the crown prince, Sultan-Hamza Mirza, started to dream about his grandsons' becoming state rulers. Amir Khan Mawsillu was also credited by a contemporary chronicler with an ambition to succeed Shah Tahmasp by virtue of being the husband of the shah's sister.[25]

According to the traditional Turkic pattern of succession, still popular in Safavid Iran, all male members of the family, including those descending from the female line, had in theory the right to the throne, despite the existence of a rival Iranian tradition of succession by the eldest son and of the Sufi custom of designating a successor according to arbitrary spiritual criteria.

Children of Safavid princesses were considered members of the ruling family. Male descendants of Safavid mothers had the right to the title of *mirza,* which, when appearing after the personal name, designated a royal prince. Certainly they did inherit from their mother membership in the Safavid house, which accounted for the special social status they enjoyed. In Safavid dynastic strategies of the sixteenth century, these children had the unquestionable right to lay claim to the legacy of their father too, often a local throne or leadership of a tribal group. By the end of the sixteenth century, Shah Abbas I finally incorporated Mazandaran into the Safavid state and considered it as his hereditary domain coming to him from his maternal side. In the second part of the seventeenth century, Chardin reports the same law of succession still in existence or at least commonly believed to be.[26]

Constructing Personalities

Not withstanding their special social position, Safavid royal and elite women were offered other means to enable them to engage eventually in political activities. Education on more than an elementary level gave princesses mastery of intellectual tools matching those of their brothers or husbands. Physical exercise was not forgotten, and such activities as horse riding and archery were promoted. Possession of their own fortunes including land revenue ensured an important degree of financial independence. It also enabled them to finance charitable and pious foundations and to keep their own court with its administrative staff, followers, and sometimes troops. All this resulted in a particular construction of female personalities mastering literary or artistic creation, intellectually able to address complex court and state politics, and physically ready to take part in battle if the necessity arose. The sixteenth century especially produced several outstanding characters whose ambition and understanding of state issues and the power and knowledge of the rules of politics propelled them among top-level players.

Education, Intellectual and Physical

The *Sharaf-nama* of Sharaf Khan Bidlisi, written in the second half of the sixteenth century, gives some details on the education of Safavid princes and sons of amirs and dignitaries who were brought up at court. No such text is known for the education of female children, but it is worth comparing what Sharaf Khan Bidlisi noted on the upbringing of young mirzas to what we can gather from various sources concerning their sisters.

According to Bidlisi, young princes and amirs' sons were encouraged to study the Qur'an, principles of shari'a, piety, and purification. They were entrusted to the care of pious (*dindar*) men, religious and secular scholars (*ulama va fuzala*), in order to protect them from the corrupt and wicked. When they grew up, they were taught military arts such as archery, horse riding, and the use of arms, as well as the game of polo. They learned rules of civility and social behavior. It was considered useful for them to know the art of painting in order to favor their formation of good taste (*saliqa*).[27]

The education of royal daughters does not seem to have been basically different from that described above. Safavid sources indicate that princesses were given a guardian or tutor (*dada, lala*). Both terms had special meaning in the Sufi milieu of the Safavid order. The role of these dignitaries, who were always chosen from among Qizilbash amirs, was to act *in loco parentis*. The royal family's male children were also entrusted to a lala and were usually brought up by him away from court. This was not the case with princesses who were brought up in court; perhaps the office of tutor of princesses was not merely an honorary one. The guardianship of Pari-Khan Khanum II was entrusted just after her birth in 1548 to an Afshar amir, Fathi Beg. Another amir, Basharat Afshar, became in 1578 the guardian of Shah Begum, newborn daughter of Shah Muhammad Khudabanda.[28]

It is difficult to ascertain the duties of guardians and tutors. Were these two offices really distinct from one another? One function of a princess's lala was to accompany his royal charge when she, having married, traveled to her husband's domains. Amir Khan Mawsillu, tutor of Khadija Begum, escorted her to Gilan to her husband, Jamshid Khan. Maryam Begum was also conducted by her tutor to Gilan to join the court of her husband, Khan-Ahmad Khan.[29]

Particular teachers were charged by the shah with girls' education. They taught reading, writing, and calligraphy as well as the Qur'an, all of which was considered basic knowledge. The art of writing, calligraphy, and com-posing letters was probably common among women of the royal court. Tajlu Khanum, chief wife of Shah Isma'il I, wrote missives to her relative, the Qizil-bash governor of Baghdad, while Zaynab Begum exchanged letters with her sister Maryam Begum and their mother, Huri-Khan Khanum.[30] During the struggle after Shah Tahmasp's death, Sultan-Haydar Mirza produced a will of Shah Tahmasp in which he was named heir and successor, but enemy amirs "muttered that the will was not in Tahmasp's handwriting, but in that of one of the harem's women whose hand resembled Tahmasp's."[31]

That women could read and write is not unusual in itself, because the education of girls was by no means an unknown concept. The mixed *mak-*

tab (elementary schools), many of which also had female teachers, had been known in Iran since the tenth or eleventh century.[32] A chronicle notes that during Shah Tahmasp's reign, "in those cities where Shi'ism was particularly strong (Mashhad, Sabzevar, Astarabad, Qom, Kashan, Yazd, Tabriz and Ardabil), forty orphan boys and forty orphan girls were provided with clothes and other necessities. Male and female Shi'i teachers (*mu'allim va mu'allima*) were appointed to instruct them, and servants to attend them, until they reached the age of puberty. Then they were married off to one another and their places taken by younger children."[33]

Shahzada Sultanum, beloved sister of Shah Tahmasp, was taught the rules of grammar and the Persian language by Nur al-Din Kashi. Her second teacher was a religious scholar, Mawlana Imad al-Din Ali Astarabadi, with whom she studied Qur'anic sciences. The mawlana, who must have been an important interlocutor for her, stayed in the princess's entourage until the end of her life and was among people quoted in her will. Shahzada Sultanum was also a pupil of the famous master Dust-Muhammad of Herat, a calligrapher, illuminator, and most probably painter belonging to the royal scriptorium (*kitabkhana*). The princess was known for her intelligence and for passing her time in learned discussions.[34]

Several daughters of Shah Tahmasp are especially singled out in Safavid sources for their knowledge and abilities. Authors and poets of the period dedicated their literary or scientific works to the royal princesses who in some cases acted as patrons.[35] Gawhar-Sultan Khanum I (d. 1577), wife of Sultan-Ibrahim Mirza Safavi, one of the most famous Safavid patrons of art, is praised not only for her piety but also for her learning. Safavid tradition says that after the death of her husband, executed by the order of Shah Isma'il II, she destroyed the books in his library to avoid their falling into the shah's hands. A variant or complementary story states that she assembled in one volume all the poems composed by her husband, and she wrote an introduction to the book. Copies were sent "all over Iran and Turan, all over Rum and India."[36]

Close scrutiny of sources from the Safavid period also reveals that other educated women engaged in intellectual activities. A text called *Javahir al-aja'yib* (Jewels of wonder), written in the mid-sixteenth century in Herat by Fakhri Haravi, is a small biographical anthology of women poets of Herat and Khurasan. Out of twenty-three entries, nineteen concern the late-fifteenth and the first half of the sixteenth centuries (late Timurid and Safavid periods), the period more or less contemporary with the author. Among the Khurasani female poets, many have Timurid (Turko-Mongol) origins, and some even wrote in Chaghatay Turki (eastern Turkic). Fakhri Haravi says that they were all well-known authors and that he himself read the *Divan* of several of them. Women poets often belonged to families from the literary or religious-elite milieu. Apparently marriage was not an obstacle to composing verses, as nearly all of them are described as married (many to older husbands). One of them, known by the pen name of Jamali, was a daughter of the celebrated poet of Herat, Mawlana Hilali (d. 1529/30), while another, Bidili, was married to Shaykh Abdullah Divana, also a well-known poet of Herat. Still another, Nisa'i (or Nisati), came from a Khurasani sayyid family.[37]

Many of these women are specifically described as cultivated, intelligent, and knowledgeable in other fields of learning. Bija (or Bega?) Munajjima, an astrologer, was well known in late-fifteenth-century Herat not only for her science of computing calendars but also as a rival of Jami (d. 1492) in literary creation and charitable foundations.[38] In the seventeenth century, Chardin notes that under Shah Abbas I, a woman physician exercised her art in the harem. Her husband was also a court physician, but Chardin insists that this woman worked independently from him and in virtue of her own science.[39]

Horse riding was an important aspect of female education. In the six-teenth century, it was the main way of moving and traveling. In 1540, Mem-brè describes Qizilbash women riders in Tabriz and during the usual migra-tion of the royal camp, who "ride like men." "Sometimes they galloped and performed marvels with their horses, making them jump and do many oth-er skilful tricks."[40] Shahzada Sultanum accompanied Shah Tahmasp on horse-back during hunting expeditions. The emperor Humayun of the Great Mo-ghuls of India, who took part in several of such parties while sojourning at Tahmasp's court in 1543–44, noticed her presence alongside the shah.[41] An-other Safavid woman followed by her slave-girls took part in a military cav-alry charge.[42] The will of Shahzada Sultanum quotes among her possessions some military equipment and horses.[43]

Women still went hunting on horseback during the Shah Abbas I peri-od, but by then hunting had become a court amusement where gender seg-regation would be strictly applied. Women employed trained hunting birds (hawks and falcons) and shot game with bow and arrows and bullets; they were also armed with swords. Although the closed litter would by the seven-teenth century become the principal means of transport for traveling court women, they still mounted horses on such official occasions as the ceremo-nial entry of Shah Abbas I to Isfahan in 1618. The chief woman of the harem, then aged Zaynab Begum, paternal aunt of the shah, headed the mounted procession of royal women. Women accompanying the shah not only rode horses but also bore arms and moved about with their veils lifted.[44]

Fortunes and Financial Independence

Personal fortune was key for the financial independence of women. It could be composed of gold, silver, jewelry, slaves, houses, land revenue, and commercial profits. Part of these fortunes was habitually used for pious and charitable foundations, which was a consecrated way of leaving a good name. Patronage was also the means of manifesting one's importance and status in a most evident and visible way.

Tajlu Khanum, wife of Shah Isma'il I, possessed arable land, gardens, and villages in central Iran, which she gave as pious endowments (vaqf) to different mausolea. She financed decorative works in the mausoleum of Safavid shaykhs in Ardabil and the renovation of the Dukhtar bridge near Miyana. She was known for encouraging the establishment of pious foundations.[45] When Tajlu Khanum was banished from the court in 1540, her personal possessions, "a great treasure," were confiscated.[46] Toward the mid-sixteenth century, a sister (or daughter) of Shah Isma'il I was given a village in Shirvan province as tiyul (regular revenue land) for a military action that had saved a battle.[47]

Shahzada Sultanum was rich. Her will, preserved in the text of a chronicle in a fragmentary way, enumerates many personal possessions that she donated to different people and pious institutions. She personally owned extensive real estate in various regions of Iran. At her death in 1562, all these lands were turned into vaqf endowments. She made other donations, particularly to Mashhad, Kerbala, and Najaf.[48] She is also known to have founded a garden in Qazvin, named after her the Bagh-i Mahin Banu (her personal name). It was part of the royal residential quarter founded by Shah Tahmasp.[49]

According to a contemporary chronicler, the fortune of Pari-Khan Khanum II in silver and gold coins was estimated at her death in 1578 to be from 10,000 to 15,000 tumans. Her court was composed of four to five hundred servants who followed her on official occasions.[50] Not much is known about her landed property, but it is impossible to believe that she did not possess any. We know that she had her own house outside the harem quarters in Qazvin.[51]

We have less information about the property other princesses owned. Khanish Khanum I, sister of Shah Isma'il I, financed a mosque in Taft in Yazd province. It was built next to the well-known khanaqah (college of dervishes) of the Ni'matullahi Sufi order.[52] In the second half of the century, Sultanum Begum, main wife of Shah Tahmasp, owned the tiyul and muqarrariyat (perpetual fixed assignation) payable on lands in western Khurasan.[53]

Zaynab Begum, daughter of Shah Tahmasp, possessed a prosperous village in the region of Yazd, which constituted only a part of her real estate. She sold it to Khan Begum, probably her sister Khanish Khanum II (sometimes called Khanish Begum). The honorific title of Khan Begum indicates that she was probably of royal blood, and about a hundred years later the village was in the hands of descendants of the Safavid princess Khanish Khanum II.[54] Zaynab Begum also owned a caravanserai and the bazaar Amir Chaqmaq, both in Yazd; at her death, the latter was transformed into vaqf to support her mausoleum in Mashhad. She devoted important financial means to the purpose of charitable foundations. Among others she financed many public buildings and renovation works.[55]

The Courts and Entourage of the Safavid Princesses

Princesses and royal spouses maintained their own courts and administrative staffs and were surrounded by their own followers and clients. In many cases, they were their relatives and people of the same origin. For instance, Circassians grouped mostly around Pari-Khan Khanum II, whose mother was a Circassian, and Georgians gathered around Sultanzada Khanum, who was one of many Georgian women of the court and mother of the royal prince Sultan-Haydar.

Khayr al-Nisa Begum, wife of Shah Muhammad Khudabanda, openly favored her Mazandarani relatives and followers in the granting of important offices. Several Mazandarani dignitaries who had served with her father arrived with her at the Safavid court in 1565–66.[56] Some probably went with her to Herat and Shiraz, where her husband was residing. When in 1578 Shah Muhammad Khudabanda was enthroned in Qazvin, these officials returned to the service of Khayr al-Nisa Begum, who had control of state affairs. Next to the Mazandarani followers who were especially privileged, Khayr al-Nisa Begum and her eldest son, Sultan-Hamza Mirza, were surrounded by people who followed them from Herat and Shiraz.[57] Khayr al-Nisa Begum's power was so evident that several state officers were especially named as being in her service, among them Mir Khan Ghazi, accountant of the kingdom (*mustawfi al-mamalik*).[58] The tribal entourage of Khayr al-Nisa Begum was composed mainly of Shamlu but also of some Afshar. Although she was not a Turkman, at least some Qizilbash support was necessary for conducting her political designs.[59]

Obtaining an office at a royal woman's court was an important stage in an administrative career. Mir Qavam al-Din Husayn, previously accountant of the governor of Shiraz, held the office of vizier to Khayr al-Nisa Begum. Khwaja

Ibrahim Khalil was the vizier to Sultanum Begum; Khwaja Majid al-Din Ibrahim Shirazi was the vizier to Pari-Khan Khanum II; and Khwaja Pir Ahmad Yazdi was the vizier to Safiya-Sultan Khanum (known as Shahzada Khanum), daughter of Shah Ismaʿil II.[60] Some high state dignitaries had held posts in service of princesses. Zaynab Begum used the services of a vizier, Mirza Lutfullah Shirazi, who later became the grand vizier of the royal supreme divan.[61]

Politics and War

During the sixteenth century, women of the political elites participated in diplomatic missions, mainly within the extended family. They could also be seen present and active during military campaigns. Some royal princesses and spouses assumed partial or complete direction of state affairs. Each generation of sixteenth-century Safavid women could find its role models for female politicians among women of the previous generation.

Women were employed traditionally by their families as diplomatic emissaries. Already in 1488, the paternal grandmother of Shah Ismaʿil I acted as mediator between her son and her nephew, the Aq Quyunlu Sultan Yaʿqub. She traveled from Ardabil, home of the Safavids, to Qum, where the Aq Quyunlu court stayed.[62] Around 1533–34, a Kurdish rebel amir, Sharaf Khan Bidlisi, is reported to have sent his wife and brother to Shah Tahmasp's court to negotiate conditions of a peace treaty. The influence of the wife certainly counted because she had been the shah's nurse.[63] In 1546, Alqas Mirza, a rebel half brother of Shah Tahmasp, sent his mother from Shirvan to the court to plead on his behalf for royal pardon.[64]

Shahzada Sultanum, the intimate counselor of Shah Tahmasp, exchanged official letters with Hurrem Sultan, favorite wife of the Ottoman sultan Sulayman the Magnificent, as well as with an Ottoman royal princess who was probably Mihrimah Sultan, daughter of Hurrem Sultan and Sulayman.[65]

On military campaigns, according to the custom of the age, the Safavids moved about with the totality of their camp including families. Camp was usually pitched a certain distance from the actual battlefield. The famous episode of the battle of Chaldiran (1514) illustrates the obvious dangers of such an arrangement. The Safavid camp was taken and looted by the Ottomans, who took many prisoners among the women, including some Safavid royal princesses. The favorite wife of Shah Ismaʿil I, Tajlu Khanum, who managed to save herself from the camp, was afterwards found wandering lost in the countryside and taken back to the shah.[66]

A revealing military episode of 1553–54 is described by two Safavid sources.[67] The Safavid governor of Shirvan, Abdullah Khan Ustajalu, was losing a battle against Shirvani rebels. Having learned of his difficulties, a woman from his family—his mother or wife—ordered people of the camp to arm themselves, and she led them into battle. The detachment was mounted and numbered about three thousand people, two-thirds of whom were *ghulams* (slave soldiers). The remaining one thousand were composed partly of Qizilbash military and partly of slave-girls and servants. The woman-warrior is said to have put on her head the Safavid *taj* (crown) and girded herself with a sword inherited from her illustrious ancestors.[68] The arriving detachment was mistaken by the enemy for regular Qizilbash reinforcement troops. The confusion enabled Abdullah Khan to win the day. In recognition of her bravery, the Safavid woman was given an allocation of land revenue and the honorary title of Tajlu Begum.[69]

Khayr al-Nisa Begum took part in a military campaign against the Ottomans in the winter of 1578–79. Although her son, Sultan-Hamza Mirza (then aged about twelve), was the official commander-in-chief of the Safavid troops, it was she who discussed decisions with Qizilbash generals.[70] The campaign ended abruptly because of a disagreement concerning the pursuit of hostilities and the control of already conquered territories. In a violent argument, during which Khayr al-Nisa Begum sharply criticized the amirs and was criticized by them in return, she left the army camp. Despite the passes being snow covered, she marched across the mountains to reach Qazvin followed by amirs and soldiers.[71] At that stage, Khayr al-Nisa Begum was in fact governing the whole Safavid state, because Shah Muhammad Khudabanda, of contemplative disposition and suffering from eye trouble, had little interest in state matters. In the Shirvan campaign, she appeared to English contemporary observers in Astrakhan as the virtual head of the army: "Queene of Persia (the king being blind) had beene with a great armie against the Turks that were left to possesse Media [Azerbaijan] and had given them a great overthrow. . . . They gathered power together, and with the Queene of their country as chiefe, they entered the country of Media, and overrane the same with sword and fire, destroying whatsoever they founde."[72]

Khadija Begum, widow of Jamshid Khan of Gilan, followed her son during the struggle for power in Gilan in the late sixteenth century.[73] During an Uzbek invasion of Khurasan in 1527, a fortress there was defended by the wife of the absent Safavid governor Burun Sultan Rumlu. Burun Sultan, then at the royal court, had officially left responsibility to his wife for military defense in case it was necessity.[74] In the mid-sixteenth century, a battle was fought between the Safavids and a Kurdish rebel, Dawlatyar Khan. The Kurds gained the victory and took a large booty. While the looting of the Qizilbash was still going on, the aged mother of Dawlatyar Khan riding a horse with no saddle joined the battlefield. She encouraged the troops to pursue the fugitives and especially called on them to seize the enemy's kettledrums.[75]

The mother of Shah Tahmasp, Tajlu Khanum, who had influence at the court of Shah Isma'il I, gained still more importance after his death and during her son's minority. When Qizilbash amirs decided to enthrone Shah Tahmasp, who was then about ten years old, they made sure to secure Tajlu Khanum's agreement. Tajlu Khanum was banished from the court by her son in 1540, and her fortune was confiscated; she was sent to Shiraz with a small pension. The reasons for this banishment are not clear, but several years previously the shah, now an adult, had taken over the control of state affairs from the Qizilbash amirs. Membrè understood—but this supposition is not confirmed—that Tajlu Khanum was involved in a plot to replace Shah Tahmasp by his younger brother Bahram Mirza, who was also her son.[76] Membrè might have misinterpreted a remark concerning the recent rebellion of another of the shah's brothers, Sam Mirza, which indeed was most probably aimed at deposing the ruler and replacing him by his brother.[77]

The place of influence at the shah's side was immediately taken by his sister, Shahzada Sultanum, also born of Tajlu Khanum. Not only was she the privileged adviser of the sovereign, who consulted her on every decision, but she also directed many state affairs.[78] She especially played the key role as a mediator in negotiations between Shah Tahmasp and the emperor Humayun of India. Having found refuge with the Safavids, Humayun sought their military support to win back the Moghul throne. Shah Tahmasp was not particularly in favor of granting him the necessary troops, but Shahzada Sultanum held the contrary opinion. Having secured the support of their brother Bahram Mirza, she saw that an army was formed and sent to regain Humayun's throne. The Safavids were to retain the province of Qandahar in return for their aid.[79]

Pari-Khan Khanum II

Shahzada Sultanum was regarded as a role model by her niece, Pari-Khan Khanum II, daughter of Shah Tahmasp, by whom she was replaced as his counselor and lieutenant (*sahib al-amr*).[80] After Shah Tahmasp's death, she headed a political party of Qizilbash and court dignitaries, which succeeded in bringing to power Shah Isma'il II (r. 1576–77) and in eliminating the counter-candidate, Sultan-Haydar Mirza, who was supported by another party.[81] Pari-Khan Khanum II's wish was to imitate and surpass her aunt. Under her brother Shah Isma'il II, she held the ambition to attain a position of influence greater than that of Shahzada Sultanum, who had been at Shah Tahmasp's side. It did not happen, as she fell out of favor with Shah Isma'il II. She ruled the state during the short interval of a few months from Shah Isma'il II's death to Shah Muhammad Khudabanda's arrival at the court of Qazvin. During this period, the amirs had to consult her on every matter and obtain her agreement to every decision. The Qizilbash amirs used to come daily to her apartments to receive their orders. She had at her private disposal armed followers as well as ghulam troops who passed under her command after the death of her full brother Sultan-Sulayman Mirza. The Qizilbash army and the royal ghulams obeyed her.[82]

On the death of Shah Isma'il II, Shah Muhammad (r. 1578–87) was chosen from among several possible candidates for the throne—all of whom but he were children—by the most powerful amirs and dignitaries who consulted Pari-Khan Khanum.[83] It is revealing that Shah Muhammad Khudabanda was chosen, because he had been until then considered unfit for the crown because of his near blindness, despite being the eldest son. After Shah Tahmasp's death, he was bypassed on account of his disability. Pari-Khan Khanum agreed to his candidacy exactly because she expected that his condition would prevent him from pursuing state conduct; it was also common knowledge that he was not interested in politics. In any case, the princess had the firm intention to rule herself while the new shah would be a sovereign in name only.[84] She did not take into account an unsuspected rival to power, Khayr al-Nisa Begum, wife of Shah Muhammad. Khayr al-Nisa Begum had no intention of leaving the government of the Safavid state to Pari-Khan Khanum but to exercise it herself.

Although the position of Pari-Khan Khanum II in the capital was for a time unchallenged, Khayr al-Nisa Begum controlled affairs in the entourage of her husband, by then officially the royal court, in progress toward the capital. In Qazvin, a conflict between the powerful maternal uncle of Pari-Khan Khanum, Shamkhal Sultan, and the grand vizier of the supreme divan, Mirza Salman, induced the latter to leave Qazvin and join Shah Muhammad's court. Immediately reconfirmed in his office of grand vizier, he became an important ally of Khayr al-Nisa Begum.[85] Analyzing the situation clearly, Mirza Salman perceived the special status of Pari-Khan Khanum as royal sister and daughter and the advantage she possessed by the command of the troops. Having known her for a long time, he argued at the shah's court that as long as the princess stayed alive she would not give up her power, nor would she permit Khayr al-Nisa Begum's interference in state matters.[86] A clash between the two women could not be avoided.

As the royal court approached Qazvin, many Qizilbash amirs, taking the example of Mirza Salman, left the city, thus transgressing the express orders of Pari-Khan Khanum, and went to welcome Shah Muhammad Khudaban-da. When the shah entered Qazvin, Pari-Khan Khanum went to greet him escorted only by her personal followers.[87] Taking advantage of the confusion reigning in Qazvin, Mirza Salman accused his old enemy Shamkhal Sultan, Pari-Khan Khanum's uncle, of armed rebellion and ordered him killed. The princess lost her freedom of maneuver and stayed a virtual prisoner in the royal harem. In February 1578, Pari-Khan Khanum was transferred to the house of Khalil Khan Afshar, who had been her lala in the past, and was stran-gled by his men.[88]

Khayr al-Nisa Begum

Khayr al-Nisa Begum, wife of Shah Muhammad Khudabanda, governed the state de facto from February 1578 to July 1579 when she was assassinated, to-gether with her mother and a group of her Mazandarani supporters, by Qizil-bash amirs.[89] During that period, she appeared at official occasions next to the shah accompanied by her eldest and favorite son, Sultan-Hamza Mirza, whom she wanted to be considered as heir apparent. Shah Muhammad was so self-effacing that even after the death of Khayr al-Nisa Begum, some Euro-pean travelers took Sultan-Hamza Mirza for the sovereign.[90]

Khayr al-Nisa Begum was the daughter of a local ruler from Mazanda-ran, Mir Abdullah Khan, and descended from the celebrated Mar'ashi say-yid, Qavam al-Din, known as Mir-i Buzurg (d. 1379). Different branches of her family had ruled Mazandaran since the mid-fourteenth century. After her father was killed by a rival cousin, Mir Sultan-Murad Khan, she and her brothers were given refuge at the Safavid court in 1565–66. Once there, she was quickly married to Shah Tahmasp's son.[91] Not much is known about her background. Coming from a sayyid and ruling family, she was probably well cultivated and, at least to some extent, acquainted with matters of state. She could certainly find role models of politically active women in her own ex-tended family, even if some belonged to the enemy faction.[92]

Khayr al-Nisa Begum's character must have been forged by adversities in her early life: defeat of her family in Mazandaran, escape to the Safavids, and dangers to which her husband and sons were exposed during Shah

Isma'il II's period when Safavid princes were being executed. The power she did finally achieve was certainly viewed by her as the best compensation for the humiliations of her younger days. But her desire to avenge her Mazandarani family was to be an instrument of her fall.

From the start of Shah Muhammad's assuming the throne, Khayr al-Nisa Begum made political, administrative, and military decisions and approved royal decrees; in short, "no affair was conducted without her advice."[93] She was kept informed about political matters in the same way as were the shah and the prince Sultan-Hamza Mirza. Amirs and civil dignitaries acknowledged her high position. They went to her quarters every day to receive their daily orders, and after New Year's celebrations in 1579 they visited the harem garden to present their greetings to her.[94] She controlled the central and provincial administration by the traditional means of distributing offices to her relatives and trustworthy supporters and money from the royal treasure to others.[95] Although she was supported by the grand vizier Mirza Salman and some amirs, her relationship with the majority of Qizilbash amirs was growing difficult. A chronicler of the time writes about her prejudice toward the Qizilbash and her desire to prevent amirs from interfering with political and administrative decisions. She was known for her severe criticisms of amirs, for she argued with and threatened them, and for her disdain toward their advice and opinion.[96]

By the summer of 1579, several moves of Khayr al-Nisa Begum angered and humiliated the amirs, already exasperated by the obstinacy she and her Mazandarani party displayed in order to block their access to decision-making and power circles and to limit their economic strength. About that time, Safavids seized her Mazandarani enemy, Mirza Khan, son of Mir Sultan-Murad Khan who had been responsible for her father's death. She ordered Mirza Khan's execution, despite his surrendering because he trusted the solemn oath of Qizilbash amirs that his life would be spared.[97] Another of her decisions removed the government of the important Kashan province from Muhammad Khan Turkman. This economically and politically important province was thus lost to the Qizilbash, for she transferred it to the category of crown land.[98] This decision struck the Turkmans directly, but indirectly it affected all the tribes, and a coup was hatched among Qizilbash amirs. Only when the conspirators were joined by Mirza Salman, whose administration was being submerged by the Mazandaranis, did it become possible to bring the begum down.

The rebellion spread among Qizilbash soldiers who, led by amirs claiming the "dismissal of the Mazandaranis," protested that the shah was present and that therefore "he should rule by himself and not delegate his power to a woman."[99] The shah received a delegation of amirs who expressed their grievances. Surprisingly or not, the begum was also present and spoke harshly to the amirs. The shah promised to send Khayr al-Nisa Begum back to Mazandaran, but he was powerless to save her. The situation had gone so far that the amirs could not ask for less than her death. Many rumors were spread about her, including one pretending that she had transferred the royal treasury to Mazandaran and another that she was having a love affair with a Tatar prince residing at court. Khayr al-Nisa Begum and her mother were strangled in the royal harem in July 1579.[100]

Khayr al-Nisa Begum's strong personal power managed for a short while to keep in check the centrifugal trends agitating the Safavid state since Shah Tahmasp's death. Her murder and the absence of a strong ruler led to a revival of Qizilbash tribal wars, which were to last until the assumption of power by Shah Abbas I in 1587.

The "rule" of Khayr al-Nisa Begum and, before that, the clash between her and the princess Pari-Khan Khanum II are among the best-known episodes of the period's history. It is easy to understand why both of them are the most famous female politicians of Safavid history. However exceptional they were in the extent of power they exercised, they were not the only Safavid women engaged in politics. Before and after them others were active in promoting their families' interests or in serving their own ambitions. This happened not only at the royal court but also in provincial courts. For example, in Shirvan around 1535 a Safavid princess tried to protect Safavid interests in a succession war after her husband's death.[101]

During the period of Shah Abbas I's reign, Zaynab Begum was again among the shah's most intimate counselors. She was kept informed of political and administrative affairs. In 1606, she was the only woman present at a session of the royal council debating military questions. Despite accidental disagreement with the shah and even a short period of disgrace, Zaynab Begum continued to participate in the management of state affairs until the successor of Shah Abbas I, Shah Safi I (r. 1629–42), banished her from the court.[102]

Conclusion

The great majority of politically and socially active women appearing in the sources were either of royal Safavid (paternal or maternal) or Turkman Qizilbash descent. The outstanding exception was Khayr al-Nisa Begum, of Iranian Mazandarani origin, who was connected to the Safavids by marriage and not by blood. Certainly an exceptional character herself, she found within the early Safavid social and political system an opportunity to develop her capacities and fulfill her ambitions. A closer scrutiny of local sources shows that some other noble women of Mazandaran and Gilan actively took part in the military and political conflicts shattering these northern provinces of Iran during the sixteenth century.

Virtually no information can be found on the urban Iranian female population, and the sources scarcely mention female poets, artists, or religious scholars. We should not be deceived by this approach of historiographers of the period, who conformed to the conventional style of writing. Although little primary source information is available, it seems clear that literary, artistic, and to some extent religious spheres of life were domains in which women could take part and even attain a certain level of prominence. Education was accessible to elite women and on a much lesser level to other social groups.

Women of the Safavid dynasty enjoyed a particular status. Not only did they receive a comparatively good education but they also enjoyed much financial independence, which enabled them to maintain their own courts and to act as patrons of art and architecture and of charitable foundations. It was socially permissible for princesses to participate in hunting parties, military expeditions, and state affairs. The role of a privileged confidante and counselor to the shah fell within their domain and was considered a normal occupation. Turkic nomadic traditions of warrior steppe societies were reflected in the cultural background of the Safavids. The famous collection of Turkic heroic stories known as the *Book of Dede Korkut* contains examples of women competing with men (who are often their fiancés) in horse riding, arrow shooting, and wrestling. While a woman's help in battle was welcome, she was not supposed to boast about her victories.[103]

Twice in Safavid history, women stepped beyond the limits of their role and achieved the highest executive power in the state. Both Pari-Khan Khanum II and Khayr al-Nisa Begum found, for slightly different reasons, that however unchallenged their power momentarily was, it was impossible for them to keep it for long. The idea of a woman openly active on the political scene and even governing the state in a period of crisis was fully accepted by Safavid elites. The same woman holding power on a permanent basis, especially when a male ruler was available, was perceived as transgressing the admitted social and political rules. It is revealing that female counselors and lieutenants of Safavid shahs kept their important positions for years on end.

This was the case of Shahzada Sultanum and Zaynab Begum as well as of Tajlu Khanum during her husband's lifetime and her son's minority, and of Pari-Khan Khanum II until Shah Tahmasp's death. Neither these latter two nor Khayr al-Nisa Begum were accepted on a permanent basis. Tajlu Khanum was banished quickly after her son's coming of age. Khayr al-Nisa Begum was murdered after eighteen months of openly exercising power. Pari-Khan Khanum II, eliminated in apparently different circumstances and for different reasons, fell victim to the same process.[104]

In sixteenth-century Safavid Iran, society was prepared to give greater space to women from the royal family and from the elite political group. They could administer their property, engage in cultural activities, and participate in certain spheres of life where traditionally women were few, such as hunting and war. To an unexpected degree, royal women were perceived as partners. They could and even were supposed to exercise some political power but on condition of keeping to their status of second-in-command. Only in exceptional circumstances and until return to normality could they effectively assume the leading role.

This situation evolved by the beginning of the seventeenth century when the influence of the Irano-Islamic tradition of settled people grew stronger with the ruler's encouragement. While Safavid upper society drifted away from its Turkic heritage, the status and spheres of activity of women were becoming modified toward more confinement within the harem enclosure.

NOTES

This chapter is largely extracted from my two-part article, "La participation des femmes de la famille royale à l'exercice du pouvoir en Iran safavide au XVIe siècle," pt. 1, *Studia Iranica* 23 (2) (1994): 211–58; pt. 2, *Studia Iranica* 24 (1) (1995): 61–122, with some revision and additional material. I thank Andrew Newman for his critical reading of the chapter's English version and for his suggestions.

1. See A. K. S. Lambton, "al-Mar'a," pt. 3, *Encyclopedia of Islam* (1954); also see W. Walther, *Women in Islam from Medieval to Modern Times* (Princeton: Markus Wiener, 1993), 103–27, for a general survey of women in Islamic history.

2. Ruy González de Clavijo, *Embassy to Tamerlane, 1403–1406*, trans. G. Le Strange (London: Routledge, 1928), 244–45. Another feast is described (258–61), where Timur's main wife appeared magnificently dressed wearing "before her face a thin white veil," a beautiful embroidered, bejeweled, and befeathered headgear, and her jet black hair "all loose, hanging down over her shoulders."

3. B. O'Kane, "From Tents to Pavilions: Royal Mobility and Persian Palace Design," *Ars Orientalis* 23 (1993), 250, 256.

4. See T. W. Lentz and G. D. Lowry, *Timur and the Princely Vision: Persian Art and*

Culture in the Fifteenth Century, Los Angeles Museum of Art (Washington, D.C.: Smithsonian Institution Press, 1989), 74, 81, 84–86, 106, 225, 255 (photo and description of Gawhar-Shad's seal).

5. See Fadlullah b. Ruzbihan Khunji-Isfahani, *Tarikh-i alam-ara-yi Amini,* ed. John Woods (London: Royal Asiatic Society, 1992), 100, 142–43, 427–30; John Woods, *The Aq Quyunlu: Clan, Confederation, Empire: A Study in Fifteenth/Ninth Century Turko-Iranian Politics* (Minneapolis: Bibliotheca Islamica, 1976), 139–40, 144.

6. Michele Membrè, *Mission to the Lord Sophy of Persia (1539–1542),* trans. A. H. Morton (London: School of Oriental and African Studies, 1993), 31.

7. Ibid., 25.

8. Vincenzo d'Alessandri, "Narrative of the Most Noble Vincentio d'Alessandri," in *A Narrative of Italian Travels in Persia in the Fifteenth and Sixteenth Centuries* (London: Hakluyt Society, 1873), 217. The woman in question was certainly Zahra Baji, a Georgian spouse of the shah; see Szuppe, "Participation," pt. 2, appendix 2, no. 47.

9. For example, see Iskandar Beg Turkman, *Tarikh-i alam-ara-yi Abbasi,* ed. Iraj Afshar (Tehran: Amir Kabir, 1955), 203; Qazi Ahmad Qumi, *Khulasat al-tavarikh,* ed. I. Ishraqi (Tehran: Danishkada-yi Tehran, 1980–84), 2:693.

10. Francesco Romano, "Travels of a Merchant in Persia," in *A Narrative of Italian Travels to Persia in the Fifteenth and Sixteenth Centuries* (London: Hakluyt Society, 1873), 172. The author, appearing as Anonymous in *A Narrative,* which is an English translation of the Italian original of 1559, is identified by Jean Aubin, "Chroniques persanes et relations italiennes: Notes sur les sources narratives du règne de Chah Esma'il," *Studia Iranica* 24 (2) (1995), 247–59, especially 254–58.

11. D'Alessandri, "Narrative," 223.

12. Adam Olearius, *Vermehrte Neue Beschreibung der Muscowitischen und Persischen Reyse* (Schleswig: J. Holwein, 1656), 480.

13. See Szuppe, "Participation," pt. 1, 214, 227–28, 238–39; also see Szuppe, "Kinship Ties with the Safavids among the Qizilbash Amirs in Late Sixteenth Century Iran: A Case Study of the Political Career of the Sharaf al-Din Oghi Tekelu Family," in *Safavid Persia: The History and Politics of an Islamic Society,* ed. Charles Melville (London: I. B. Tauris, 1996), 79–104.

14. Szuppe, "Participation," pt. 1, 215–40; Szuppe, "Kinship Ties," 79–104.

15. Szuppe, "Participation," pt. 1, 235n.107.

16. See Hasan Beg Rumlu, *Ahsan al-tavarikh,* ed. Abd al-Husayn (Tehran: Babak, 1978), 2:14, 16, 21–22; Bijan, untitled history of Shah Isma'il I, MS British Library, Or. 3248, fol. 29b, 31a; Fazli Khuzani, *Afzal al-tavarikh,* MS British Library, Or. 4678, fol. 58a–b; Iskandar Beg, *Tarikh,* 25.

17. Szuppe, "Participation," pt. 1, 220–23n.47, for sources, table 1. Also see Amir Mahmud b. Khwandamir, *Iran dar ruzgar-i Shah Isma'il va Shah Tahmasp,* ed. Gholam-Reza Tabataba'i (Tehran: Bonyad-i mowqufat-i Doktor-i Mahmud Afshar Yazdi, 1991), 287.

18. For both terms, see *Tadhkirat al-Muluk: A Manual of Safavid Administration,* trans. V. Minorsky (Cambridge: Cambridge University Press, 1943), 117, 119. For the office of *amir al-umara,* see also R. M. Savory, "The Principal Offices of the Safawid State during the Reign of Isma'il I (907–30/1501–24)," *Bulletin of the School of Oriental and African Studies* 24 (1960): 91–101; and "The Principal Offices of the Safa-

wid State during the Reign of Tahmasp I (930–84/1524–76)," *Bulletin of the School of Oriental and African Studies* 24 (1961): 71–79.

19. Iskandar Beg, *Tarikh*, 1022; see also Szuppe, "Participation," pt. 1, 223, for more details.

20. Szuppe, "Participation," pt. 1, 229–32, tables 3, 4.

21. Mir Timur Mar'ashi, *Tarikh-i khandan-i Mar'ashi-yi Mazandaran*, ed. M. Sutuda (Tehran: Ittila'at, 1961), 173, 174, 182, 184–85. Mah-Parvar Khanum was also known in Mazandaran as *khatun-i Turk* (Turkish princess) and *arus-i Turk* (Turkish bride). See Szuppe, "The Jewels of Wonder: Learned Ladies and Princess Politicians in the Provinces of Early Safavid Iran," in *Women in the Medieval Islamic World: Power, Patronage, and Piety*, ed. Gavin Hambly (New York: St. Martin's, 1998), 335.

22. Abdi Beg Shirazi Navidi, *Takmilat al-akhbar, tarikh-i Safaviyya az aghaz ta 978*, ed. Abd al-Husayn Nava'i (Tehran: Nay, 1990), 128; Qumi, *Khulasat*, 454; Iskandar Beg, *Tarikh*, 126. *Mahd-i uliya* was the traditional title of royal women in use at least since the Aq Quyunlu (see Khunji, *Tarikh*, 142–43, on Saljuq-Shah Begum) until the Qajar period.

23. On Shamkhal Sultan, who held the office of keeper of the seal (*muhrdar*), see Qumi, *Khulasat*, 558, 601, 627; Rumlu, *Ahsan*, 2:568, 600–601, 633; Iskandar Beg, *Tarikh*, 206.

24. Nasrullah Falsafi, *Zindigani-yi Shah Abbas-i avval* (Tehran: Ilmi, 1960), 2:198–201; L. Lockhart, *The Fall of the Safavid Dynasty and the Afghan Occupation of Persia* (Cambridge: Cambridge University Press, 1958), genealogical table following p. 472; Szuppe, "Participation," pt. 1, 226–28, table 2; J. Aubin, "De Kuhbanan à Bidar: La famille Ni'matullahi," *Studia Iranica* 20 (2) (1991): 1–130, on the Ni'matullahis before the Safavid period. J. Chardin reports in the second half of the seventeenth century that "on les [princesses] marie à un ecclésiastique bien fait et de bonne famille, mais jamais à un homme d'épée, ni à un homme d'état, de peur que cette grande alliance ne lui fit former des desseins contraires au gouvernement"; *Voyages* (Paris: Langlès, 1811), 5:247.

25. Szuppe, "Participation," pt. 1, 214–15.

26. Chardin, *Voyages*, 5:240. In the eighteenth century, among the many pretenders who were proclaimed shah by different tribal amirs, several were descended from the Safavids through the female line. See Lockhart, *The Fall*, genealogical table following p. 472. Also see Szuppe, "Kinship Ties," 79ff. For a comparison with Timurid practices, see M. E. Subtelny, "Babur's Rival Relations: A Study on Kinship and Conflict in Fifteenth–Sixteenth Century Central Asia," *Der Islam* 66 (1) (1989): 102–18. For the importance of the son-in-law (damad) at the Ottoman court and the succession problem, see L. Peirce, *Imperial Harem: Women and Sovereignty in the Ottoman Empire* (Oxford: Oxford University Press, 1993), 65–90.

27. Amir Sharaf Khan Bidlisi, *Sharaf-nama, tarikh-i mufassal-i Kurdistan*, ed. M. Abbasi (Tehran: Ilmi, 1985), 576–77. Chardin's comments on the education of Safavid princes in the mid-seventeenth century are similar (Chardin, *Voyages*, 5:246). Several Safavid princes were highly cultivated and sometimes accomplished artists as well as patrons of art. Shah Tahmasp was known as a good painter; see Qazi Ahmad Qumi, *Gulistan-i hunar*, ed. A. Suhayli Khwansari (Tehran: B.F.I., 1973), 138. His brother Sam Mirza, who was the author of a biography (tadhkira) of poets (*Tuhfa-*

yi Sami), and another brother, Bahram Mirza, were also good calligraphers and con-noisseurs of painting. The most famous of the early Safavid princes was Sultan-Ibra-him Mirza, son of Bahram Mirza, governor of Mashhad, whose patronage of artists and poets rivaled and perhaps surpassed that of the royal court. On royal and princely Safavid patrons, see A. Welch, *Artists for the Shah: Late Sixteenth-Century Painting at the Imperial Court of Iran* (New Haven: Yale University Press, 1976), 150–88. See also Rumlu, *Ahsan*, 2:712–13.

28. Qumi, *Khulasat*, 668, 967. Basharat Afshar was an officer of the protocol of the harem administration (*ishiq aqasi*).

29. Abdi Beg, *Takmilat*, 130, for Khadija Begum; Qumi, *Khulasat*, 664, for Maryam Begum; her tutor was Pir-Ali Beg Chavushlu.

30. Qumi, *Khulasat*, 176, for Tajlu Khanum; *Shah Tahmasp Safavi, majmuʻa-yi as-nad va mukatibat-i tarikh hamrah ba yaddashtha-yi tafsili*, ed. Abd al-Husayn Navaʼi (Tehran: Arghavan, 1972), 14, 18, for Zaynab Begum's correspondence.

31. Iskandar Beg, *Tarikh*, 193.

32. See Ehsan Naraghi, *Enseignement et changements sociaux en Iran du VIIᵉ au XXᵉ siècle* (Paris: Maison des Sciences de l'Homme, 1992), 36.

33. Iskandar Beg, *Tarikh*, 123.

34. Shahzada Sultanum's first and second teachers and her disposition for learn-ing are mentioned by Qumi, *Khulasat*, 430; Qazi Ahmad Ghaffari, *Tarikh-i jahan-ara* (Tehran: Hafiz, 1964), 307. For Dust-Muhammad of Herat, see Budaq Qazvini, *Java-hir al-akhbar* (St. Petersburg: National Library), MS Dorn 288, fol. 111a; Chahryar Adle, "Les artistes nommés Dust-Muhammad au XVIᵉ siècle," *Studia Iranica* 22 (2) (1993): 226–28.

35. Shahzada Sultanum had works dedicated to her, including by religious schol-ars. See Qumi, *Khulasat*, 404, 980; C. A. Storey, *Persian Literature: A Bio-Bibliographical Survey* (London: Luzac, 1927), 1197. Abdi Beg dedicated his chronicle *Takmilat al-akhbar* to Pari-Khan Khanum II; Abdi Beg, *Takmilat*, 99. When the poet Mawlana Mohtasham Kashi dedicated a *qasida* to Pari-Khan Khanum II and another one to Shah Tahmasp, he was reminded by the princess that he should rather write poems celebrating Imam Ali (Iskandar Beg, *Tarikh*, 178). See also Welch, *Artists*, 170–71.

36. Qumi, *Khulasat*, 637.

37. Fakhri Haravi, *Javahir al-ajaʼyib*, lithographed text, Lucknow, 1873, 20–21 for Jamali, 15 for Bidili, and 16–17 for Nisaʼi.

38. Fakhri Haravi, *Javahir*, 14; she knew Jami personally.

39. Chardin, *Voyages*, 8:27–28. Their son Mirza Ibrahim was a physician at the court of Shah Safi, successor of Shah Abbas I.

40. Membrè, *Mission*, 25. See also the quotation heading the chapter.

41. Gulbadan Begum, *The History of Humayun*, ed. Annette Beveridge (London: Royal Asiatic Society, 1902), 69, 169–70.

42. Khuzani, *Afzal*, fol. 203b–204b; Qumi, *Khulasat*, 372.

43. Qumi, *Khulasat*, 430.

44. Olearius, *Reyse*, 529. Pietro Della Valle, *Viaggi di Pietro della Valle il Pellegrino, descritti da lui medesimo in lettere all'eurdito suo amico Mario Schipano: La Persia* (Rome: Vitale Mascardi, 1658), 1:295–97, 2:12–14. Also see Falsafi, *Zindigani*, 2:225; Szuppe, "Participation," pt. 1, 245–47.

45. For example, nine villages or parts of villages with fields and land in the Qum area were given as vaqf to the sanctuary of Fatima in Qum in 1522; Qumi, *Khulasat,* 290; *Turbat-i Pakan,* ed. H. Tabataba'i (Qum, 1976), 1:132, 133–41. In Qazvin, Tajlu Khanum made vaqf donations of arable land (in 1531–32) and part of a village (in 1536) to the mausoleum of Shahzada Husayn; H. Mudarrisi Tabataba'i, *Barghi az tarikh-i Qazvin: Tarikhcha'i az Astana-yi Shahzada Husayn va dudman-i sadat-i Marʿashi Qazvini* (Qum: Kitabkhana-yi Umumi-yi Hazrat Ayatullah al-Uzma Najafi Marʿashi, 1972), 131–34, 142–47. The bridge near Miyana was repaired in 1526–27; Qumi, *Khulasat,* 290. Also see J. Aubin, "L'avènement des Safavides reconsidéré," *Moyen Orient et Océan Indien* 5 (1988): 67.
    46. Membrè, *Mission,* 31.
    47. Khuzani, *Afzal,* fol. 203b.
    48. Qumi, *Khulasat,* 430–31, 974. She also set free her slave-girls.
    49. Abdi Beg Shirazi, *Rawzat al-sifat,* ed. A. Ragimov (Moscow: Nauka, 1974), 57–59.
    50. Qumi, *Khulasat,* 662. Iskandar Beg, *Tarikh,* 225–26, gives the amount of 2,000 tumans. To compare, in 1578 a normal salary of an army judge who was an important official was 30 tumans per year; Qumi, *Khulasat,* 671.
    51. Qumi, *Khulasat,* 606.
    52. See Muhammad Mufid Mustawfi Bafqi, *Jamiʿ-yi Mufidi,* ed. Iraj Afshar (Tehran: Asadi, 1961), 3:60, 686.
    53. Qumi, *Khulasat,* 883.
    54. The village, Ahmadabad-i Taft, was known for its excellent air, many gardens, orchards, and flowers; Muhammad Mufid, *Mufidi,* 3:701. In Szuppe, "Participation," pt. 1, 250, the name of Maryam Begum should be amended to read Khan[ish] Begum.
    55. Muhammad Mufid, *Mufidi,* 3:173; *Shah Tahmasp,* 16–17. The bazaar had an excellent location in a commercial and residential quarter of Yazd. Della Valle (*Viaggi,* 1:457) lodged in a caravanserai of Zaynab Begum on the route from Qazvin to Sava in 1618. An inscription dated 1040 (1630) commemorates the renovation of the Shahzada Husayn mausoleum in Qazvin and names the princess Zaynab Begum; see Mudarrisi Tabataba'i, *Barghi,* 30, 43–44. For the charitable foundations of Ottoman women, see Peirce, *Imperial Harem,* 198–218; Ü. Bates, "Women as Patrons of Architecture in Turkey," in *Women in the Muslim World,* ed. Lois Beck and Nikki Keddie (Cambridge: Harvard University Press, 1978), 245–60.
    56. Qumi, *Khulasat,* 695, 697; Mulla Jalal al-Din Muhammad Munajjim Yazdi, *Tarikh-i Abbasi ya ruznama-yi Mulla Jalal,* ed. S. Vahidniya (Tehran: Vahid, 1987), 48; Mir Timur, *Tarikh,* 156.
    57. Szuppe, "Participation," pt. 2, 70.
    58. Qumi, *Khulasat,* 671, 696, 697, 699; Mulla Jalal, *Tarikh,* 34.
    59. The Shamlu of Herat (Abdilu Shamlu) were related to the Safavid house by the marriage of Shah Ismaʿil I's sister to Abdi Beg Shamlu (see above). See also Szuppe, "Participation," pt. 2, 68–69n.180.
    60. Qumi, *Khulasat,* 658, 696, 700, for Mir Qavam al-Din; Mulla Jalal, *Tarikh,* 123, for Ibrahim Khalil; Qumi, *Gulistan,* 52–53, for Majid al-Din Shirazi; and Muhammad Mufid, *Mufidi,* 3:487, for Pir Ahmad Yazdi.

61. Qumi, *Khulasat,* 889, 1074; Iskandar Beg, *Tarikh,* 1090.

62. Khunji, *Tarikh,* 280. This was not a new or exclusively Safavid tradition but a generally acknowledged diplomatic custom. See Peirce, *Imperial Harem,* 219, for its occurrence among the Aq Quyunlu and Ottomans. It is also recorded in seventeenth-century Georgia dealing with the Safavids; see Szuppe, "Participation," pt. 2, n. 8.

63. Bidlisi, *Sharaf-nama,* 541. The link with the nurse (*daya*) and her relatives, especially her own children, was an essential social link. For other examples of the daya's importance in Turko-Iranian societies, see Szuppe, "Participation," pt. 1, nn. 118, 164; Szuppe, "Participation," pt. 2, 69; Szuppe, "The Female Intellectual Milieu in Timurid and Post-Timurid Herat: Faxri Haravi's Biography of Poetesses, *Javaher al-Aja'yeb,*" *Oriente Moderno,* n.s. 15 (2) (1996): n. 10; Peirce, *Imperial Harem,* 131; Bates, "Women as Patrons," 249; Gulbadan, *Humayun,* 58–62; and Abu al-Fazl Allami, *The A'in-i Akbari,* ed. D. C. Phillot (1927; reprint, New Dehli: Atlantic, 1989), 1:331, 340–41, 347.

64. Qumi, *Khulasat,* 315–16; Khuzani, *Afzal,* fol. 129a; Ghaffari, *Tarikh,* 296; Abdi, *Takmilat,* 56; Khurshah b. Qubad al-Husayn Ilchi, *Tarikh-i Ilchi-yi Nizamshah,* MS British Library, Or. 153, fol. 70a, fol. 61b.

65. Tahmasp Safavi, *Tadhkira-yi Shah Tahmasp,* MS British Library, Or. 5880, fol. 67b; Ilchi, *Tarikh,* folio 70a. Hurrem Sultan's letter and the reply are published in *Shah Tahmasp,* 343–48.

66. On this episode of Safavid history, see Aubin, "L'avènement," 66.

67. Khuzani, *Afzal,* fol. 202b–203b; Qumi, *Khulasat,* 372. See Szuppe, "Participation," pt. 1, 215, 221; Szuppe, "Participation," pt. 2, 64–65, 72–75.

68. Only in Khuzani, *Afzal,* fol. 203a. Here, the taj is a headgear particular to the Safavids and Qizilbash. See its contemporary description and drawing by Membrè, *Mission,* 26, 97.

69. Khuzani, *Afzal,* fol. 203b. Abdullah Khan received an official robe of honor, *khil'at.*

70. Qumi, *Khulasat,* 680; Iskandar Beg, *Tarikh,* 235–39; *Don Juan of Persia: A Shi'a Catholic, 1560–1604,* ed. G. Le Strange (London: Routledge, 1926), 150; Falsafi, *Zindigani,* 1:50–53. See also Szuppe, "Participation," pt. 2, 95.

71. Qumi, *Khulasat,* 685–87; Iskandar Beg, *Tarikh,* 235–39.

72. Quoted from the report of Banister and Duckett, agents of the Company of Muscovy in Astrakhan, in Anthony Jenkinson, *Early Voyages and Travels to Russia and Persia* (London: Hakluyt Society, 1886), 447–48, 462.

73. Mulla Abd al-Fattah Fumani, *Tarikh-i Gilan dar vaqayi-yi salha-yi 923–1038,* ed. M. Sutuda (Tehran: B.F.I., 1970), 85, 102, 104, passim.

74. Ilchi, *Tarikh,* fol. 35b.

75. Bidlisi, *Sharaf-nama,* 427.

76. Qumi, *Khulasat,* 155, 289–90, and a variant reading, 954–55; Membrè, *Mission,* 31. See also Szuppe, "Participation," pt. 1, 71–72.

77. See M. B. Dickson, "Shah Tahmasb and the Uzbegs: The Duel for Khurasan with Ubayd Khan" (Ph.D. diss., Princeton University, 1958), 289–95, on the rebellion of Sam Mirza and his Shamlu tutor Aghzivar Khan in Khurasan, 1533–34.

78. Qumi, *Khulasat,* 430; Ghaffari, *Tarikh,* 307; Rumlu, *Ahsan,* 2:536.

79. On this subject, see Riazul Islam, *Indo-Persian Relations: A Study of the Politi-*

168 MARIA SZUPPE

cal and Diplomatic Relations between the Mughal Empire and Iran (Tehran: Iranian Culture Foundation, 1970), 33, 37.

80. Khuzani, *Afzal,* fol. 274b. Pari-Khan Khanum II could also have had another role model in the person of her other paternal aunt, Pari-Khan Khanum I, who was active in Shirvan; see Szuppe, "Jewels of Wonder," 333–34.

81. See W. Hinz, "Schah Isma'il II: Ein Beitrag zur Geschichte der Safaviden," *Mitteilungen des Seminars für Orientalische Sprachen an der Friedrich-Wilhelms-Universität zu Berlin* 36 (2) (1933), 47; Szuppe, "Participation," pt. 2, 79–89; and S. Golsorkhi, "Pari Khan Khanum: A Masterful Safavid Princess," *Iranian Studies* 28 (1995): 143–56.

82. Two chroniclers give particular attention to the life of Pari-Khan Khanum II: Qumi, *Khulasat,* 622, 660, 662, passim; and Iskandar Beg, *Tarikh,* 201, 219–20, 223, passim.

83. Qumi, *Khulasat,* 656; Iskandar Beg, *Tarikh,* 219–20. *Don Juan of Persia,* 132–33, gives some variant versions. Apart from Shah Muhammad, his sons, and his brother Sultan-Ali Mirza (who was blinded), all other Safavid princes (royal brothers, nephews, uncles, and cousins) had been executed by order of Shah Isma'il II during his short reign between 1576 and 1577.

84. Qumi, *Khulasat,* 656; Iskandar Beg, *Tarikh,* 219–20.

85. Qumi, *Khulasat,* 657–58; Iskandar Beg, *Tarikh,* 222, 224; Mulla Jalal, *Tarikh,* 42. On Mirza Salman, see R. M. Savory, "The Significance of the Political Murder of Mirza Salman," in his *Studies on the History of Safawid Iran* (London: Variorum Reprints, 1987); Falsafi, *Zindigani,* 1:39–40.

86. Qumi, *Khulasat,* 660; Iskandar Beg, *Tarikh,* 224; Mulla Jalal, *Tarikh,* 42.

87. Qumi, *Khulasat,* 660; Iskandar Beg, *Tarikh,* 225. Nevertheless, they were four to five hundred people.

88. Rumlu, *Ahsan,* 2:655; Qumi, *Khulasat,* 660, 662; Iskandar Beg, *Tarikh,* 225–26; Mulla Jalal, *Tarikh,* 42–43.

89. Qumi, *Khulasat,* 697. See also Szuppe, "Participation," pt. 2, 90–100.

90. See H. Horst, "Der Safawide Hamza Mirza," *Der Islam* 39 (1964): 90–94. Sultan-Hamza Mirza was officially proclaimed crown prince after her death; Qumi, *Khulasat,* 700; Iskandar Beg, *Tarikh,* 251. *Don Juan of Persia,* 135, says that the prince ruled in his father's name.

91. See Abdi Beg, *Takmilat,* 128; Qumi, *Khulasat,* 454; Mir Timur, *Tarikh,* 157.

92. See Szuppe, "Participation," pt. 2, 90–100. Also see Szuppe, "Jewels of Wonder," 334–35, on the extended Mazandarani family of Khayr al-Nisa Begum, especially Bibi Zuhra and Titi Begum. The main source is Mir Timur, *Tarikh,* 121, 160, 174–76, 191–92, 275, 284–85.

93. Qumi, *Khulasat,* 658, 662.

94. Ibid., 662, 690; Iskandar Beg, *Tarikh,* 226.

95. Rumlu, *Ahsan,* 656–57; Qumi, *Khulasat,* 662–66, 688; Iskandar Beg, *Tarikh,* 227.

96. See Szuppe, "Participation," pt. 2, n. 187. Also on Khayr al-Nisa Begum's distribution of money to the Qizilbash amirs, see Qumi, *Khulasat,* 668.

97. Qumi, *Khulasat,* 693–94; Iskandar Beg, *Tarikh,* 210–11, 240–41.

98. Qumi, *Khulasat,* 696; Iskandar Beg, *Tarikh,* 248. This was done on the pretext

that its governor, Muhammad Khan Turkman, was accused by the inhabitants of misconduct and incompetence.

99. Abdi, *Takmilat,* 125; Qumi, *Khulasat,* 695–96; Iskandar Beg, *Tarikh,* 237, 248–49.

100. Qumi, *Khulasat,* 696–97; Iskandar Beg, *Tarikh,* 249, 251; *Don Juan of Persia,* 152. See also Falsafi, *Zindigani,* 1:57–58. The Tatar prince in question was Adil Giray Khan of Crimea who was taken as prisoner in a war and who became an honorary hostage at the Safavid court.

101. She was Pari-Khan Khanum I, daughter of Shah Isma'il I; see Szuppe, "Participation," pt. 2, 72–76; Szuppe, "Jewels of Wonder," 333–34.

102. Della Valle, *Viaggi,* 1:457, 488; 2:12. See also Falsafi, *Zindigani,* 2:205–7; Szuppe, "Participation," pt. 2, 100–102; *Shah Abbas Safavi, majmu'a-yi asnad va mukatibat-i tarikhi hamrah ba yaddashtaha-yi tafsili,* ed. Abd al-Husayn Nava'i (Tehran: Zarrin, 1987), 3:27n.1. For more on her and the female personalities of the later Safavid period, such as Zubayda Begum, daughter of Shah Abbas I, or Maryam Begum, daughter of Shah Safi I, in different social and political conditions of seventeenth-century Iran, see K. Babayan, "The Aqa'id al-Nisa': A Glimpse at Safavid Women in Local Isfahani Culture," in *Women in the Medieval Islamic World: Power, Patronage, and Piety,* ed. Gavin Hambly (New York: St. Martin's, 1998), 349–81. See also Chardin, *Voyages,* 5:455, describing the seal ring of the princess Maryam Begum, daughter of Shah Safi; Chardin, *Voyages,* 6:6, passim, for a description of the late-seventeenth-century harem.

103. *Dede Korkut Kitabi,* ed. M. Ergin (Ankara: Turk Dil Kurumu, 1963), 29–30, 68, 78–79; G. Lewis, "Heroines and Others in the Heroic Age of the Turks," in *Women in the Medieval Islamic World: Power, Patronage, and Piety,* ed. Gavin Hambly (New York: St. Martin's, 1998), 147–60.

104. It was also the case with the Timurid Gawhar-Shad Begum at Herat as well as the Aq Quyunlu Seljuq-Shah Begum at Tabriz in the fifteenth century.

8   Waters and Women, Maidens and Might: The Passage of Royal Authority in the *Shahnama*

MAHMOUD OMIDSALAR

THE *SHAHNAMA*, Iran's national epic, is the legendary history of Iran from the beginning to the Muslim conquest of the area in the seventh century. The poet Ferdowsi (d. ca. 411/1020) versified it from a prose original in the latter part of the tenth century. By European standards, the *Shahnama* is a massive epic made of some hundred thousand lines of poetry arranged in nearly fifty thousand distichs. It is about four times the size of the *Iliad* and the *Odyssey* combined. Traditionally the *Shahnama* is divided into three parts. The first, usually called the mythological section, tells of the creation of civilization by early kings and culture-heroes. The second or legendary part is chiefly concerned with Iran's wars with its enemy land Turan, and the final portion is a legendary telling of the rule of historical kings. Although many scholars refer to this last section as its historical part, the rules and adventures of historical kings detailed in this part of the poem are legendary renditions of historical personages and events and should not be confused with history in the strictest sense.

The existing literature on women in the *Shahnama* is meager. The best work on the subject is still Khaleghi-Motlagh's *Die Frauen im Schahname*. Afshar lists books and articles in his bibliography, *Kitabshinasi-yi Firdawsi*. These works are chiefly descriptive rather than analytic. Other articles and books concerning this topic have appeared since the publication of Afshar's bibliography. These are either primarily descriptive nontheoretical essays or reprints of older studies.[1] Nöldeke notes, "Women do not play in the *Shahnama* any overactive role. They practically appear only as a subject of desire or love."[2] Careful reading of the epic, however, yields a different impression of its women than he indicates. In this chapter, I make the case against his view and introduce evidence in support of the vital role that the feminine idea in general and women in particular play in driving the poem's narrative flow. Rather than saving my views until the end when they can be revealed with full dramatic effect—a tactic more suitable for mystery novels than for expository essays—allow me to present them at the outset. By doing so, I hope to help the reader see the details of my evidence and judge its merit.

Within the narrative of the *Shahnama,* significant political transition often involves the mediation of women or feminine symbols that arbitrate all *significant* instances of transfer of power, be they royal, heroic, or magical. This rule is so well entrenched in evidence that apparent deviations from it are likely to be cases of underanalysis. Indeed traces of the transitional feminine may be found in the surviving pre-*Shahnama* heroic and mythological narratives.

The feminine stands at the dawn of creation in Iranian mythology. Zoroastrian myth tells of the creation of a primordial man and a primordial cow. The pair live in a state of peace for a time until the evil spirit and his hosts attack and kill them. The world is then made from the bodies of the primordial man and his bovine companion. Among the miscreations of the evil spirit, a female demon named Jeh is sometimes called the primordial whore and is instrumental in causing the first man's downfall and by implication the creation of the world as we know it. That Jeh may be merely the female aspect of the evil spirit himself should not be surprising because a measure of dual sexuality is sometimes implied for both good and evil creators in the religious tradition of Zoroastrians. For instance, the Zoroastrian text *Bundahishn* speaks of how the god Ahura Mazda carried the ideal form of the world in his body "like a mother her child."[3] It also tells of the deity being both the *mother* and the *father* of creation.[4] The same duality of gender is evident among demons. According to at least one myth, the evil spirit created his host of demons by impregnating himself through anal intercourse with himself.[5] This suggests that the evil spirit possesses a "feminine" aspect that manifests itself in different ways. If this argument is correct, then the demon Jeh may represent the female aspect of the evil spirit. Jeh sets in motion the process of the corruption of the primordial man, which results in his death. Possibly life began by the mediating effects of Jeh's activities in destroying the original state of *innocent stagnation.* Jeh does not stand alone at the beginning of all life. Beside her stands the earth goddess Spandarmadh, who first receives the ejected sperm of the dying Gayomart into the protection of her motherly folds and gives the divine forces time to collect it for purification.

Once purified, this seed is again planted in her, and from it the original human pair grows in the form of two rhubarb stalks. All humanity emanates from this pair. Thus, transition from stagnation to vitality and from proto-human to human is mediated by the feminine in Zoroastrian tradition.

Female entities roam not only at the morning of creation but also beyond the grave. In pre-Islamic Iranian eschatology and in the epic tradition alike, when a person dies his or her soul comes to a bridge called Chinwat.[6] This bridge stretches between the world of the living and that of the dead. Every soul must cross it on its way to the hereafter. At this bridge the soul meets a female entity whose form depends on the soul's character. If the soul belongs to the pious, it encounters a maiden of lovely form and heavenly scent. If it belongs to the impious, it meets an old hag of evil countenance and foul smell. These two women lead the soul to its place of rest or damnation.[7] A woman stands at the point of transition between life and death.

The presence of the feminine at such moments may be motivated by at least two factors. First is man's jealous knowledge of the indispensability of women in bringing forth new life.[8] The inescapable implication of this knowledge is the realization that the birth of all new orders presupposes the existence of some feminine entity (often portrayed symbolically) to act as the mother out of whom the new order is born. These episodic changes are also births of new states for which the mediating presence of the feminine is essential. Second, all points of crossing and frontiers of action are also loci of fear and anxiety because they involve the unknown. Since man has a dire psychological need to master this fear, he achieves this mastery either by stylized repetition of the trauma (hence the recurrence of the pattern) or by providing himself with a reassuring presence to alleviate his anxiety. Both of these strategies are symbolically expressed in myth and folklore. Lofty rites of passage celebrated amid great pomp as well as the more mundane beliefs of daily life (such as superstitions about thresholds) are to various extents ingenious ways of mastering anxiety about this state. The appearance of the feminine at such points of crossing reflects the need to seek the comforting presence of the prototype of all protection, namely that of the mother. "Civilization originates in delayed infancy and its function is security. It is a huge network of more or less successful attempts to protect mankind against the danger of object-loss, the colossal efforts made by a baby who is afraid of being left alone in the dark."[9] If Róheim is right in this interpretation, then the presence of feminine symbols at anxiety points may be an expression of man's need to run to the security of the maternal embrace when faced with danger.

This need is so powerful in Iranian epic tradition that in the rare instances when a male entity helps with the process of transition, he is effeminized.[10] Except during the reign of all but the last of the creator-kings or culture-heroes, almost every important transition of power in the *Shahnama* involves either a woman or a feminine symbol. If she is not a queen, mother, or lover, then she is a blatantly feminine symbol.

The involvement of women with transitions of political power begins with the reign of the last culture-hero, Jamshid, who is responsible for the invention of many arts and crafts of civilization. Toward the end of his reign, he grows arrogant and claims to be god. God punishes his arrogance by withdrawing divine protection, and in time Jamshid is succeeded by the dragon-king Zahhak. All creative activity has been concluded at the time of this transition. The king has sinned and fallen from a creator-king's position to that of a human one. A period of chaos ensues, ending in the ascension of the dragon-king Zahhak to the Iranian throne.[11]

According to the *Shahnama,* some time before ascending the throne, the Arab prince Zahhak was enticed by the devil to kill his father and become king in his place. Meanwhile, Iranian nobles who rebelled against Jamshid's excesses send an emissary to Zahhak to invite him to assume the throne. The dragon-king quickly moves to Iran and takes the reins of power. Once in Iran, Zahhak legitimizes his authority by marrying two daughters of the deposed king Jamshid.[12] The passage of royal authority from Jamshid to Zahhak is thus signaled by the tyrant's marriage to the princesses.

An intriguing account of Zahhak's adventures in the folk versions of this tale is left out of the *Shahnama.* Zahhak's career begins with his incestuous love for his stepmother.[13] The oral version of the tale is more detailed than the Middle Persian account. According to the oral version, Zahhak kills his father because he is in love with his beautiful stepmother. After that, he proclaims his love and asks her to marry him. Desperately trying to avoid her stepson's amorous advances, the woman responds that she will be his wife only if he goes to King Jamshid and asks to be appointed to his father's office. Zahhak succeeds and returns to renew his demands. Rather than succumbing to her lecherous stepson's advances, the woman commits suicide in despair.[14] In this folktale, her ample charms launch Zahhak on a path of parricide, and her demand that he obtain his father's office paves the way for his eventual kingship over Iran. By asking Zahhak to gain his father's office, the woman demands that the son grow up and become the father. Symbolically she creates Zahhak the king out of a love-sick whimpering parricide.

Women play prominent roles throughout Zahhak's career. His adventures

begin and end under their influence. One of the tyrant's distinguishing characteristics in Persian and Arabic texts is his sexual avarice.[15] The dragon-king's
impending doom is revealed to him in a nightmare while he is in bed with
his two wives. Zahhak stirs with a cry of terror and much like a scared young
boy seeks refuge in his wives' arms. Fear paralyzes him, but one of his wives
persuades him to ask the dream interpreters for the meaning of his nightmare before choosing a course of action. The interpreters tell him that his
dream portends the birth of a prince and that this prince, who is named
Fereydun, will one day overcome and unseat him. The tyrant is alarmed and
orders that all newborn males in his realm be slain. But neither his Phara-
onic cruelty nor his agents' ruthlessness can alter his fate. What is more, his
agents kill Fereydun's father, thus giving Fereydun an additional cause to rise
against Zahhak.[16] Fereydun's mother was instrumental in the king's downfall. Having lost his father to Zahhak's murderous agents, Fereydun begins
life in the exclusive company of his mother, Faranak. With her infant son this
resourceful woman escapes the despot's wrath. In the meantime, a magical
cow born at the same time as our hero serves as the infant's wet nurse. Zahhak's agents soon kill the cow, Barmaya, during a raid. Barmaya is more than
an animal-nurse in the folk and literary versions of the story. According to
one folktale, it not only nurses the hero but also teaches him to walk and plays
with him on the grass.[17] When Fereydun is enumerating the reasons he in-
tends to kill Zahhak, he says that he does so in order to avenge the murder
of his bovine wet nurse. No other instance in the epic occurs where a king
or hero seeks to avenge an animal's murder.

Just before he moves against the tyrant, Fereydun orders his blacksmiths
to make him a "cow-headed" mace.[18] The weapon's form is practically a reproduction of Barmaya's head. The matter is plainly stated in the poem:

> [Zahhak killed] that cow Barmaya, which was my wet nurse,
> and of which the body was beautifully adorned.
> What use was the slaying of that harmless animal to that evil-minded man?
> I have therefore girded myself seeking war.
> Having come from Iran for vengeance,
> I shall smash his head by this cow-headed mace.
> I shall show neither forgiveness nor mercy.[19]

True to his promise, Fereydun defeats Zahhak in the royal harem by a single
blow of the mace.[20]

Fereydun used a cow-headed weapon in this confrontation because he
wanted to destroy the killer of his wet nurse with a weapon that would make

the vengeful nature of the action clear. Also, the shape of the hero's weapon, by virtue of being fashioned after a female animal's head, reiterates that feminine forces mediate the transition of power from Zahhak to Fereydun. Despite this evidence, Fereydun's cow-headed club is always referred to in translations as a bull-headed mace. The androcentric point of view of epic scholarship considers the mace of the hero *manlier* if it is bull-headed rather than cow-headed. Manly or not, a firm blow of a cow-headed mace can kill a man just as the strike of a bull-headed one could, and the textual evidence in favor of the cow's head is incontestable.

Fereydun begins life in almost exclusively female company. He is fatherless before birth and raised by his mother on the milk of the magical cow Barmaya.[21] Throughout Fereydun's perilous infancy, his mother saves his life by constantly moving him, often only steps ahead of Zahhak's agents of death. His education, although conducted by three ascetics in remote places, is designed and managed only by his mother, Faranak, who chooses the ascetics as her son's mentors and guardians. Later when he triumphantly enters Zahhak's palace, he romances the dragon-king's two wives, who must be at least as old as his mother.[22] The symbolism of Fereydun's maternal attachment is unmistakable. That his first amorous encounter with the dragon-king's wives occurs when Zahhak is away in India recreates the conditions of the hero's birth. He was, after all, born to a widowed mother whose husband was killed (that is, absent). Fereydun's assumption of kingship (his birth *qua* king), symbolized by his victorious entry into the royal palace and his takeover of the royal women, is remarkably symmetrical with the circumstances of his actual birth, and his mastery of these women is similar to what Zahhak himself did when he assumed Jamshid's throne. The importance of feminine forces in Fereydun's career is not limited to his contact with and nurturing by women.

According to a folk version of the tale, Fereydun is the son of Jamshid.[23] Before his death, Jamshid tells his pregnant wife to go to the city gate. There she will meet a half-white, half-yellow cow. He states, "Ride the cow! It will take you across a river that no one else can cross. On the other side [you will find] people who will help you, and you will give birth to a boy. This boy will avenge my death one day." The woman follows her husband's advice, and Fereydun is born. Zahhak's agents know the young prince's whereabouts but cannot cross the river and capture him. They try in vain to entice him to cross and come to his doom, but he is not fooled. The river stands as a protective barrier between Fereydun and his enemies.[24] This powerful symbol, namely the river, appears once again in the tale of Fereydun's adventures.

According to the *Shahnama,* Fereydun must cross a frontier river before he can enter Iran. This aquatic passage from one stage to the next is a rite of passage for many kings and warriors. Water is a powerful feminine symbol. In Iranian heroic and mythic traditions, the deity presiding over the waters is not a god, as he is in Greco-Roman tradition, but a goddess. What is more, the Iranian goddess of waters, Anahita, happens to be on excellent terms with kings and warriors. Heroes appeal to her more often than they do to the war god one would normally expect to be the object of these heroic supplications.[25]

After arriving at the riverside, Fereydun meets a boatman who has been ordered to demand a special permit from all who wish to cross. When our young prince is unable to produce it, the ferryman refuses to carry him. Strangely enough, rather than flying into a fit of rage at the rogue's refusal, Fereydun decides to cross the vast river on horseback. Such passivity is uncharacteristic of the hero who during his royal career demonstrates a terrifying cruelty by ordering the slaying of two of his own sons for their fratricidal opposition to his will.[26] One expects the mighty hero to deal severely with the scoundrel. Instead he chooses simply to brave the raging torrent.[27] His unusual mildness toward the boatman underscores the symbolic significance of the scene and sets up the dynamics of the narrative's progress. Fereydun's passage through the torrent is the test of the legitimacy of his royal authority and the symbolic birth of his political success. This time the river, that powerful feminine presence that once flowed forbiddingly between the boy Fereydun and his persecutor's murderous agents, runs at the border of two stages in his life: powerlessness, which he is leaving behind, and dominion, to which he goes. Once the river prevented assassins from harming the boy; now it yields to the man who would be king. This pattern occurs again in the epic during another prince's entrance to Iran. This time, the dramatis personae are Prince Kaykhosrow, his mother, Farangis, and the warrior Giv.

Kaykhosrow is the most pious king of the *Shahnama*. His father, Siyavakhsh, is the Iranian crown prince who is forced to go into exile in Turan. The details of the events leading to his exile do not concern us here, although the amorous advances of his stepmother Sudaba were instrumental in bringing them about. He is offered safe passage by the Turanian king Afrasiyab, who also gives him his daughter Farangis in marriage. He lives in Turan until court intrigue compels Afrasiyab to kill him. At the time of Siyavakhsh's death, his wife is pregnant with his son Kaykhosrow. Kaykhosrow is therefore a prince of singular royal qualifications. He is grandson of the Iranian monarch Kaykavus and the Turanian ruler Afrasiyab.

After commanding Siyavakhsh's murder, Afrasiyab attempts to destroy

Kaykhosrow by ordering his pregnant mother flogged in the hope that she will abort. Luckily the great warlord Piran intercedes on behalf of the princess, and Afrasiyab relents. He agrees to leave her with Piran until she gives birth. When Kaykhosrow is born, Piran once again manages to persuade Afrasiyab not to kill the child. He assures the king that menials will raise Kaykhosrow as a shepherd. He argues that with such an upbringing Kaykhosrow will have no awareness of the princely code of honor that requires him to avenge his father's murder, and therefore the king has nothing to fear from his grandson. This arrangement works, and Kaykhosrow is allowed to live in Piran's care. Unbeknownst to Afrasiyab, Piran provides Kaykhosrow with a princely education.

Several years later, when Kaykhosrow has grown into a comely and brave youth, the Iranian warlord Gudarz is informed of his existence in a dream and sends his son Giv to Turan to find the prince. After several years of hardship, Giv locates Kaykhosrow and his mother, Farangis. The three set out for Iran. The Turanians give chase, but their force is beaten back by Giv. On their way to Iran, the fugitives come to a river separating the two territories. The future king must cross the water before he can enter Iran.

As in the story of Fereydun, the boatman refuses to allow the prince the use of his vessels. He demands an offensive payment before the three are permitted to board his ships. The price the boatman demands is the prince himself as a slave, the prince's mother for his pleasure, the prince's black stallion, or the prince's father's armor (at the time donned by the hero Giv). Instead of killing the man in a pitch of heroic anger, Giv advises the prince to put his trust in god and cross the great river on horseback. He argues that if Kaykhosrow is destined to be king, god will facilitate his passage just as he facilitated Fereydun's. Giv's strange nonviolence in this scene stands out in view of his typical ruthlessness. Just beforehand, Giv has single-handedly vanquished a great force of Turanian horsemen. Yet the warrior, who ordinarily would not allow a lowly ferryman to disobey his will and demand either payment or permit, inexplicably reverts to unusual meekness at the riverside.[28]

The fugitives' successful passage clearly depends upon the prince's mother. If she has not been chaste, that is, if the prince is a bastard, they cannot cross. A rather odd requirement indeed, unless the mother's role is viewed as symbolic of the feminine's influence in transitional states. This symbolism is reiterated in another version of the tale. When the three emerge on the Iranian side of the river, neither the king nor the court heroes have come to receive them but rather Banugushasp, the Amazon daughter of the hero Rustam.[29] The presence of Banugushasp underscores the type of patterning in the epic's narrative that requires females or feminine symbols at transitional moments. Could we not reasonably interpret this episode as a symbolic rebirth of Kaykhosrow? Is he not baptized the king by his passage through the waters?

Like Fereydun, Kaykhosrow is a fatherless prince who is raised by his mother in a foreign land.[30] He sets out for Iran in order to assume his place on the royal throne. Like Fereydun, he comes to a body of water that he crosses although he is hindered by the boatman. Like Fereydun, neither he nor his attending hero attempt to punish the impertinent man. The motif of importance is the miraculous passage of a prince through a body of water symbolizing a new ruler's birth. These waters flow at the frontier of two orders of existence. As the prince passes through them, he is baptized ruler. He enters a boy, a mere claimant to the throne, and exits a king. In this respect, he is like a fetus emerging from the flood of amniotic fluid as a newborn life.

Passage of the hero/king through water (female/mother) as a symbol of transformation, rebirth, and transition of power in the *Shahnama* is not limited to the vitae of these two kings. The same pattern with slight modifications occurs in the episode of Ardasher-e Babakan's career. Although an actual scene of aquatic passage does not occur in this variant of the episode, both of its important elements, namely the woman and the water as mediators of the passage of royal authority, are plainly present.

According to the *Shahnama*, Ardasher, born to the daughter of a provincial prince, is sent by his maternal grandfather to the court of King Ardavan in order to continue his princely education. Before long, he angers his royal host and as punishment is assigned to service in the stables. Meanwhile, Golnar, a lovely consort of the king, falls in love with him, and the two begin an illicit liaison. Like Fereydun and Kaykhosrow, Ardasher finds himself away from his homeland. Rather than being in a foreign land, however, the hero is merely away from his birthplace. Like the two heroes/kings before him, Ardasher is befriended by a woman. In this case, she is not his mother but the king's favorite concubine. By virtue of being the sovereign's choice, Golnar is also a mother figure. If we allow that the king may be interpreted as a symbolic father, then his woman could symbolically represent the mother. Consider the Persian expression *pedar-e tajdar,* "the crowned father," a euphemism for king.

Ardasher's love affair with Golnar proves crucial for the young man's future success because it is she who discovers a secret that places Ardasher on the path to power. Royal astrologers have told Ardavan that should a prince rebel against him during a certain time, the heavenly forces are such that the rebellion may succeed. Golnar imparts this vital information to her young lover, who consequently decides to defy the king and escape his unpleasant assignment at the royal stables. Golnar decides to flee with her paramour and comes to him at night bringing riches from the king's treasury. According to the tale's Middle Persian variant, the young woman steals several items from the king's storehouse and gives them to Ardasher, including a fine sword, golden saddle, royal sash, golden reins, suit of armor, and fine weapons.[31] Such items, the insignia of kingship, are found in other cognate tales within wider Iranian epic tales, including Herodotus's account of the legend of the origin of another Iranian group, the Scythians.[32]

By giving Ardasher these insignia of royal rank, Golnar symbolically invests her lover with kingship. She gives him not only the knowledge that he needs before he can move against Ardavan but also the trappings of kingship. The divine origin of kingship is indicated by the royal astrologers' warning to Ardavan that heavens will favor any prince who might challenge him for the throne. Although they warn their king of the perilous position of the heavenly bodies, they tell him nothing about his challenger's identity. By her actions, Golnar determines his identity. Ardasher owes his rule to her, and Ardavan his demise. Golnar's crucial role in causing the transition of political power in this story is further conveyed by the following detail. Golnar was loved by Ardavan not only for her charms but also because the unfortunate monarch had developed a superstitious attachment to her. He considered her beautiful countenance to be so auspicious that he had ordered her to wake him up every morning so that her face would be the first sight he beheld. This, Ardavan thought, was an insurance against ill fortune. Thus, by investing her with extra attraction, the epic tradition expresses the symbolic equality of the young woman and royal fortune. On the day of the lovers' escape, Ardavan remains in bed as is his custom and waits for his beautiful concubine to ask him to rise. She does not appear because she has already escaped with Ardasher. Once she leaves Ardavan, the king loses his royal fortune and is replaced by his young rival. Kingship follows Golnar.

Shortly after the lovers' escape, news of their departure reaches Ardavan, who sets out in hot pursuit. According to the tale's Middle Persian variant, in the course of their flight the fugitives meet two women who call out and address the hero: "Fear not O Ardasher of the line of Sasan, descendant of King Dara. You are safe from harm. No one can catch you. You will lord over the land of Iran for many years. . . . Do not relent until you reach the sea, because when your eyes behold it, you will have naught to fear from your enemies."[33]

Who are these women who suddenly appear on the fugitives' path? How do they know Ardasher's name and lineage? After all, his true descent (an impeccably royal one) was kept secret all along. His father, Sasan, was afraid of revealing it and confessed it only after solemn assurance that his secret would be safe.[34] What enables these women to forecast his future so clearly? Might one suggest that they are another manifestation of the feminine bequeathers of royal authority? Note that until these women loudly proclaim Ardasher's royal descent and hence the legitimacy of his claim to the throne, he is only a boy fleeing from the royal court. By enunciating the rebel's true lineage, these women transform him and make his kingship public. They speak the unspoken, namely that he is not Ardasher, son of Babak.[35] Later he defeats and kills Ardavan and goes on to start a new dynasty.

Throughout this story, no explanation is offered as to why reaching water would nullify Ardavan's efforts in stopping Ardasher's rebellion. Reaching or crossing a body of water by a contender for the throne in the *Shahnama* symbolizes the passage of royal authority from one person to another. Unlike Fereydun and Kaykhosrow, Ardasher does not have to cross rivers because he is not coming from abroad. Like the two kings before him, however, his safety is assured only when he reaches water.

Golnar was instrumental in bringing about her lover's success, but once Ardasher achieves kingship, no further mention is made of her. This conspicuous absence emphasizes her symbolic importance in the early part of Ardasher's career. Her individual identity and the question of her future destiny are no more relevant than are the identities of the two prophesying women of the tale's Middle Persian variant. Great literature speaks in symbolic language, not in the idiom of daily concerns. Her involvement with Ardasher cannot be reasonably interpreted as merely an expression of the hero's manly charms. I do not argue that our hero is helped by a woman rather than a man because being a hero—an idealized expression of manhood—he is so handsome and charming that hardly any woman can withstand his appeal. We are dealing with an artistic and symbolic pattern of expression of ideas, not a mere reflection of reality. To the extent that the *Shahnama* is a great literary epic, it utilizes an artistic and symbolic manner of expression. Female bestowers of authority and kingship in the *Shahnama* appear in many different forms. One of the most intriguing is found in the story of Shapur II.

Shapur is captured by his Roman foe in the latter's camp and is condemned to slow death by being sewn into an animal's skin. The tale of his rescue has two versions. Some "historical" sources state that the prince is sewn into a cow's skin and is rescued by Persian captives who pour oil on him and thus soften the skin to enable him to slide out.[36] The story's literary version

is of a higher order of symbolization and is preserved in the *Shahnama*.[37]
There, the captive prince is sewn into the skin of a jackass, and a woman
comes to his rescue.[38] She frees him by pouring warm milk on the skin.[39] The
symbolism of the milk-giving woman and of the young man encased in a skin
pouch is hardly subtle, particularly because the text explicitly states that when
the prince slides out, his body is covered with blood. The scene expresses a
deposed king's symbolic rebirth and resumption of rule. Can a king be more
deposed than one who is captured by his enemies and sewn into an ass's skin?

Once arrested by the Romans, rather than being placed under heavy guard
or imprisoned, Shapur is taken to the women's quarters where he is sewn into
the skin of a jackass and placed under the care of female custodians.[40] Devoid
of political power and helpless, Shapur is symbolically infantilized. Because
he is first taken to the women and sewn into a skin pouch there, he is more
than infantilized; he is fetalized.[41] The womb in which he is placed, however,
is displaced out of the "mother's" body and symbolically expressed as the skin
sack. The woman who comes to Shapur's assistance and delivers him from
the asinine womb can only be a maternal symbol. Giving milk and releasing
the monarch from the engulfing skin symbolize maternal care and rebirth in
an inverted order.[42] Once the king is rescued, the woman brings him horses
and weapons. Like Golnar who helped Ardasher, she brings her beloved the
insignia of rule and makes him king again.[43] Like Golnar, this woman is never heard of again. She is an important symbol with a function to perform.
Once she performs it, her raison d'être is exhausted, and she quietly disap-
pears so that the economy of the epic narrative is not disturbed. As a type, she
will reappear in the guise of other helpful maidens who bear help for other
heroes. In a few instances, the helpful maiden meets a tragic end.

The cruelest example of disposing of a female bestower of victory in the
Shahnama is also found in the story of Shapur. Ta'ir, father of an Arab princess, is holding out in a fortified castle against Shapur. The princess chances to
see the handsome king and falls in love. She sends a message promising to
deliver her father's castle into his hands if he agrees to marry her.[44] The king
agrees and, following the directions provided by the young woman, conquers
Ta'ir's castle and marries the girl. Shortly afterwards, the king puts her to death
in a horrifying manner because he fears that since she was unfaithful to her
father she might also be unfaithful to him.[45] The outrageousness of the act
notwithstanding, the death of this helpful maiden is structurally the same as
the sudden disappearance of other like-minded women in the *Shahnama*.

The androcentric universe of Iranian heroic tales treats powerful females
in one of three ways. Some, such as Golnar and the young woman who helped

Shapur, disappear unceremoniously. Some, especially those who betray or challenge men, are not tolerated at all. They are usually killed after being accused of some crime or treachery.[46] And others, namely those powerful women who are neither killed nor made to disappear, consist of masculinized women. They are robbed of every shred of femininity and transformed into female men. Their defeminization is the mirror image of symbolic castration for men.[47] One of the Amazon daughters of the hero Rustam is so robbed of her femininity that she cannot even engage in normal sexual behavior. During her wedding night, rather than respond to the amorous advances of her husband, she attacks and ties him up and then throws him into the corner of the nuptial chamber where he remains bound until morning. Not until her father, Rustam, intercedes on the groom's behalf does she allow him to consummate their marriage.[48]

A similar idea is expressed in Persian Sufi texts. Attar (d. ca. 672/1221) writes, "When women conduct themselves in a manly fashion on the path of [service to] god, they cannot be called women. . . . [It is said] that on the day of judgment when the call is sounded, [saying] '[Arise] O men,' the first who steps forth in the line of men is the [virgin] Mary."[49]

In the *Shahnama*, the forms of feminine bestowers of power range from the highly disguised and symbolic to the blatantly obvious. In the story of the rebel-general Bahram-i Chubina, we encounter an undisguised manifestation of the empowering female. Bahram's alienation from the court begins when the king publicly affronts him by sending a suit of women's clothes and a spindle case as a gift. Bahram dons the feminine accoutrements and appears before his troops in that guise. The troops who love their general are equally insulted and persuade him to rebel against the king.[50] The birth of a rebel is thus symbolized by putting him through the mediating state of feminization. Shortly afterwards, Bahram is led to a palace in the desert where he meets his fortune, which appears to him in the form of a beautiful woman. The two talk privately before Bahram decides to rebel openly by assuming the regalia of rule.[51] His donning of feminine clothing is the beginning of his alienation from court, while his meeting with his fortune in the desert is symbolic of this alienation's completion and a sign of his rebellion's absoluteness.

·   ·   ·

All transition of power in the *Shahnama* is mediated by the feminine either manifestly or symbolically. Although my presentation of the evidence for this claim has been limited to what can be included in a brief essay, it is enough to reject the notion that women do not play an important role in the Iranian national epic. The transitional importance of women is rooted in the ambivalent relationship between men and women that characterizes the patriarchal culture of Iran. In societies such as Iran, where women are the primary caregivers and providers of discipline during the formative years, it is every infant's destiny to experience his or her encounter with power in a nurturing woman.[52] The infantile memory of the feminine as the source of comfort and discipline is not lost with age. The passage of time only mythologizes it. As a result, men unconsciously and psychologically live in a perpetual state of matriarchy. This inner psychological universe contradicts their practical environment in which men hold the lion's share of power. The contradiction is resolved by means of what psychoanalysts call a compromise formation. They create a fantasy universe in which the experience of infancy, during which power was essentially a feminine prerogative, is replicated. This is why, although the universe of Iranian epic literature is manifestly patriarchal, its patriarchal fabric is disrupted at transitional moments by powerful women or feminine symbols. These female entities hold the patriarchal narrative together at its seams and thus give it coherence.

NOTES

1. D. J. Khaleghi-Motlagh, *Die Frauen im Schahname* (Freiburg: K. Schwarz, 1971); I. Afshar, *Kitabshinasi-yi Firdawsi*, 2d ed. (Tehran: Anjoman-e alhar-e melli, 1976); *Hayat-i ijtima'i-yi zan dar tarikh-i Iran* (Women's social life in Iranian history) (Tehran: Amir Kabir, 1369/1991); cf. T. Bassari, *Zanan-i Shahnama* (Women of the Shahnama) (Tehran: Daneshsara-ye Ali, 1971); N. Hariri, *Firdawsi, zan, va tirazhidi* (Ferdowsi, women, and tragedy) (Tehran: Babul, 1365/1987). The edition of the *Shahnama* I use in this chapter is Ferdowsi, *The Shahnameh*, vols. 1–5, ed. D. J. Khaleghi-Motlagh (Costa Mesa, Calif.: Mazda Press, 1988–97). Volumes 6–8 are in preparation. When I quote from the *Shahnama*, the translations are my own. When I refer in this essay to "folk versions" of the *Shahnama* stories, I mean the oral versions. These folk versions are collected in three volumes by A. Injavi, two of which I cite in this chapter: *Mardom va Shahnama* (People and the *Shahnama*) (Tehran: Farhang-e mardom, 1975) and *Mardom va qahramanan-e Shahnama* (People and the *Shahnama* heroes) (Tehran: Amir Kabir, 1985). Ferdowsi's *Shahnama* is separated from these oral traditions by at least four generations of textual antecedents.

2. T. Nöldeke, *The Iranian National Epic*, trans. L. T. Bogdanov (1930; reprint, Philadelphia: Porcupine Press, 1979), 88–89.

3. J. Duchesne-Guillemin, *Religion of Ancient Iran* (Bombay: Tata Press, 1973), 213; cf. M. Bahar, trans., *Bundahishn* (Tehran: Tus, 1369), 51–54.

4. Bahar, *Bundahishn*, 38.

5. *Darab Hormazyar's Rivayat*, ed. Ervard Manockji Rustamji Unvala (Bombay: British India Press, 1922), 274.

6. H. Yaghma'i, ed., *Garshaspnamah* (Tehran: Tahoori, 1976), 137, 402.

7. Bahar, *Bundahishn*, 129–31.

8. Alan Dundes, "Earth-Diver: Creation of the Mythopoeic Male," in *Analytic Essays in Folklore* (The Hague: Mouton, 1975), 130–45; B. Bettelheim, *Symbolic Wounds: Puberty Rites and the Envious Male* (New York: Collier Books, 1962).

9. G. Róheim, *The Origin and Function of Culture* (New York: n.p., 1943), 100.

10. M. Omidsalar, "Invulnerable Armour as a Compromise Formation in Persian Folklore," *International Review of Psychoanalysis* 11 (1984): 448–49.

11. Zahhak sports two serpents on his shoulders. He is also the anthropomorphized remnant of a ravaging tricephalic dragon that plagued the rivers of ancient Iranian lore. See M. Omidsalar, "The Beast Babr-e Bayan: Contributions to Iranian Folklore and Etymology," *Studia Iranica* 13 (1) (1984): 129–42.

12. Zahhak, line 6. References to the text of the *Shahnama* are given by the name of the story followed by the verse (*bayt*) number. Thus, "Zahhak, line 6" means verse 6 in the story of Zahhak. This manner of reference makes it easy to locate verses in almost any standard edition of the epic. Whereas the verse number would not be exact in every edition of the *Shahnama*, the reader can easily find the verse close to verse 6.

13. The folk version may represent an older tradition according to which Zahhak was guilty of incest. In the Middle Persian accounts of the dragon-king's vita, Zahhak commits incest with his own mother, Vadhak, and is even known by the matronymic *vadhakan shah*, "king of the line of Vadhak." See E. W. West, *Pahlavi Texts Part III: Dina-i mainog-i khirad* [*sic*] (Sage and spirit of wisdom), in *Sacred Books of the East*, vol. 24, ed. Max Muller (Delhi: Motilal Banarsidass, 1965), 103.

14. Injavi, *Mardom va Shahnama*, 301–2, 307–8.

15. S.v. "Azhdahag," *Encyclopedia Iranica*.

16. Zahhak, lines 106, 125–28, 170–72.

17. Injavi, *Mardom va qahramanan-i Shahnama*, 31–32.

18. Zahhak, lines 286–90.

19. Ibid., lines 379–82; cf. Injavi, *Mardom va Shahnama*, 314.

20. Zahhak, line 483.

21. Ibid., lines 131–35.

22. Ibid., lines 440–44.

23. This is quite different from the *Shahnama* version in which Fereydun is Abtin's son.

24. Injavi, *Mardom va qahramanan*, 31–33.

25. J. Darmesteter, *Le Zend Avesta*, vol. 2 (Paris: A. Maisonneuve, 1960), 63; M. Omidsalar, "The Beast Babr-e Bayan," 131–35.

26. Fereydun, lines 711–43.

27. It is only in the Avestan version of the tale that the hero punishes the boatman by turning him into a bird condemned to perpetual flight. Even there, the man is saved through the goddess Anahita's kindness. See *Yasht-ha*, ed. E. Poordavood, 2d ed. (Tehran: Tahoori, 1347/1969), 61–66.

28. Injavi, *Mardom va qahramanan*, 148–49.

29. Ibid., 151.

30. Fereydun's biography falls in what is called the "hero pattern." For a theoretical discussion of the pattern and ample bibliography, see Alan Dundes, "The Hero

Pattern and the Life of Jesus," in *Interpreting Folklore* (Bloomington: Indiana University Press, 1980), 223–63.

31. *Karnamag-i artakhsher-i papkan* (Deeds of Ardasher, son of Babak), ed. B. Farahwashi (Tehran: Tehran University Press, 1356/1976), 12–13.

32. *Herodotus,* vol. 4, trans. and ed. A. D. Godley (Cambridge: Harvard University Press, 1946), 5.

33. *Karnamag,* 17–18.

34. Ibid., 14–16; cf. Ashkaniyan, lines 96–107.

35. Ashkaniyan, lines 320–21.

36. Al-Tha'alibi, *Ghurar akhbar muluk al-furs wa siyarihim,* ed. H. Zotenberg (Paris: Imprimerie Nationale, 1900), 524–25; Mas'udi, *Muruj al-dhahab wa ma'adin al-jawahir,* ed. C. Pellat (Beirut: Manshurat al-jami'ah al-Lubnaniya, 1965), 1:299; Bal'ami, *Tarikh-i Bal'ami* (Bal'ami's history), ed. M. T. Bahar (Tehran: Zawwar, 1975), 2:916–17.

37. Cf. H. Jason, *Ethnopoetry: Form, Content, Function* (Bonn: Linguistica Biblica, 1977), 30–31.

38. Shapur II, lines 189–90.

39. Ibid., lines 229–35.

40. Ibid., lines 191–200.

41. Ibid., line 187.

42. Ibid., lines 227–35.

43. Ibid., lines 239–55.

44. Ibid., lines 216–17.

45. Tabari, *Tarikh al-umam wa al-muluk* (Cairo: n.p., 1939), 2:50; Tha'alibi, *Ghurar akhbar muluk,* 491–92; Ibn al-Balkhi, *Farsnamah,* ed. G. Le Strange and R. A. Nicholson (Tehran: Tahoori, 1363/1985), 62.

46. Shapur's murder of the Arab princess was motivated by his fear of her potential ability to harm him. He must have believed her capable of bestowing his kingdom on another man just as she was able to bestow her father's kingdom on him. The princess's name *malika* (queen) onomastically implies that whomever has the queen must be king. Females have the power to grant princely authority and to take it away. See *Bahman Nama* (ascribed to Iranshah ibn Abi al-Khayr), ed. R. Afifi (Tehran: Scientific and Cultural Publications, 1370/1991), 178–79, for another example of such women.

47. For example, Khosrow Parviz, lines 3126–60; *Bahman Nama,* lines 8703–7, 8809–10, 8719–20. It may be partly the source of the idea of the breastless Amazons and other female warriors in the Iranian epic tradition.

48. *Faramarznamah* (Bombay: n.p., 1906), 74; Injavi, *Mardom va Shahnama,* 76–78. These manly women are treated as honorary men in all androcentric epochs and cultures.

49. Attar, *Tdhkirat al-awliya,* ed. M. Qazwini (Tehran: Eqbal, 1968), 1:64.

50. Hurmuzd, lines 1390–1420.

51. Ibid., lines 1427–70, 1474–95.

52. The greater the subjugation of women in reality, the more powerful the female deities and forces that roam the fields of fantasy. See P. Slater, *The Glory of Hera* (Boston: Beacon Press, 1968), 4–23, 131–36, 220.

9 Taming the Unruly King: Nizami's Shirin as Lover and Educator

FATEMEH KESHAVARZ

TRAVELING ON HORSEBACK from country to country, inheriting the throne, rejecting a king's proposal of marriage and keeping him at her doorstep, advising a master mason on finishing a seemingly impossible project, and counseling a young and ill-behaved king in matters of ethics and rulership are not traditional female tasks in any premodern society. They are certainly not what we would consider a medieval Muslim poet's vision of routine activity for an ideal female protagonist. We have to reexamine our expectations at least in relation to Nizami's (d. 1209) celebrated romantic epic *Khusrau u Shirin,* since the activities mentioned fit comfortably in the diverse daily routine of the female protagonist, Shirin.[1] Some questions arise. Was Shirin a completely mythical creation? Are heroes so much "larger than life" that they bear no relation to the social realities of their time? Was Shirin a taboo for the Muslim society of Nizami's time or a shock to the literary tradition in which she was created? This chapter tackles these questions while investigating the personality of Shirin.

Ilyas ibn Yusuf—known as Nizami of Ganjah—was born in 1140. Famed for his erudition, poetic mastery, and subtle story-telling techniques, Nizami has evoked much admiration from his classical and modern critics. "The acknowledged master of romantic *mathnavi* [rhyming couplet]," "the most brilliant poet of the romantic epic," and "a master of thought and word whose freshness and vigor have not been effaced throughout the centuries" are a few expressions of such sentiment.[2] Little is known about Nizami's personal life beyond passing references in his own poetry to a few family members. Of his career, we can speak with more certainty. We know that despite being a prolific poet and dedicating five major compositions to contemporary rulers, he avoided writing panegyrics and becoming a court celebrity. He was and remains a mainstream poet of widespread acceptance, and this acknowledged mastery rests not on a patron's favor but on literary talent demonstrated in a vast poetic corpus.[3]

Heroes and Reality

Was Shirin a mythical heroine who bore no relation to the social realities of her time? Generations of new readers will have to provide fresh perspectives on the epic to forge their answers. The question could also be posed as a broad theoretical query concerning the construction of literary heroes and heroines in general. Let us leave the answer to the former, the nature of Shirin's identity, to be formulated in the course of this chapter and concentrate on the latter: do heroes and heroines of literature represent the cultures in which they are created?

Literary memory of cultures may not reflect the hard and fast realities of their diverse and changing social environments in a concrete manner. The artist may be uninterested in such facts or subordinate them to more pleasant ones for political or artistic considerations. Medieval Persian literary works are no exception. Nevertheless, epic works provide us with the authors' ideals embodied in the hero and heroine. Such heroes may be rebels "who go beyond the verdict of society in their search for appropriate action" with a "non-conformist element" at the heart of their creative instinct. Yet such heroes influence "the collective cultural imagination" of a people. Their images are thoroughly absorbed and remain part of that culture's "understanding of the past and present."[4] Such ideal/idealized figures will not pass the credibility test with the reader unless a bridge connects their impeccable goodness to the realities of their time. No good storyteller will present his or her audience with protagonists whose actions—good or bad—will be impossible to believe or recognize. Renard affirms this observation in *Islam and the Heroic Image* in relation to Rustam, hero of the most celebrated Persian epic, the *Shahnamah*.[5] He describes the hero's responses as "larger than life" but maintains that such responses nevertheless reflect the "affective needs and capabilities" of his creator and his fans alike.[6] The need to recognize an ordinary human dimension in a hero's or heroine's personality is echoed in Campbell's work on a hero's various faces. He argues that our fascination for a potent individual capable of achieving extraordinary feats is rooted in the feeling that he [or she] is ultimately each of us.[7] Thus, authors' exaggerations of their protagonists' actions and achievements are limited. Such redefinitions of reality are necessary to express fresh thoughts, even alter generic features. After all, as Calder notes, the idea of a hero is based on the notion that heights can be reached in courage and commitment that go beyond the ordinary.[8] The authorial alterations of reality will not be successful if they change literary conventions or heroic figures beyond recognition.

The presence of a strong, dynamic, and complex figure in the person of Shirin, the heroine of Nizami's *Khusrau u Shirin*, deserves attention for reasons other than those exclusive to literary inquiries. The creation and acceptance of Shirin demonstrate that the necessary cultural space for a female character of her magnitude and complexity exists. Furthermore, the epic's author did not come from an obscure or unconventional background. In his productive career, Nizami produced a series of romantic epics such as *Haft Paykar* and *Khusrau u Shirin* that came to be among the most influential compositions in the Persian literary canon. What many of these works share is the creation of prototypical female heroic figures such as Layli in the tragic romance of *Layli u Majnun* and Shirin in the romantic epic *Khusrau u Shirin*.[9] Among Nizami's heroines, Shirin is arguably the strongest and most vibrant. Her depth of personality, practical intellect, and social conduct contradict and challenge the generally held stereotype of the ideal medieval Muslim woman of the author's time. Such ideals are thought to include silence, passivity, and absence from the social scene. Not only is Shirin beautiful, loyal, and pious, but she also thinks well and acts on her thoughts even when this involves extreme mastery of thought processes or mobility in physical space. She is assertive with words and deeds to the point of keeping Khusrau—the man who is also the king—at her doorstep in order to express dissatisfaction with his conduct.[10] Creating a figure as bold and complex as Shirin has no doubt entailed assistance from Nizami's imagination and talent for expanding reality. His creation testifies to at least two significant facts. First, a man of Nizami's traditional stance considered action, intelligence, and dynamism—instead of passivity, submission, and silence—to be the necessary components for creating an attractive heroic woman. Second, in so doing, Nizami did not shock or disappoint his readers but presented them with an enchanting figure who "reflected the affective needs and capabilities" of such readers.[11] Shirin has remained visible ever since her creation not only in the ensuing barrage of romantic epics that mimicked Nizami and kept her as their central protagonist but also as the mythical embodiment of beauty and strength evoked in various lyric genres.[12] For the character of Shirin to be embraced to the degree that it has been, it must have resonated with recognizable as well as desirable traits worthy of love and respect. If we view heroes, as Calder suggests, as "the symbolic embodiments of a collective will, a shared culture" or "a traditional creativity,"[13] then Shirin can easily be viewed as one model for the symbolic embodiment of the ideal womanhood shared by the Persianate cultures of the Islamicate world.

Contemporary criticism of classical Persian literature presents the classical period as wholly male-dominated. Milani gives voice to a shared sentiment when she declares that "the literature of Iran has long possessed a predominantly masculine character. Conspicuously absent from it has been the presence of women as writers or critics." This female absence is sometimes taken out of its universal context and overemphasized.[14] While in terms of authorship the absence of women is a conspicuous pattern, the portrayal of female figures by male authors is yet to be explored. This neglect is due to a general newness of critical efforts in the field as well as to an unquestioned acceptance by critics (indigenous or otherwise) of the Orientalist stereotype of Muslim women as idle, faceless, passive, and dormant beings not worthy of much attention.[15] Nizami's portrayal of Shirin, a figure he compared to his own wife Afaq, demonstrates that some medieval Muslim men espoused a different view of the ideal woman, one who was endowed with strength, courage for self-expression, and mobility in mental as well as physical realms. Shirin not only defies the Orientalist invention of Muslim womanhood but in many ways goes beyond models of feminine virtue and heroic humility articulated by medieval European writers, for whom women are "marked by the absence of self-assertion."[16]

A Plot Summary

Because this study explores facets of Shirin's personality, let us first construct a summary of the epic's plot. *Khusrau u Shirin* tells the story of the love between the Persian king Khusrau and Princess Shirin from the land of Armenia (Arman). Despite her Armenian background and pre-Islamic historical origin, Nizami's princess is not presented as foreign or as practicing a religion different from that of Khusrau. In fact, the author's admiration for

Shirin and the analogy he draws between her and his wife indicate the intimacy between the author and his creation. Shirin, expected to succeed to the throne of her aunt Mahin Banu, falls in love with Khusrau after seeing a portrait of him that was painted and deliberately placed where it would attract her attention. She journeys to the land of Persia (henceforth referred to as Iran) in pursuit of her love, where on the way she stops to bathe in a spring. During this bathing scene, among the most beautifully described in Persian literature, Khusrau gazes at her from behind a bush without knowing her true identity. From the time of Shirin's arrival in Iran and the confession of mutual love between Shirin and Khusrau, the story unfolds in an eventful narrative sequence presenting one obstacle after another on the slow road to the lovers' union. Obstacles are created by Khusrau's mistakes, his stubborn nature, and his kingly pride, such as marrying the Roman emperor's daughter after conquering Constantinople. Along the way, a new character is introduced, the master mason Farhad. Brought in to design a passageway, Farhad falls in love with Shirin's irresistible charm. His love, however, is of a different kind: full and selfless devotion. The only concrete expressions of Farhad's desire for Shirin are the pieces of stone expertly carved into exotic shapes and patterns. His love's enormity is demonstrated when he nearly succeeds in digging a tunnel in the impenetrable Bistoon mountain. This superb metaphorical expression of the desire to find a way to the beloved's heart remains incomplete when the master is tricked by Khusrau's envoy to kill himself under the shock of the false rumor of Shirin's death. From the moment that Farhad is introduced in the story, Shirin is placed between two magnetic yet irreconcilable characters. As a king, lover, and warrior, Khusrau embodies all that the carnal world has to offer. He is handsome, passionate, powerful, and blinded with arrogance, whereas Farhad is cordial, modest, perceptive, imbued with artistic sensitivity, and endowed with an original mind. While admiring Farhad's rare qualities, Shirin remains loyal in her love for Khusrau. In the meantime, Khusrau goes through a metamorphosis. By the end of the story, his untamed personality is transformed through Shirin's companionship and guidance. Our promiscuous prince and ruler changes into a loyal husband and a just, god-fearing king. The story ends tragically. Unlike Khusrau and Farhad, Shirin is not tricked or betrayed. In a premeditated scene, which Nizami describes with affection, Shirin's self-destruction resembles lovemaking more than death. After stabbing herself with a dagger in exactly the same spot where Khusrau's body had received his injury, Shirin

> then embraced the king tight,
> Lip to lip and shoulder to shoulder.
> Raised her voice high,
> So high that those outside the chamber could hear:
> A soul has united with a soul, a body with a body
> Liberated from harsh judgment and from separation.[17]

Shirin's Heroic Cycle

Let us now explore various stages of the maturation of Shirin's heroic personality. A conceptual framework can bestow a meaningful order on investigation; the infrastructure I offer is a modified version of the organization that Heath, in his study of the popular Arabic epic *Sirat Antar*, recovers from that text. It demonstrates a clear pattern in isolated events and renders visible the "general configurations of storytelling structures that govern the organization of these individual motifs." He terms this general sequence of events "the heroic cycle," which pertains to a popular epic work, one with unidentified authorship and largely addressed to a different audience.[18] Still, it corresponds to general heroic patterns observed in classical Islamic compositions and proves equally useful in its application to *Khusrau u Shirin*. Applying the heroic cycle, I demonstrate a distinct characteristic in the composition of Shirin's persona and establish that she is a hero in her own right and not another replica of most female protagonists, the reversal of the male hero.[19]

Rise of the Heroine

The first stage of the heroic cycle, the rise of the hero, describes the unusual circumstances of the hero's birth (unusual social status, physical attributes, or extraordinary accoutrements). It is often connected with singular acts of courage and generosity leading to widespread public acceptance. Although the circumstances of Shirin's birth are not told, she comes from a royal lineage in an exotic land, a land other than Iran. Described as Armenia, this geographical entity possesses mythical qualities. It is ruled by women (currently Shirin's aunt Mahin Banu), its inhabitants have no occupation but merrymaking, and the evil eye has no effect there.[20] Nizami endows Shirin with at least two of the extraordinary accoutrements that great heroes usually possess: unusual helpers and a wonderful horse. Shirin has seventy unrivaled beauties at her service who are equally peerless in martial arts and capable of fighting lions and elephants. Her black horse Shabdiz is even more important in that Nizami devotes several independent sections to describing its merits. This unique black steed, running on its "iron hooves" faster than the "philosopher's mind," later becomes Khusrau's. The agency of the king's physical mobility and military victories in fact belongs to Shirin.[21] Shirin proves her heroic abilities in many ways including her solitary journey on horseback to Iran. She is strong enough to remain mounted and brave enough to dismount in the wilderness and bathe in clear, inviting water. The princess and the spring become metaphors for one another. They are both unique, inaccessible, brilliant, and full of life. To rid herself of weariness, Shirin does not just wash her flower-like body in the spring; she grows in it in the manner of water lilies on the surface of ponds.[22] Shirin's delicate beauty does not detract from her heroic ability to survive. The metaphorical organic bond between her and the spring serves more than to indicate her brilliant beauty, for it also endows her with the life-giving power of a clear spring at a long journey's end.

The Heroine's Love Story

The heroic cycle's second stage is the love story. Nizami pays meticulous attention to details about the way Shirin falls in love. Khusrau surrenders his heart after hearing a verbal description of Shirin and admits to it shortly afterwards. For Shirin, a full portrait of Khusrau is painted to accompany verbal praise and secure her attention. Even so, it takes three viewings and a long conversation with the painter Shapur for Shirin to confess openly her feelings.[23] This delay cannot be seen as the result of a woman's weak and hesitant nature, for when she is certain of her feelings for Khusrau, the daring decision to ride alone to Iran takes little deliberation. Shirin's arrival in Iran does not lead to the lovers' encounter back in her country. A long process of courting begins in which Shirin and her female attendants prove their riding and shooting skills as much as Khusrau demonstrates his bravery by engaging a lion in bare-handed combat. Nizami uses the metaphor of "the master hunter" capturing the beloved's heart for Shirin and that of a helpless prey to allude to Khusrau:

> The king watched Shirin secretly.
> [He realized] what her hunting would in the end bring!
> He saw a gazelle appearing out of nowhere,

Intent on pursuit and capturing of the king.
In the hands of that master hunter, that world-conqueror [Shirin],
A world-conqueror such as Khusrau became a helpless prey.[24]

Khusrau has equally to charm Shirin, not just by good story-telling skills and defeating lions but by quelling the riot in his homeland and recapturing what is claimed by his rebellious officer Bahram Chubin but is legitimately his. Disagreements between the lovers occur mostly because of Shirin's loyalty to her principles. Although she is desperately in love, love can be fulfilled for her under one condition alone: turning Khusrau into the virtuous man and worthy king that he has the potential to be. To defy Shirin's exacting standards, Khusrau uses every device he can muster. He begs in humility, frowns, departs in anger, and even marries other women (including Maryam, the emperor's daughter) to intimidate Shirin. Shirin takes each incident with dignity and does not allow her love to shake her will, for she knows that Khusrau will return apologetic and regretful. On one such occasion, Khusrau camps at the threshold of Shirin's palace and begs her to show at least a glimpse of her face by appearing on the terrace if she chooses not to open the door for him to enter:

Open the door, after all this is the king!
He has come on foot to apologize to you.
You know that in my furthest thoughts
I would not dream of doing you any wrong.
You have to sit with me for a while!
I cannot go before seeing your face.
But if you so wish I leave this place in haste,
Allow me [at least] to take one look at you head to foot![25]

Shirin appears on the terrace and speaks to the king in humility. Her heart is broken but her will is not. Despite her humility and loving words, the palace's doors remain closed. Khusrau's promiscuity is as unacceptable to Shirin as his kingly negligence in abandoning his throne to the rebellious Bahram. She seeks the affection of the faithful lover and the honorable king that Khusrau deserves to be. Shirin's iron will and closed doors triumph over the king's stubborn nature. This personal transformation of an overbearing, aristocratic young man into a just and respectable king is the greatest of Shirin's heroic services.

Introducing a new lover, Farhad, Nizami puts Shirin on equal footing with Khusrau by demonstrating that as he enjoys the attention of other women, she is capable of having devoted lovers other than the king. Farhad is not the champion of a worldly kingdom but holds authority in another—equally fascinating—realm, art. Farhad is a master mason who enters the story in order to carve a stony passageway for milk to flow to Shirin's palace. This carefully selected metaphor highlights a fundamental difference between Farhad's love for Shirin as compared to Khusrau's passion: its gentle and nurturing dimension. Once the author uses the adjective *farzanah* (wise) for Farhad and describes the artist's mastery of geometry and sculpting skills, we are certain that this lover will not be found drunken begging at the door-step of Shirin's palace. If giving Shirin a devoted second lover to make her equal to Khusrau was one justification for Farhad's creation, this difference in personality is another significant reason why a second lover is needed in the story. Farhad is added because Shirin's exquisite beauty and complex personality call for a lover who is deeper and more perceptive than Khus-rau. Until Khusrau's passionate and concrete desires mature into a fuller love to correspond to Shirin's, Farhad's artistic sensitivity functions as the mir-ror reflecting Shirin's more evolved understanding of love. As Daleski dem-onstrates for English literature, love triangles, in addition to heightening the sense of drama, give the author a chance to introduce a "second self," a dif-ferent side of the hero's or heroine's personality. The second lover serves as a mirror reflecting qualities that have not attracted or been reflected in the first lover.[26] Nowhere is the sharp contrast between the personalities of Far-had and Khusrau more apparent than in their confrontation and ensuing verbal contest over possessing Shirin's affection. A curious Khusrau, shocked by the fact that Shirin may reciprocate his style of pursuing other lovers to arouse jealousy and threatened by Farhad's reputation for artistic mastery and personal charisma, arranges for him to be brought to the palace. In the ensuing conversation, the king's tone is sarcastic, guileful, and interrogative. Farhad's responses, while not audacious, are imbued with reverence for love and indifference to royalty. Whereas Khusrau attempts to keep the conver-sation concrete, Farhad moves in the direction of ambiguity and abstraction. Curious about the whereabouts of Farhad's homeland, the king hears "the land of companionship." Concerning the skills most common in that part of the world, he receives the riddle: "selling one's life to buy sorrow." Know-ing full well that he cannot contest the king's worldly authority, Farhad strives to show that kings have little authority in the realm of love. The opportuni-ty to assert this point comes when Khusrau attempts to dismiss Farhad's devotion by pointing to the strange nature of "selling one's life." Farhad re-

minds him that all conventions including royal decrees crumble in the domain of love, in which no incident could be considered strange:

The first thing, "Where are you from?" said the king.
"From the land of companionship," answered he.
"What is the occupation of the people in that land?" the king asked.
"They trade their lives for sorrow," he replied.
"But selling lives is not appropriate," said the king [sarcastically].
"It is not unexpected for true lovers," he answered.
"Did your heart get you so deep in love?" was the king's next reaction.
"You talk of heart," said Farhad; "for me this is a matter of life [or death]."[27]

Shirin is not heedless of this refined and artistic soul, yet neither is she
indifferent to his selfless love. When his passageway is prepared, she is so
impressed with the work's aesthetic quality that she removes her earrings to
reward the artist's mastery. In a later visit to his work area, she gives the exchange a new and personal dimension by offering him a glass of milk from
her own hands. Her visit to Farhad first sparks Khusrau's jealousy. The true
state of her appreciation for Farhad, however, emerges only after the master's bitter and untimely death:

Shirin's heart was pained with his loss.
A rare bird had disappeared from her garden.
She shed many a tear like the spring clouds
At the loss of that lonesome cypress tree grown on the stream's side.
She had his body dressed in exquisite vestment as did the nobles,
Then returned him to the earth and [herself] returned empty-handed.
She built a dome over his burial place,
Making his tomb a site for regular visits.[28]

Yet at no point in the story is Shirin overwhelmed by having the full devotion of these two extraordinary lovers; neither does she ever attempt to use
one against the other. She loves Khusrau, cherishes Farhad's artistic expressions of love, and yet stands confidently between the two strong love currents
because she has a part of each lover in her own complex character: Khusrau's
beauty, noble lineage, and passion combined with Farhad's sensitivity and
wisdom.[29] Her choice of Khusrau over Farhad is not due to her preference
for material power as opposed to wisdom. She chooses because she is loyal
to the one she loved first and is aware of her ability to educate Khusrau and
correct his erroneous ways.[30]

The Heroic Service

The heroic cycle's third stage is the heroic service. Although Shirin's heroic nature endows her with a rebellious dimension that motivates her for an act as daring as her solitary journey on horseback, she is in many ways a traditional royal figure prepared to fulfill personal and patriotic obligations. When her aunt Mahin Banu dies, Shirin follows her responsibility by ascending to the throne. Her heart is broken, for Khusrau has left her in anger and married another woman. Yet she rules with the utmost care and justice. She frees prisoners, abolishes unfair taxes, and attends to seekers of justice. When she leaves her kingdom to a trusted friend and sets out to seek Khusrau again, her abdication is motivated by the fear that her preoccupation with Khusrau's love might affect her ability to be a just ruler.[31]

Shirin's greatest heroic service is to tame Khusrau's untamed personality. In the story, through her words and deeds, Shirin maintains a dialogue with him. This effective dialogue, ranging from pleading to reproach, has a transforming quality. Whether through keeping Khusrau behind closed doors, blaming him for drunkenness, or instructing him concerning the significance of learning, Shirin diverts the king's attention from a constant search for pleasure to higher goals. This transformation is not surprising where the overall aspirations of the story are concerned. On the contrary, it is essential that Khusrau's personality improve if he is to remain the epic's central male protagonist. As Calder observes, heroes may have ups and downs but as individuals who supposedly contain "the best of the mass," they must never be allowed to act against the collective interest.[32] Khusrau's drinking habit, neglect of some duties, and promiscuity, perhaps tolerable for a young prince, have to be changed for him to become a proper king. In that sense, Nizami's desire to improve Khusrau's personality is not in itself unexpected or unique. What makes his approach worthy of mention is the agent of this change. In most epic tales, a wise old man, a mythical creature, or a good (male) companion are placed beside the hero to become a source of wisdom and set him on the right track when he deviates from the appropriate course of action. Here Nizami's choice of a young and attractive woman as the instrument of the change is both intriguing and unusual. Educators and sources of wisdom are traditionally, universally male, while women are at best good learners. The methods of training leave much to be desired too. Shakespeare and Shaw are two out of innumerable writers who employ strong male educators to tame shrews and shape uncouth women into refined ladies. In each case, the teacher is a male, the apprentice is a female, and the harshness of the teaching method—despite some surface criticism—is ultimately justified through the glorification of the magical final transformation. By contrast, Shirin is a woman in love trying to educate a man who is at the same time the king. Considering the situation, she moves with admirable certainty and force. If at times she feels trepidation, it is due to fear of risking his love rather than being subjected to kingly wrath. She combines her lessons with gentleness and humility and considers herself neither better nor worse than her student. Her propriety is due to her kind nature rather than to any sense of hesitation with using power to tame him. Thus, Shirin reminds Khusrau of the need to free Iran from the rebellious Bahram Chubin instead of spending his time seeking her:

> You have youth, bravery, and kingship.
> You are the head [of the land], your head adorned with the crown.
> Free the limbs of this land from the confines of chaos.
> For once demonstrate your [kingly] skills
> To this Hindu who has pillaged your personal belongings,
> To this Turk who has taken over your royal office.
> Destroy his body with a flash of your sword.
> Break the spell that he has cast [on Iran].
> For the hands of kings in seeking the king's pleasure
> Should, at times, carry a wine cup, at other times a sword.[33]

An intriguing characteristic of Shirin's wise and stable personality is its apparent lack of conflict with sexual desire and attraction. All major belief systems demonstrate suspicion toward female sexuality and at best consider it a source of distraction and temptation. This sexual potency is equally exaggerated in literary traditions. Women's sexually magnetic power can make men lose their ability to judge and leave them susceptible to committing irreversible errors. It is not surprising that such dangerous beings have not often been portrayed as educators or sources of wisdom and knowledge—or have achieved that status only after aging and losing their initial physical attraction.[34] Shirin, however, is beautiful and desirable. Her ruby lips, dark hair, and fragrant body are frequently and graphically described. Bird, flower, and other imagery from nature form a substantial part of these descriptions, filled with playful, deliberate exaggerations. They are not meant to have any mystical or spiritual connotation and at times are clearly and unquestionably erotic. The best example of Nizami's attention to Shirin's sexuality (and its attributes essential to making the heroine's character) occurs during the lovers' wedding night. As demanding as ever, Shirin asks Khusrau not to drink that particular

evening so that they can have a sober and full appreciation of their first intimate contact. Knowing Khusrau's ways, she then puts an elderly woman in
her place to measure his sobriety and test his promise of self-restraint. Pre-
dictably unable to keep his word, Khusrau discovers the ruse despite being
drunk. Then, after thirty verses devoted to yet another description of her beauty, Shirin finally enters the nuptial chamber. The description of the lovers' first
intimacy is probably the most lavishly detailed erotic description of lovemaking in classical Persian literature. Despite possessing female carnal charm,
Shirin retains her role as counselor and source of wisdom.

Death of the Heroine

The heroic cycle's last stage is the hero's death. Farhad, who killed himself
after hearing the false rumor of Shirin's death, has been dead for some time.
Shirin and Khusrau are united in marriage, resulting in a transformation of
Khusrau's restless personality. In fact, Khusrau's devotion to learning and
worship gives his son Shiruyeh a chance to confine his father and place himself on the throne. Shiruyeh's greed is further fueled by his love for Shirin,
whom he has admired since the age of nine when she married his father.
Hoping to possess Shirin, he stabs Khusrau to death in his sleep in his
confinement chamber, and Khusrau dies without waking Shirin.[35] Shiruyeh's
message of love and promise of union with Shirin follow. Shirin has two
choices: to live with a murderous usurper whom she disdains or to die with
the just king and caring husband she loves. Like any proper heroic figure, she
chooses the latter. Nizami seizes the opportunity to give her a royal farewell,
one more prominent than any other protagonist in the story.

Shirin is the survivor, in control and able to restrain her personal grief
to bury her lover with the full respect he deserves (as she did earlier for Farhad). She has the king's body placed in a bejeweled coffin and carried by the
nobility to his burial site. Dressed in red silk with her face made up like a
bride's, Shirin follows the body with light, seemingly happy steps. In this way,
she hides her sorrow from the murderous Shiruyeh and gives a hint of the
joyous nature of the union that is going to follow after her self-destruction
next to Khusrau's body. She then stabs herself and dies with her body upon
his as in a loving embrace.

This gracious but sorrowful end has a deeper wisdom than is first apparent. That Khusrau's own son Shiruyeh murders him is not a mere coincidence
or a result of sheer bad luck. Shiruyeh is the outcome of Khusrau's marriage
to the Roman emperor's daughter Maryam, an act motivated by political am-

bition as well as disloyalty to Shirin. Khusrau has committed much wrong in his own time. He may be forgiven for excessive drinking and promiscuity as a young prince, but other sins are less forgivable. At his command, the false rumor of Shirin's death was spread with the explicit aim of harming Farhad. That his son should now kill him may be seen as punishment for the unjust and jealous act of trickery that triggered Farhad's suicide. What destroys Khusrau in the end is the consequence of his earlier acts of jealousy and betrayal.

If Farhad is a victim of the trickery of others and Khusrau of his own mistakes, Shirin demonstrates full agency in her own death. She takes her life in a premeditated plan with full awareness of its goal: to deny Shiruyeh's will to possess her after Khusrau's demise. Nizami does not bemoan Shirin's death, for he presents it as a courageous act and a way for her to reunite with the deceased king. In the loss of this legendary heroine, nature cries instead. A storm darkens the horizon, and a cloud rises from "the sea of sorrow" to rain a flood that covers all mountaintops.[36]

Nizami and Shirin

The degree of Nizami's attachment to Shirin and his insistence on breathing life into this fabulous figure find a touching personal explanation in the closing verses of the romantic epic *Khusrau u Shirin*. Just as we consider the story concluded, we observe the author emerging from the text to shed his garb as the detached storyteller and ask us to observe and acknowledge his personal stake in the composition. He wants us to know that Shirin comes not only from his creative imagination but also from his life, that he knows her because he was married to a woman like her, one named Afaq:

> O you! Who do not take heed from this story:
> What do you think, that you are reading a fabulous tale?
> O, this tale begs for tears,
> Tears as bitter as rosewater to be shed for Shirin.
> For the life of that short-lived one
> Was scattered to the wind as are flowers in their prime.
> She left early like my Kipchak idol.
> O, it was as if she was my Afaq herself.
> A royal figure in beauty and in wisdom
> Sent to me by the prince of Darband.
> Silk was an armor on her body, stronger than armor.
> Her dresses tight-sleeved like a man's garment.

> She was capable of pulling heads by their ears
> Yet gave me a pillow of companionship to rest on.
> Like all Turks, she needed to emigrate [and left].
> In her Turkish ways she ravished all that I possessed.[37]

Sent to the poet by the prince of Darband, Afaq was a Kipchak slave-girl who according to Nizami's biographers became a fundamental turning point in his life. Through Afaq, he "experienced true love, its ecstasy and also, within a short time, its sorrow." In the moving passage above, Nizami not only mourns the loss of his beloved wife Afaq but also reveals her as the woman who was the inspiration for Shirin's creation.[38]

Nizami paid his greatest respect to Shirin, and by extension to Afaq, through not making the heroine of his epic the shadow (or the reverse) of a male hero but a powerful individual in her own right. The individuality and centrality of Shirin's figure stand out in contrast to the universal characteristic of premodern heroines who were an "image of antithesis" in relation to the hero. Edwards describes female heroes as "leading a fugitive existence" with their presence "overlooked" and identities "obscured." "Western culture, for example, has represented heroes typically as military leaders: commanding, conquering, and above all male. . . . Within this context—patriarchal, hostile, preoccupied with rank—the woman hero is an image of antithesis. Different from the male—her sex her sign—she threatens his authority and the system he sustains."[39]

Shirin is given the attention that male heroes usually receive in that she "dances in the spotlight" instead of being "eclipsed" and "upstaged in darkness," and the centrality of her figure to the overall story is equally significant.[40] A male hero is universally the primary figure who inspires and therefore requires followers. The heroine obeys, falls into line, and takes second place. Although a hero can theoretically exist in a narrative without a heroine, the reverse is not the case.[41] Far from being a shadow of Khusrau or Farhad, Shirin forms a necessary pillar without which the story would collapse. Nizami demonstrates awareness of the centrality that he bestows on Shirin. In the closing verses of the story, the second and third, as quoted above, are of particular relevance here:

> O, this tale begs for tears,
> Tears as bitter as rosewater to be shed for Shirin.
> For the life of that short-lived one
> Was scattered to the wind as are flowers in their prime.

In these lines, the only reason given for the sadness of "this tale" is Shirin's untimely death. Although such an allusion does not mean that other deaths in the story are insignificant, by singling out Shirin's demise to close the narrative and by describing it as begging for tears, Nizami makes her fate the embodiment of the tragic essence in the story. She is beyond doubt the most central figure.[42]

Shirin's Resonance in Literary Memory

Was Shirin a taboo for the Muslim society of Nizami's time or a shock to the literary tradition in which she was created? How did readers come to terms with a woman who was a powerful hero? An ideal way of assessing the popularity of a figure in a literary tradition would be to look for studies evaluating the character. Classical Persian verse and its critics did not focus their attention on character development. Their view of literature was in one sense holistic and in another acutely conscious of details. The holistic approach focused on the overall aim of the literature to teach, entertain, and praise. The particularistic aspect of the critical approach to poetry concerned itself with mastery of verbal expression, the fine details at the sonic surface of poems. Although no premodern writer is known to have analyzed Shirin's character, the fact that Nizami passed the test on both general and particular levels is apparent from some unambiguous facts. *Khusrau u Shirin* acquired canonical status immediately after its composition and activated a process of literary imitation that continued to modern times. The long, impressive list of those who imitated Nizami includes Amir Khusrau (d. 1325), Khaju (d. 1352), and Jami (d. 1492). Imitation of authoritative texts was a familiar literary device enabling a poet to adopt a known classical text and use it as a forum to express his or her creative impulse by producing variations on the familiar themes. This process was by no means a blind repetition of the old but rather a complex and dynamic process of interaction with a vast and resonant body of literature to revive for personal use what reverberated intertextually in the readers' cultural memory. That so many poets retold the story of *Khusrau u Shirin* is a sign of widespread admiration for the work.[43]

Another, more specific way exists to measure the resonance of Shirin's image in the Persian literary memory. The *ghazal,* the most common vehicle for lyric expression in classical Persian literature, did not usually employ thematic expression. Instead of having a narrative line run through its various elements, the ghazal made use of an effective method of juxtaposing vivid images and concepts, each alluding to diverse poetic figures and events. In this way, it freed itself from the confines of one story and acquired a striking resonance by employing many stories circulating in the culture's literary memory. Shirin is beyond doubt one of the most frequent topics of such allusions in Persian literature. In the intertextual journey taking her through eight centuries of writing, she remains a symbol of life, beauty, youth, and love. She is the archetypal beloved of classical Persian poetry.[44]

Western literary influence has brought new perspectives to the Iranian literary scene. Going beyond allusions to pay close attention to storytelling and character development has, in modern times, occupied Iranian critics too. As a result, we can now observe the more direct cultural reactions of the unconventional force and independence of a female character such as Shirin. An example is the comparative study of the personalities of Layli and Shirin in *Sima-yi du zan* (Portraits of two women) by the Iranian critic Sirjani.[45] Layli, the female protagonist in Nizami's other celebrated romantic tragedy, *Layli u Majnun*, differs from Shirin. Not only does she not travel to seek the one she loves, she is married to a person against her will. Sirjani explores the reasons for the difference between these women's personalities in Nizami's work. Favorably impressed by Shirin's strong will and harshly critical of Layli's weakness, he considers the difference to be the result of varying circumstances in the two stories' composition. Nizami created a woman of his personal choice in the figure of Shirin, whereas Layli's personality was already shaped, and the poet put her preexisting story into verse only at his patron's request. Sirjani's study is not without conceptual flaws. For example, he does not indicate that Layli and Majnun's love is meant to exemplify different sentiments than Khusrau and Shirin's. Everyone in the story—not just Layli—thinks and acts in a more restrained, introverted manner. Sirjani's essay serves an immediate political purpose in that it provides social commentary directed at the ideal of womanhood in postrevolutionary Iran. He offers contemporary Iranian women a classical model of self-assertion when he praises Shirin for boldly pursuing her love. The fact remains that a twentieth-century Iranian male critic endorses eight hundred years of admiration for Shirin by giving her assertive personality his unconditional approval.

Scholars could sift through the vast body of romantic tales in classical Persian literature to see how many Shirins, as opposed to Laylis, are found. Did Afaq's decisive personality prompt Nizami to create a dynamic and assertive Shirin? Did his idealized vision of the "other" in the exotic, faraway land of Armenia give free rein to his imagination? Or did the nature of the story, a happy retelling of a tale of love requiring immediate and concrete fulfillment as opposed to belated spiritual reward, warrant Shirin's creation? Whatever justification may be found for the conception of this lively and influential woman in classical Persian literature, her continuing presence may not be explained by any factor other than her full acceptance in the culture. We are advised to examine carefully our notion of an "ideal woman" in premodern traditional societies. As Edwards observes, "sex, class, status, and occupation have great historical and social resonance, but not inherent meaning. A culture's heroes reflect a culture's values."[46]

NOTES

1. This romantic epic was composed in 6,500 verses during the years 1177–81 and was dedicated to Atabak Shams al-Din Muhammad Jahan Pahlavan, the Seljuq ruler. I use the Persian edition, Nizami Ganjavi, *Kulliyat-i khamsah-i Nizami-i Ganjavi,* ed. Muin Far (Tehran: Zarrin, 1362/1983). All English translations are mine.

2. The former quote is from Edward Browne's *A Literary History of Persian Literature* (Cambridge: Cambridge University Press, 1906), 2:400, and the latter two are from Jan Rypka, *History of Persian Literature,* trans. P. van Popta-Hope (Dordrecht, Holland: D. Reidel, 1968), 210.

3. Browne, *Literary History,* 400–402.

4. Jennie Calder, *Heroes: From Byron to Guevara* (London: Hamish Hamilton, 1977), xii.

5. Composed by Abu al-Qasim Firdausi most probably during 975–94. See Rypka, *Persian Literature,* 155; and Mahmoud Omidsalar's chapter in this volume.

6. John Renard, *Islam and the Heroic Image: Themes in Literature and the Visual Arts* (Columbia: University of South Carolina Press, 1993), 233.

7. Joseph Campbell, *The Hero with a Thousand Faces* (New York: Pantheon, 1949), 365. Linda Hunt uses the same argument to justify the criticized silence and passivity of Jane Austen's Fanny Price; "A Woman's Portion: Jane Austen and the Female Character," in *Fetter'd or Free: British Women Novelists, 1670–1815,* ed. Mary Anne Schofield and Cecilia Macheski (Athens: Ohio University Press, 1986), 8.

8. Calder, *Heroes,* ix.

9. Nizami's versified romantic epics total five and have come to be known as the *panj ganj* (five treasures). In order of composition they are: *Makhzan al-asrar, Khusrau u Shirin, Layli u Majnun, Bahraminamah* or *Haftpaykar,* and *Iskandar-namah.* For an account of Nizami's life and information on these masnavis (rhyming couplets), see Zabih Allah Safa, *Tarikh-i adabiyat dar Iran: Az miyanah-i qarn-i panjum ta aghaz-i haftum-i Hijri* (Tehran: Firdausi, 1369/1980), 2:198–824. For existing manuscript copies, early printed editions, and critical editions, see François De Blois, *Persian Literature: A Bio-Bibliographical Survey* (London: Royal Asiatic Society of Great Britain and Ireland, 1994), vol. 5, pt. 2, 438–95.

10. Nizami, 253–79.

11. Renard, *Islam and the Heroic Image,* 233.

12. The persistence of the lyrical resonance in Shirin's personality over a long time span is remarkable. Just as for the poet Hafiz (d. 1390), Farhad's fall for Shirin serves as the archetypal motif of the lover's total surrender to love; Hafiz, *Divan-i khvajah Shams al-Din Muhammad Hafiz*, ed. Husayn Niknam (Tehran: Alburz, 1374/1995), 59, verse 5. The contemporary Iranian poet Shahriyar hears Farhad's complaint of separation from Shirin in the sorrowful flute's song; Muhammad Husayn Shahriyar, *Divan-i Shahriyar*, 16th ed. (Tehran: Zarrin, 1374/1995), 1:203, verse 9.

13. Calder, *Heroes*, ix.

14. Farzaneh Milani, *Veils and Words: The Emerging Voices of Iranian Women Writers* (Syracuse: Syracuse University Press, 1992), 1. Overlooking the universality of female absence in the world's written literature is exemplified in Michael Hillmann's study of the contemporary Iranian poet Forugh Farrokhzad. He opens the book's preface with the statement, "Iranian history is of men and their exploits," which implies that the history of other societies is of women and their own exploits; *A Lonely Woman: Forugh Farrokhzad and Her Poetry* (Washington, D.C.: Mage Publishers and Three Continents Press, 1987), 1.

15. For an Orientalist portrayal of Arab/Muslim women, see Malika Mehdid, "A Western Invention of Arab Womanhood: The 'Oriental' Female," in *Women in the Middle East: Perceptions, Realities, and Struggles of Liberation*, ed. Haleh Afshar (New York: St. Martin's Press, 1993), 18–58. Mehdid notes that even Edward Said, critical observer (*Orientalism*, London: Routledge and Kegan Paul, 1978), does not tackle the gender issue.

16. Chaucer's treatment of Constance's life in *The Man of Law's Prologue and Tale* is an example. Juliette Dor, "Humilis Exaltetur: Constance of Humility Rewarded," in *Heroes and Heroines in Medieval English Literature*, ed. Leo Carruthers (Cambridge, U.K.: D. S. Brewer, 1994), 74–75. The comparison between Shirin and Nizami's wife Afaq focuses on the strength of personality and length of life; Nizami, 331.

17. Nizami, 327.

18. Peter Heath, *The Thirsty Sword: Sirat 'Antar and the Arabic Popular Epic* (Salt Lake City: University of Utah Press, 1996), 68–69.

19. That heroines are often the reverse of heroes demonstrating little more than patience and suffering has been observed in many studies. Richard Jordan describes Donne's heroine Elizabeth Drury as a "heroic figure who did little more than die" in *The Quiet Hero: Figures of Temperance in Spenser, Donne, Milton, and Joyce* (Washington, D.C.: Catholic University of America Press, 1989), 62. Cf. heroines in Carruthers, *Heroes and Heroines.*

20. Nizami, 125.

21. Ibid.

22. Ibid., 140.

23. Ibid., 126–30.

24. Ibid., 164.

25. Ibid., 256–57.

26. Hillel Matthew Daleski, *The Divided Heroine: A Recurrent Pattern in Six English Novels* (New York: Holmes and Meier, 1984), 18.

27. Nizami, 219.

28. Ibid., 233.

29. Nizami's positive attitude toward his heroine Shirin must not be taken as a categorical absence of misogynistic assertions in his writings. Such negative comments are often expressed by his protagonists, not Nizami himself. One example is the reaction of Khusrau's wife Maryam to Khusrau's desire to see Shirin. She objects to the visit by commenting on women's unreliability; see Nizami, 202.

30. The fact that Nizami and his royal patrons would most probably not approve of a union between a princess and a stonemason is another factor in directing the story line.

31. Nizami, 193–94.

32. Calder, *Heroes*, xii.

33. Nizami, 181.

34. Cf. Jose Ignacio Cabezon, ed., *Buddhism, Sexuality, and Gender* (Albany: State University of New York Press, 1985); Uta Ranke-Heinemann, *Eunuchs for the Kingdom of Heaven: Women, Sexuality, and the Catholic Church*, trans. Peter Heinegg (New York: Penguin, 1990). Fedwa Malti-Douglas examines Islamic literary tradition in *Woman's Body, Woman's Word: Gender and Discourse in Arabo-Islamic Writing* (Princeton: Princeton University Press, 1991).

35. Nizami, 320–24.

36. Ibid., 327–28.

37. Ibid., 331.

38. For information on Nizami's wife Afaq, see Rypka, *Persian Literature*, 211.

39. Lee R. Edwards, *Psyche As Hero: Female Heroine and Fictional Form* (Middletown: Wesleyan University Press, 1984), 4.

40. Ibid.

41. Ibid., 5–6.

42. Nizami, 331.

43. Safa, *Tarikh-i adabiyat*, 809.

44. The Persian ghazal has often been criticized for being fragmentary because of its lack of narrative line and use of allusions. For discussion of this misconception, see Fatemeh Keshavarz, *Reading Mystical Lyric: The Case of Jalal al-Din Rumi* (Columbia: University of South Carolina Press, 1988), 141–45. For premodern and modern examples of allusion to Shirin, see Renard, *Islam and the Heroic Image*.

45. Saidi Sirjani, *Sima-yi du zan: Shirin va Layli dar khamsah-i Nizami-i Ganjavi* (Tehran: Nau, 1368/1989).

46. Edwards, *Psyche As Hero*, 4.

10 Lifting the Veil from the Face
of Depiction: The Representation
of Women in Persian Painting

LAYLA S. DIBA

EVEN A CURSORY SURVEY of Persian painting—lifting the veil from the face
of depiction, in the words of a sixteenth-century chronicler—reveals the significance, richness, and variety of representations of women. What would Khusraw be without Shirin, Bahram Gur without Azadeh, Giv without Farangis,
paradise without *paris* (angels), and the heavens without *khurshid khanum*
(maiden sun)? In contrast to public life, where women are largely absent—or
if present, heavily veiled—many representations of women in Persian painting (as in literature and poetry) provide considerable evidence for investigating the origins and broader social and cultural implications of such imagery.
Nevertheless, the subject has rarely been the focus of scholarly attention.[1]

This chapter proposes to begin by considering general questions regarding Persian painting as they relate to the depiction of women and to proceed
to a preliminary overview of the topic by examining the subject of women
from three perspectives: power, love, and society.

Persian Painting and the Representation of Women

In the course of the history of Persian art, representations of women are
found in a wide variety of media. For the Sasanian period (A.D. 224–628),

textual sources refer to illustrated manuscripts of Manichean origin and, by implication, to representations of women. In addition, extant depictions of female divinities and entertainers in mural painting, representations of the goddess Anahita in the rock reliefs of Taq-i Bustan, and maenads and dancers on silver objects attest to the widespread use of female imagery in pre-Islamic times.[2]

From the early Islamic period in Iran onward (mid-seventh to thirteenth centuries) and particularly during Seljuq rule (A.D. 1030–1190), depictions of women are found as decorative motifs and individual images as well as elements of narrative compositions. These representations were utilized for ceramics, metalwork, tilework, textiles, and stucco.[3] From the mid-fourteenth century onward, manuscript illustration and to a lesser degree mural painting became the preeminent media for Persian painters, although the decorative arts continued to feature fine designs with representations of women related to those produced for illustrated manuscripts. For the purposes of this chapter, I confine my investigation to the arts of the book and architectural decoration. The chronological range considered herein—with one exception, the earliest-known illustrated manuscript, dated to the early thirteenth century—will be the mid-fourteenth century to circa 1900.

This study also examines in successive order the links between innovations in the representation of women and the material contexts such representations were intended for. These contexts included narrative painting, that is, illustrations for manuscripts of historical, epic, and lyrical texts; detached single-page paintings; lacquerwork and oil on canvas or mural paintings for architectural decoration; and caricatures for lithographed newspapers.

The widespread use of such imagery would appear to contradict the well-known Islamic aversion to figural imagery frequently expressed in the traditions (hadith) of the Prophet Muhammad and to a lesser extent in the Qur'an itself. The importance of this prohibition has been somewhat overstated in the past, since it was often applied sporadically and was largely limited to public spheres and religious contexts. The prohibition—inherited from the Judaic tradition against the making of graven images—was primarily directed against sculpture and the making of idols. It does not seem to have inhibited the depiction of women in the decorative arts or painting per se, any more than it did the development of Persian painting as a whole. Painting was commonly produced for use only within the context of private life and was traditionally commissioned by ruling and merchant classes for the embellishment of interior spaces— accessible to only a select few—and the decoration of luxury manuscripts.[4]

Women were portrayed according to established canons in an idealized fashion with little expression of emotion. Negative aspects of women's personalities, such as the salaciousness, deviousness, and capriciousness often found in literature and satire, are largely absent from Persian painting.[5] The range of activities and social roles played by women in society and history, however, is reflected only in the most limited sense. For instance, the important role of women mystics is never recorded, although representations of mystics and sufis were a popular theme with Persian painters. Concurrently, few images are found of women engaged in traditionally male activities such as writing and reading poetry.[6]

A defining characteristic of Persian painting is the repetition of compositions: once a compositional type or portrait genre was originated, painters prided themselves on the creative replication of the original. For the portrayal of women, painters invented stock types such as youthful beauties or old crones, formulae that continued to be repeated with variations by generations of painters according to the aesthetic canons and stylistic criteria of successive historical periods.

As a rule, few differences exist between the stock types of men and women; similar figural proportions, scale, and physiognomy prevail, and often the only distinguishing characteristics are the type of headgear worn (turbans for men, veils for women), elements of clothing, or facial hair. In certain schools of Persian painting, including paintings of the Seljuq period and late-sixteenth-century Safavid painting, depictions of the human form were unequivocally androgynous.

These stock types, while originally invented to illustrate specific episodes of a text or to enhance the decorative program of a three-dimensional object, also illustrated broader cultural themes associated with women. Images of women often reflect contemporary reality and provide valuable visual evidence of aspects of women's lives and the ways they were viewed by society.

Women and Power: Literary Heroines and Consorts

Among the most frequent representations of women are images of heroines from literary texts. The composition of Firdawsi's *Shah-nameh*, the Persian national epic compiled circa A.D. 1000, and other related works resulted in the production of illustrated manuscripts of epic poetry. Romantic epics such as Nizami's *Khamseh* (Quintet), composed in the fourteenth century, became equally popular with painters and patrons as well.

The formative period of manuscript illustration (ca. 1225 to 1400) witnessed the evolution of the image from narrow "wall-painting" format illustrations with a single ground line and solid or illuminated backgrounds to full-page compositions depicting complex actions set against fully developed architectural and landscape settings. From simplified cartoon-like illustrations complementing the text, Persian painting evolved into a lyrical and at times expressive art form going well beyond the strict interpretation of the text.

The compositions invented by Persian painters of this period set the standard for the succeeding two centuries. A mid-sixteenth-century chronicler, the calligrapher and painter Dust Muhammad, describes this seminal moment in the formative period of Persian painting (during the rule of Abu Sa'id, the Ilkhanid sultan, r. 1317–35): "Master Ahmed Musa, who was his father's pupil, lifted the veil from the face of depiction, and [the style] of depiction that is now current was invented by him."[7]

Ideally, a comprehensive analysis of our subject would consider not only individual manuscript illustrations depicting women but also the relationship of such scenes to the text and the illustrative program of the whole. Such an analysis is feasible in only a few cases, since systematic studies of individual Persian illustrated manuscripts are few in number. Here I briefly discuss two that have been studied in depth: a thirteenth-century *Warqa and Gulsha* and a dispersed mid-fourteenth-century royal Mongol manuscript (formerly known as the "Demotte *Shah-Nameh*").

The earliest complete illustrated Persian manuscript, a copy of the romance of *Warqa and Gulsha* by Ayuqqi, composed in the eleventh century, transcribed circa 1225, features many depictions of the female heroine Gulsha (fig. 1).[8] Of the seventy-one illustrations to this manuscript, twenty-three feature the heroine Gulsha. A story of star-crossed lovers taking place among tribes in Arabia during the seventh century, *Warqa and Gulsha* recounts the tale of the separation, trials, and eventual reunion after the two lovers' death.

In this illustration, Gulsha is shown engaged in a battle to rescue her lover, Warqa, from a rival Arab clan. Mounted on horseback and unveiled, Gulsha pierces with her spear a rival claimant for her hand, Rabi ibn Adnan. Warqa can be seen on foot, being led in chains, to the right of the painting. The heroine, identified by the inscription in olive-gold pigment to her right, is portrayed in three-quarters view, with the same scale and similar proportions to that of the male protagonists.

Her head, like that of all other figures, is encircled by a golden halo commonly used by Persian painters of this period to set off figures against the background. She wears male clothing with boots and trousers and can be

Figure 1. "Gulsha Rescues Warqa." Illustration to a manuscript of *Warqa and Gulsha* by Ayuqqi. Western Iran or Baghdad, ca. 1225, illustrated by Abd al Mumin ibn Muhammad Naqqash al-Khuy. (H.841, fol. 22r. Courtesy of the Topkapı Palace Museum.)

distinguished from her male counterparts only by the coronet on her head. Her face is round, framed by bangs and long braids, with a small rosebud mouth and red cheeks, arched eyebrows, and almond-shaped eyes.

Formally, the paintings are characterized by the stylization of figures, simplification of landscape elements, symmetrical disposition of figures, and use of backgrounds either left plain or decorated with oversized vegetal arabesques. Often the painter embellishes the text or even contradicts it. In the case of this illustration, for instance, Ayuqqi's text states that Gulsha's horse is gray and that Warqa was bound to Rabi. The painter depicts Gulsha on a gold steed, and Warqa is led not by Rabi but by another horseman to the extreme right of the image.[9]

The painter follows the poet's description of Gulsha, which states that she is moon-faced and cypress-like. Other poetic conventions used by Ayuqqi to portray Gulsha, such as comparison with idols, figurines, and the narcissus, clearly provided few literary clues to guide painters in their representation of the heroine. While the painter derived his aesthetic canon for the portrayal of Gulsha from Ayuqqi's text, other aspects of his portrayal are based on prototypes from the decorative arts of the Seljuq period and contemporary manuscripts of other texts. Some authors have also noted a similarity of the narrow format with that of wall paintings.[10]

Thus, the earliest image of a woman we encounter in the pages of Persian manuscripts is that of a female warrior, a medieval action heroine. Her stance, proportions, attire, and actions are not commensurate with the chaste, passive, and submissive image of Persian women commonly held. Gulsha's appearance as a principal protagonist in twenty-three of the seventy-one episodes selected for illustration underlines the importance of the portrayal of women in the illustrative program of this manuscript.

Manuscripts of the *Shah-nameh*—which became the favored text for illustration after the thirteenth century—also featured numerous depictions of women.[11] Firdawsi's epic poem provided opportunities for inventive compositions for painters and was the most suitable text for rulers and the nobility to commission for their libraries because it recounted the heroic deeds of legendary and historical kings (and, I may add, queens and princesses). The role of women as active protagonists in the forward progression of the epic's action can be traced throughout the following centuries in illustrated manuscripts of the *Shah-nameh*. In Firdawsi's text, both positive and negative images of women abound: heroines, mothers, and warriors but also traitors and schemers.[12] Women are portrayed as well in their traditional passive roles of prize or booty for the male conqueror.

While as a rule manuscript painters chose to portray the heroic qualities of these women, it has been suggested that in one instance negative aspects of the use of power were emphasized in episodes selected for illustration: the royal Mongol *Shah-nameh* manuscript, generally assigned to circa 1330 at Tabriz, the capital of the Ilkhan Mongol rulers of Iran (1220–1380). The manuscript is undated, restored, incomplete, and dispersed yet nevertheless constitutes a great monument to Persian painting.[13] In their study of this manuscript, Grabar and Blair single out the critical role of women as mediators in the establishment of royal power as one of the five principal themes of the illustrative program of the manuscript.[14] Additionally, they argue that the manuscript's illustrative program reflects contemporary events at the Mongol court. According to this hypothesis, the eight illustrations featuring women were chosen to reflect the conspiracies of powerful and ruthless Mongol consorts and princesses.[15]

The attempted reconstruction of the manuscript cannot conclusively determine the range of subjects chosen for illustration or their total number, and hence these arguments, while tantalizing, remain inconclusive. While the authors emphasize the rarity of certain illustrations, others—such as Zal and Rudabeh—are among the universally favored themes, and others still are open to a less negative interpretation than the authors propose. Nevertheless, the hypothesis is intriguing that special royal manuscript commissions such as this one, as distinct from the less luxurious manuscript production for the general market, reflect historical events of their time.

It may be argued that a number of images from other fourteenth-century manuscripts depicting enthroned royal couples reflect the political importance and relative freedom from the laws of seclusion of Seljuq and Mongol princesses.[16] Examples include the double-page frontispiece of a manuscript of the poetic anthology *Munis al-ahrar* (Free men's companion to the subtleties of poems), copied in 741/1341 and most recently assigned to Isfahan (fig. 2).[17] The right-hand side depicts a hunting scene; on the left, a royal couple is enthroned. The couple is shown seated, facing each other, on a high-backed, carved, and painted wooden throne draped with a red textile; the ruler offers his queen a drink from a stemmed goblet. Around them, attendants stand at attention, prepare refreshments, and fan the consort. The painter has given equal importance to both central figures, while the attendants are smaller in scale; the two figures share the same scale, proportions, and rich attire. The ruler is distinguished by his elaborate Mongol feathered headgear, and his consort—whose veil is barely perceptible—holds a handkerchief in her hand, sometimes interpreted as a symbol of power. Key figures in compositions were often rendered in larger scale than the other protagonists. In this instance, the portrayal of the woman enthroned, holding an attribute of power, may indicate that at certain periods royal women were considered equal to their consorts and could be portrayed as legitimate symbols of authority. This frontispiece was clearly intended to represent historical figures of the time, although the identification of the figures remains inconclusive.

The frontispiece is related to a number of examples of detached court scenes in albums in the Topkapu Saray Library in Istanbul and the Islamic Museum in Berlin. These depict comparable scenes of Mongol queens wearing a distinctive headgear known as *buqtaq* and seated with rulers and surrounded by princesses and court attendants; they provide further examples of images of women in power in fourteenth-century Persian painting.[18]

Manuscript illustration evolved considerably under the subsequent reigns of the Timurids (1380–1500) and Safavids (1500–1722) into full-page complex compositions of a lyrical character with fully elaborated landscapes executed in highly polished jewel-like colors. Representations of men and women continued to follow the stock types used during the preceding periods while exhibiting a reduced scale in relation to the overall composition. Also characteristic are increasingly elegant silhouettes and proportions that reflect the sophisticated court taste and evolving aesthetic canons of the period.

Many images of powerful women occur in the lavishly illustrated manuscripts of sixteenth-century Persian painting produced in the centers of

Figure 2. "Royal Couple Enthroned." Illustration to a manuscript of the *Munis al-ahrar*. Isfahan, 741/1341. (LNS 9 MS, fols. 1v–2r. Copyright © Dar al-Athar al-Islam-iyyah, Kuwait National Museum.)

artistic production, principally Tabriz and Shiraz. An illustration of Kay Khusraw crossing the Oxus with Farangis and Giv (fig. 3) may serve as a striking example. Framed by text panels, it depicts the moment when the future ruler, Kay Khusraw, returns to Iran from Turan. He is accompanied by his mother, Farangis, who protected him and gave him a princely education, and the hero Giv. The three protagonists are shown fording the river Oxus on horseback, as fish gambol in the waves beneath their horses and onlookers watch from shore. The dominant role played by queen mothers throughout Iranian history is reflected in this composition. The painter has chosen to emphasize Farangis's importance by placing her at the center of the composition, between her son Kay Khusraw and Giv. The heroine is modestly veiled; she is placed on an equal plane and rendered in the same scale as the male protagonists. According to the stylistic conventions of Safavid painting, Farangis is shown as elegant and ethereal, far from a flesh-and-blood woman. Nevertheless, her proud stance and forceful gestures imply an amazon-like quality despite these delicate proportions and silhouette. Farangis also plays a key role in the group's safe negotiation of the river torrents, a metaphor for the assumption of political power.[19] According to Firdawsi's text, the three figures could cross by boat only if they met the insulting conditions of a boatman (not shown in the illustration) and therefore decide to ford the river on horseback. Omidsalar states that folk versions of this tale emphasize that the safe crossing is contingent upon Farangis's purity.[20]

Farangis represents only one of many such figures in Persian poetry. In the Safavid period, when royal princesses and queens held land, acted as cultural patrons and donors, and were known for their excellent horsemanship, depictions such as this one may have reflected a contemporary reality as well.

Women and Love: Beloved, Huri, Nude, and Entertainer

A second category of female representation was the "ideal beauty" of the romantic and mystical poetic texts. The *Khamseh* of Nizami was a favorite text for Persian patrons and painters, particularly in the fifteenth and sixteenth centuries. This romantic epic devoted to the adventures of legendary Persian heroes and their love affairs inspired some of the most lyrical representations of women in Persian painting.

One of Nizami's most beloved heroines is Shirin, queen of Armenia and paramour of the Persian ruler Khusraw Parviz, depicted in the previous

Figure 3. "Kay Khusraw Crossing the Oxus with Farangis and Giv." Detached illustration to a manuscript of Firdawsi's *Shahnameh.* Shiraz, late fifteenth to early sixteenth century. (No. 86.227.173. Courtesy of the Brooklyn Museum of Art, gift of the Ernest Erickson Foundation, Inc.)

episode from the *Shah-nameh*. Of the many episodes from their story, we may single out the scene where Khusraw first glimpses Shirin, from a manuscript of the *Khamseh* produced by order of Shah Tahmasp, the second Safavid ruler, circa 1539 in Tabriz (fig. 4). This rendering is one of the masterpieces of Persian painting and bears the inscription "work of Sultan Muhammad," the preeminent court painter of the period.

Shirin is depicted at the epicenter of the composition as an elegant, ethereal being floating on a silver pool (now tarnished to darkest gray), her long black braids chastely covering her torso. Her alabaster limbs, moon-shaped face, and long black hair illustrate the ideal of feminine beauty in Nizami's poetry. Nizami describes Shirin as a flower and an angel, combing her hair as she sits in a royal-blue pool rising to her waist. Although Sultan Muhammad follows Nizami's description of his heroine, the composition, a variant of many examples evolved during the Timurid period, is a personal and masterful interpretation of this classical theme. The pool is in a rocky landscape under a golden sky, painted in a palette of pastels, ranging from light green to gray-blue and beige, sprinkled with bright spring flowers, and shaded by a full-leaved plane tree. From a distance, Khusraw gazes at this vision of almost unearthly loveliness while he marks his astonishment with his finger to his lips. The intimacy of the moment is underlined by Shirin's horse, Shabdiz, who rears his head in warning at the stranger's intrusion. Sultan Muhammad's painting elaborates considerably on Nizami's text—inscribed in panels above and below the main scene—and he has admirably captured in images the magic of the moment when the two protagonists first meet.

Another idealized image of feminine beauty is that referred to in the Qur'an as the reward of faithful Muslims in paradise: "wide-eyed *huris*" (chaste maidens restraining their glances and untouched before them by any man or jinn) and in Persian poetry as *malekeh* (angel), *pari* (fairy), and huri, all related terms used in poetry as metaphors for beautiful women and the beloved.[21] Distinctions between angels and fairies (genderless beings although feminine in appearance) and huris (chaste maidens promised to the faithful in paradise) are frequently blurred in Persian painting.

Such images occur to a remarkable degree in paintings of the sixteenth and seventeenth centuries. Their frequency attests to the Persian painters' creativity in finding novel and religiously acceptable ways of portraying women. We may propose that this secret language of female beauty was directly inspired by gender separation and female seclusion in Iranian society and that, as a corollary, the Safavid painters transformed mere objects of male desire into ethereal and angelic images of beauty. Earlier, angels are found

Figure 4. "Khusraw Discovers Shirin Bathing." Illustration to a manuscript of the *Khamseh* by Nizami. Tabriz, 1539, signed by Sultan Muhammad. (MS Or.2265, fol. 23v. Reproduced by permission of The British Library.)

in narrative compositions for illustrated manuscripts, such as cosmological treatises, histories of the prophet's life, *Mi'raj Namehs*, and representations of paradise in frontispieces to *Shah-nameh* manuscripts, such as scenes of King Solomon and Balqis, Queen of Sheba.[22] In sixteenth-century Persian painting, angels and their counterparts, while continuing to be utilized in manuscript illustration, become ubiquitous in other forms of painting as well, such as lacquer bindings, illuminations (sun- and moon-faced beauties), and single-page paintings.

A typical example occurs in the binding of a well-known manuscript of the *Divan* (Anthology) of Hafiz, Tabriz, circa 1520–30, which may again be assigned to the painter Sultan Muhammad or a follower (fig. 5). The upper and lower covers are painted in polychrome colors and gold pigment under lacquer with a design of medallions with pendants and quadrants. On the upper cover, a young prince and an attendant offering refreshment are featured in a central medallion, which in turn is situated on a field embellished with pheasants and angels amid arabesques with large flowering lotuses and quadrants with lotus arabesques, the whole on a wine-red ground. The outer frame displays a complementary arabesque design. The angels are shown as androgynous beings with the youthful beauty of adolescents of indeterminate gender, not far removed from the young page who offers the prince a bowl of wine. They are gracefully posed in flight, bearing covered trays with food, their long, tapering, multicolored wings providing a sharp counterpoint to the curving arabesques and rounded floral forms of the ornate field. The design is undoubtedly an image of paradise awaiting the true believer with its gardens, beautiful maidens, wine, and fruits.

In the late sixteenth and early seventeenth centuries, as single-page paintings became increasingly widespread, isolated images of youthful beauties proliferated. Such paintings were either held loose or mounted in albums with, among others, images of loving couples of various genders and ages and samples of calligraphy. At first, they conformed to the elegant androgynous heroines of sixteenth-century painting, depicted with the decorative patterning and flatness of early Safavid painting, even though they no longer served to illustrate specific events in a text or evoked the lyrical atmosphere of Persian poetry.

As the seventeenth century progressed, women were increasingly portrayed as decorative objects for the viewer's gaze and admiration. Concurrently their function as visual metaphors for the themes of lyrical poetry became increasingly difficult to establish. A new canon of beauty appeared. The portraits of women associated with the works of Riza Abbasi and his

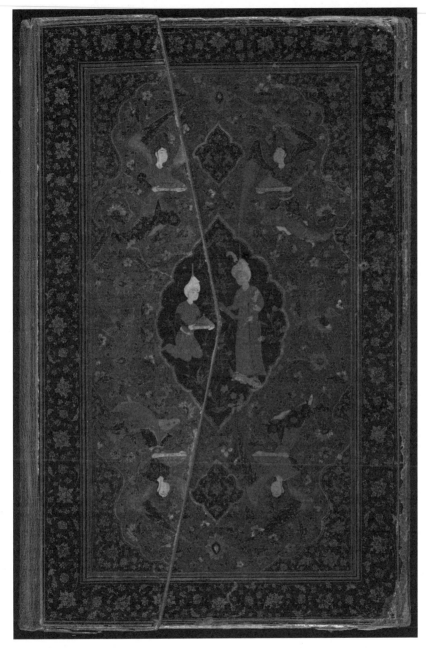

Figure 5. Upper cover of a binding to a manuscript of the *Divan* of Hafiz. Tabriz, ca. 1520–30, assigned to Sultan Muhammad or his atelier. (No. 1964.149. Photo by Allan Macintyre, © President and Fellows of Harvard College. Courtesy of the Arthur M. Sackler Museum, Harvard University Art Museums, gift of Mr. and Mrs. Stuart C. Welch Jr.)

followers were increasingly voluptuous, curvaceous, and earthy. This is also true for portrayals of young ephebes and pages shown alone or with elderly male admirers who graced the Safavid courts.

Such frank representations of female sensuality and male androgyny may be taken as indicators of the prevailing liberal sexual atmosphere in the court and upper levels of Safavid society. If painting is to be considered a reliable indicator of social conditions, it may be argued that the status of women in society (although not that of women of the ruling class) declined from the seventeenth century onward, since it became increasingly permissible to depict women with overt sexuality and eroticism. Indeed, documentary evidence exists for the presence of many brothels and tax-paying prostitutes in seventeenth-century Iran.

A masterful illustration of this trend may be seen in the detached painting of an amorous couple (fig. 6), signed Riza Abbasi and executed in 1039/1629–30. Devoid of any literary associations or accompanying explanatory verses, the formal qualities of the work itself convey the image's meaning. The lovers are placed close to the front of the picture plane, thus dominating the composition. The woman sits in her lover's lap and playfully tucks a narcissus into his fur-lined cap. Her outer veil has been thrown back and provides a thin barrier to complete intimacy with her lover. Her male companion clasps her chin with one hand and caresses her belly through the opening of her robe with the other. A wine bowl, half-empty crystal carafe, scattered fruits, and a lost slipper allude to sensual joy and physical union, the themes of the painting. The daring pose of the lovers—in which their arms symbolically intertwine, overlap, and envelop and their heavy-limbed sensuous forms fuse together—vividly conveys the union to which they seem to aspire. Yet this erotic quality is mitigated by the calligraphic qualities of the line, the impassive features of the moon-faced lovers, and the almost abstract linear form of the couple, perhaps hinting at a mystical dimension to the image. Whether describing a physical union or a mystical one, Abbasi's innovative composition nevertheless presents the woman as an object held by the man and displayed for the viewer's pleasure.

Later in the seventeenth century, textual sources chronicle another aspect of this interest of royal collectors in the taste for representations of women of different ages and races. This interest is a reflection of the later Safavid rulers' connoisseurship of painting and of the increasing pursuit of pleasure that characterized Isfahan court life. Jean-Baptiste Tavernier, a French jeweler who traveled to Iran in the latter part of the seventeenth century, records a meeting with Shah Abbas II (r. 1642–66). The ruler not only displays Persian

Figure 6. "Two Lovers." Detached single-page painting. Isfahan, 1039/1629–30, signed by Riza Abbasi. (No. 50.164. Reproduced by permission of the Metropolitan Museum of Art, Francis M. Weld Fund, 1950.)

paintings of women from his collection and engages Tavernier in a discussion of the relative qualities of beauty of European and Iranian women but also attempts to obtain an enameled portrait of Tavernier's own wife for his private collection.[23]

As painters became bolder in their depictions of the feminine form, they turned from Persian poetic texts and looked to Europe for inspiration. Depictions of modest if nude females, such as water sprites and bathers, had been found previously in isolated illustrations in manuscripts such as those of the *Manafi al-hayawan* or the *Khamseh* (see fig. 4),[24] but now Persian painters looked to European sixteenth- and seventeenth-century engravings for models for innovative, more openly erotic female types such as the sensuous nude in a landscape derived from later Italian Renaissance paintings of Giorgione and Titian and variants in Dutch engravings.[25] Painters may have been catering to the curiosity of their patrons, who had only recently been introduced to the greater freedom, both social and in dress codes, enjoyed by European women.

These engravings continued to serve as prototypes well into the eighteenth and sometimes the nineteenth centuries. A typical example is a painting of Venus with Cupid and a satyr, after an engraving of the same subject by the Dutch artist Raphael Sadeler (1561–1628),[26] by the artist Muhammad Ali (fig. 7).[27] The painting is signed prominently in the center, *mashq-i* Muhammad Ali and dated 1146/1732–33. Venus is shown in an interior, languidly resting on a stone plinth, draped in richly colored fabrics and cushions. A classical column and luxuriously painted red curtain occupy the background. Venus is accompanied by Cupid, startled by a satyr unveiling the sleeping nude's ample charms.

A comparison with the earlier painting of Khusraw and Shirin reveals that both images depict a theme of a man spying on an oblivious or otherwise unsuspecting nude woman. Whereas in the earlier version the scene is imbued with the innocence of the two protagonists, and Khusraw admires Shirin's beauty from a distance, emphasized by the rocky landscape that separates them and her "equine duenna," in Muhammad Ali's painting the hero becomes a salacious satyr in a boudoir, lifting up the bedsheets of an invitingly recumbent Venus. Shirin is all spirit and delicacy, Venus all flesh and reality.

We should note, in all fairness, that perhaps neither the Persian painter nor his patron perceived the erotic subtext of Sadeler's engraving as clearly as we do today and that they may have viewed it simply as an updated version of a traditional theme. Muhammad Ali copied an image he deemed appropriate to present an innovative version of an established theme of Safavid

Figure 7. "Venus with Cupid and a Satyr." Detached single-page painting. Iran, 1146/1732–33, signed Muhammad Ali. (Private collection, New York, N.Y.)

painting. He modified the original; electrifying jolts of intense color, only slightly modified by attempts at shading, were added to the black-and-white line drawing of the original; the quiver for Cupid's arrows is omitted, and a garland of leaves covers Cupid's genitalia. An earlier painting after the same original by the artist Muhammad Zaman, dated 1087/1676–77, exhibits a much freer interpretation of the original. The painter has situated the scene in a land-scape and omitted the satyr, a clear attempt to devise a composition based on the genre of the Italian nude in landscape. Zaman apparently had a greater familiarity with the European idiom than Muhammad Ali and the confidence to use selectively elements from the European source in a creative manner.

In the later version, the inscription on the lower blue margin of the paint-ing, probably added after the work was completed, brings an additional lev-el of meaning to the image. It states, in essence, that the image represents the body of the holy Mary facing the devil Iblis and that she has consented to his desires. By the eighteenth century, the meaning of the image, of little concern to the seventeenth-century painter who had greater familiarity with European paintings and their iconography, needed some explanation. The explanation clearly reflects the prurient interests of patrons and artist alike as well as the complete misunderstanding of a classical allegorical theme of European painting. This fanciful interpretation is based on the Persian commentator's attempt to identify this image of a "foreign" nude with one of the few known Christian females in Islamic literature. Although Mary is revered in Islam and mentioned in the Qur'an, our commentator has manufactured a fictitious episode with the devil, Iblis, *faute de mieux*—which does not take into account the role of Cupid, who is omitted from the description—to explain the meaning of this scene.

This painting and its inscription exemplify the process whereby European religious and profane imagery were conflated in later Persian painting and new portrayals of women thereby invented. It may be argued that European religious imagery was considered by Persian painters as one of the permissible or licit forms in which to portray women as the beloved, especially if they were scantily clad or nude, a process already familiar from early Safavid painters' use of angelic and paradisical imagery to depict the female form.

Our third category of representations linked to women and love is female dancers and entertainers—often depicted in scenes illustrating courtly entertainments in Persian poetic manuscripts. In the mid-seventeenth century, large-scale mural paintings of royal reception scenes, emphasizing the prestige and military prowess of rulers, were commissioned for Safavid palaces. The large reception hall of the Chihil Sutun in Isfahan was embellished with three reception scenes—Shah Tahmasp and the Mughal ruler Humayun; Shah Abbas I and Vali Muhammad Khan, ruler of Turkestan; and Shah Abbas II and Nadir Muhammad Khan, another ruler of Turkestan—which feature female entertainers in the foreground.[28] Paintings such as these served as precedents for the wall paintings of the Qajar period (1794–1924).

Under the Qajars, large-scale painting for palaces served to legitimize the new dynasty. Painters' talents were primarily devoted to creating magnificent and awe-inspiring (and all-male) images of the ruler and his court, particularly in the case of the second Qajar ruler, Fath Ali Shah (r. 1797–1834), who commissioned many portraits of himself and his sons at the hunt, engaged in battle, or enthroned.

Yet Qajar painting is equally renowned for its representations of women acrobats and entertainers. These individual portrayals are closely related to female representations in the reception scenes of Safavid palaces, but they invite closer comparison as well with paintings in oblong niches in the verandas of the Chihil Sutun. There, individual portrayals of female nudes, standing men and women, and seated couples were used for decoration.

The interpretation of these paintings, while speculative, must be framed in light of their relationship to the decorative program of the main hall. Images of women, representing different ethnic peoples such as Armenians, Europeans, and Georgians, may have conveyed the message of the cosmopolitanism of the late Safavid court and its capital. Similar paintings known to have been commissioned for the homes of wealthy Armenian merchants in Isfahan may have served a similar purpose. In the Qajar period, images of women also conveyed the message of royal power but with a different emphasis.

Certainly under the Qajars, representations of individual women increased, but they are rarely depicted as heroines of the past or idealized beauties as they had been in earlier manuscript illustration and never as recognizable individuals but rather as accoutrements of the ruler, as acrobats and entertainers. In the painted decoration of public and private reception rooms, niches were filled with sensuous images of alluring females with none of the emphasis on varied ethnicity found in Safavid painting. At times these paintings were grouped around a portrait of the ruler; such was undoubtedly the case with a painting of a maiden playing a guitar (fig. 8), one of three with a matching portrait of Fath Ali Shah, painted by Abu'l Qasim and dated 1231/ 1816. Coyly eyeing the viewer, the woman is shown emblazoned with jewels and richly patterned fabrics, her breasts exposed. Nearby a tray of fruit and wine evokes the sensual pleasures of drink and sweetness, visual equivalents for the entertainer's charms.

It is striking to note how official portraiture of the period largely omits women, when matrilineal descent from a Qajar princess was crucial to establishing the heir's right to the throne. Thus, while Qajar princesses were often powerful in their own right, maintaining their own courts and providing patronage for poets, this status was not reflected in any official imagery. Clearly, decorum would not allow depictions of female members of the royal family in public spaces. Since paintings of women were to be found in areas of public access, virtuous women and real personages could not be portrayed, so generalized images of lower-class women belonging to the category of entertainers were the only female imagery deemed suitable. It should be emphasized that Qajar painters were following tradition. The portrayal of Qajar women, even though it was more visible and larger in scale than previously, was no more realistic than in earlier periods, whether for public spaces or small-scale painting for private use. The traveler Charles Texier who visited Iran in 1838 describes a palace in Isfahan painted with portraits of the shah's (presumably Fath Ali Shah) sons and harem women dressed in French Empire style. He remarks on the "singularity" of

226

LAYLA S. DIBA

Figure 8. "Maiden Playing a Guitar." Oil on canvas painting. Dated 1231/1816 and signed by Abu'l Qasim. (Formerly Negarestan Museum, Tehran.)

the Persians who hide their women in the harem but display portraits of them to the public in revealing clothing.[29]

Women and Society: Children, Mothers, Courtesans, and Wives

Persian manuscript painters as early as the fourteenth century exhibited a fondness for depicting women in domestic situations and at their daily chores. Women are shown giving birth, spinning, and milking. Nizami's *Khamseh* provided them with opportunities to illustrate the schooling of girls as well. Bihzad, the late-fifteenth-century painter of Herat (1450–1524), is universally recognized as the most eminent artist of his time. Safavid connoisseurs praised his power of lifelike representation, drawing, figural composition, and skill at composing battle scenes. In addition, he broadened the conventions of Timurid painting to include vignettes from daily life and realistic portraiture.

Bihzad's interest in innovative subject matter is clearly reflected in his composition illustrating the episode of Layli and Qays (hereafter Majnun, "the mad one") at school, executed for a manuscript of Nizami's *Khamseh* dated 900/1494–95 (fig. 9). The school (*maktab*) is in the courtyard of a mosque or madrasa, whose façade and dome form the background of the composition. In the foreground, a pool, raised platform, and fountain frame the central scene where school activities take place. A master teaches a student the Qur'an, another student copies a text on a tablet, and a third removes his outer garments and polishes paper. In the right foreground under an immense plane tree, students wash themselves at the fountain, converse, write, and nap.

Layli—accompanied by a female companion—and Majnun are shown in the background, kneeling in front of the architectural façade and inscriptions, which frame them and isolate them from the rest of the scene. Layli is shown talking with the young Majnun, who offers her a gift, perhaps a pen box. They are separated but lean toward one another, Layli shyly bending her head and lifting her sleeve to cover her face. The composition and accompanying text convey the innocence of their love but also their ultimate tragic destiny. Qur'anic verses warn of the Day of Judgment while the orange and yellow palette of the plane tree presages the coming winter.

Although the story takes place in pre-Islamic Arabia, it is clearly set in Timurid Herat and illustrates the opportunities for education for women of royal and privileged backgrounds. Indeed, some Timurid and Safavid princesses were known for their skill as calligraphers and poets as well as for their erudition. The practice of educating boys and girls together until the onset of puberty is reflected in Bihzad's composition.

Another superb example of genre painting is a detached illustration from a *Shah-nameh* or *Khamseh* (fig. 10) of an encampment, by Mir Sayyid Ali, one of the most talented court painters of Shah Tahmasp. The composition has been cut into two sections and re-pasted, but the design's integrity has been maintained. In the foreground, a group of elders confers under a magnificently patterned tent; the remainder of the illustration is devoted to the panoply of daily life in a nomads' encampment. The painter revels in the decorative patterning and detail of fabrics and textures but also shows a

Figure 9. "Layli and Majnun in School." Illustration to a manuscript of Nizami's *Khamseh*, dated 900/1494–95. Kamal ad-Din Bihzad. (MS Or.6810, fol. 106v. Reproduced by permission of The British Library.)

Figure 10. "Scene of an Encampment." Detached illustration to a manuscript of a
Khamseh or *Shah-nameh*. Tabriz, ca. 1540. Mir Sayyid Ali. (No. 1958.75. Photo by
Katya Kallsen, © President and Fellows of Harvard College. Courtesy of the
Arthur M. Sackler Museum, Harvard University Art Museums, gift of John Goelet,
formerly in the collection of Louis J. Cartier.)

remarkably naturalistic portrayal of women washing laundry, preparing food, and suckling a baby. Rarely has the elegance and refinement of Safavid painting been allied with such a profound power of observation and sensitivity as in this work.

Certainly any discussion of women in Persian painting would be incomplete without considering issues of dress and especially the use of the chadur (veil). As can be seen in most of the previous examples, women are rarely shown veiled, or if they are it is almost as an afterthought or a bow to convention. In Mir Sayyid Ali's composition, which admittedly allowed him greater freedom because it depicts a nomads' camp and thus would not require as strict an observance of Islamic female dress codes as an urban setting, the refinement and full range of traditional women's clothing is vividly rendered.

The female personages are clothed in layered garments in luxurious fabrics, some brocaded, cut close to the figure, with long flowing lines, with a rich variety of headdresses, jewelry, and veils. Loose undergarments of transparent fabric, open in the front, are worn with diagonally patterned trousers under the outer full-length robe. Loose veils, pointed delicate kerchiefs attached to little caps with aigrettes and jeweled headbands, sometimes with floral sprays added, are worn by young women. Older women are dressed in larger head coverings (*charqat*) secured by fabric bands. Necklaces that fasten under the chin, bangles, kohl-rimmed eyes, and tattoos on the feet, hands, and faces all complete the toilette.

The composition, featuring elders in the foreground and women's activities in the background, clearly illustrates the vertical division of the sexes in Iranian society. The majority of manuscript illustrations, while less striking than this example, also reflect gender separation in their depiction of exclusively male hunting scenes, evening revels, and images of war.

On other occasions, Persian painters depicted with frankness the harsher realities of the condition of urban women. In the seventeenth century, when Persian painters increasingly turned to scenes from daily life, images of courtesans are not infrequent. These images reflect the considerable population of prostitutes in the capital Isfahan, recorded in foreign travel accounts.[30]

Persian manuscript illustration at times exhibited a subtext reflecting contemporary events. This tradition may be seen in an illustration commissioned for a magnificent manuscript of the translation of the *1001 Nights* produced for Nasir al-Din Shah (r. 1848–96). A team of forty-seven painters worked for sixteen years under the direction of the leading court painter of the time, Abu'l Hasan Ghaffari, Sani al-Mulk, to finish this ambitious project.

Although the action takes place in Baghdad during the reign of the caliph Harun al-Rashid, Persian painters, as was their custom, clothed their representations in contemporary dress.

An episode illustrating the stoning of an adulteress (fig. 11) is a vivid rendering of this barbarous act. Abu'l Hasan's depiction of the pain and agony of the culprit and the indifference of the men stoning her imparts to the work a quality of cinema verité, of newspaper reportage. This is not implausible because Abu'l Hasan had executed scenes of riots clearly based on personal observation for the court newspaper, *Ruznameh-i vaqayi ittifaqieh,* in the 1860s.

With the constitutional period at the turn of the twentieth century, the condition of women became a principal issue of social reform. This development was reflected in cartoons produced for lithographed newspapers that decried the legal inequality of women. This image of before and after the honeymoon was executed for the newspaper *Mulla Nasr al-Din,* printed in the Caucasus (fig. 12). While this image may have been the work of a Western-trained artist, it accurately reflects the tradition of caricature and social protest, which coexisted in Persian painting with the stylization and elegance of court painting.

Figure 11. "The Stoning of an Adulteress." Illustration to a manuscript of the *1001 Nights.* Tehran, 1853–57. Abu'l Hasan Ghaffari or his atelier. (Folio number not given. Courtesy of the Gulistan Palace Library.)

Figure 12. "Before and After the Honeymoon." Cartoon for the lithographed newspaper *Mulla Nasr al-Din,* published in Tiflis, 16 February 1908.

Conclusion

What factors may have accounted for the wealth of female imagery? It appears that the seclusion of women actually encouraged their depiction in illustrated manuscripts. Men were the only known patrons of manuscripts, where they could look at images of beautiful women to their hearts' content and in complete privacy. But Qajar paintings also displayed female charms in a public context. How could this be permitted, when it was forbidden to look upon women, as Texier had so perceptively noted? The answer lies in the Islamic attitude toward imagery. According to tradition, painters could never breathe life into their works and thus challenge the Creator.[31] It seems plausible, therefore, that in painting, women could be both represented and gazed at because these were only poor reflections of reality in the neoplatonic sense.

The rich Persian literary tradition and its expression in the arts of the book were also a principal factor in the development of female imagery. Heroines of literary texts, such as those of the *Khamseh* and *Shah-nameh*, belonged to Iran's pre-Islamic past. Painters had more freedom in depicting such legendary women than recognizable women of their own time. Iran's long-standing tradition of mural painting for palace decoration contributed to the acceptance of figural representation for public spaces—representations that seemed to have shocked devout Muslims as much as prudish Europeans. The somewhat daring search of Persian painters for innovative ways of depicting women within traditional formats as well as their openness to foreign artistic influences considerably enriched the range of female imagery and the media for which it was employed.

However we weigh these factors, the depiction of women in Persian painting shows that, while in reality women's lives may have been restricted, their bodies shrouded in veils and their range of activities limited, they lived fully and freely in the imagination of the Persian painter and his works—a dichotomy that is as fascinating and timely today as ever.

NOTES

1. In the field of art history, studies have focused on issues of lexicography and iconography, attribution, dating, and only rarely on subject matter. Only one study has attempted a systematic survey of subjects selected for illustration in Persian illustrated manuscripts of Firdawsi's *Shah-nameh;* Jill Norgren and Edward Davis, *Shah-nameh: Preliminary Index of Shah-Nameh Illustrations* (Ann Arbor, 1969). Nasrin Rohani's *Bibliography of Persian Miniature Painting* (Cambridge, Mass., 1982) lacks

both general and individual entries in the index. The most useful source, although based on a single collection, is Nora Titley, *Miniatures from Persian Manuscripts: Catalogue and Subject Index of Paintings from Persia and India in the British Library and British Museum* (London, 1977), which includes an extensive entry for women in the subject index, 345–46. In the field of sociology, Wiebke Walther's *Women in Islam* (Montclair, 1981) presents a comprehensive survey of the question based primarily on Arabic sources. While the book is copiously illustrated with images of women from Persian manuscripts and decorative arts, the author only briefly discusses female heroines in Persian literature (118–20, 141) and omits any discussion of women in painting in the chapter devoted to women in Islamic culture (105–9). In my chapter here, "Persian" will be used in preference to "Iranian," following standard terminology in art historical studies, except in the political or sociological context.

2. For references to illustrated manuscripts, see Guitty Azarpay, *Soghdian Painting* (Berkeley, 1981), 179; for illustrations of murals depicting a goddess, female donors, musicians, a goddess on a throne supported by *sinmurv*s (mythical winged creatures), female warriors, mourners, and the goddess Nana, see ibid., figs. 3a, 26, 34, 46, 56, 58, and color plates 3, 12, 13, 26–28; for representations of women in the decorative arts, see Prudence Harper, *The Royal Hunter* (New York, 1978); in silverwork, 48, 50, 64, 79; in stucco, 109, 115; in seals, 145–46; in ceramics, 163, 165.

3. M. S. Simpson, "Narrative Allusion and Metaphor in the Decoration of Medieval Islamic Objects," in *Pictorial Narrative in Antiquity and the Middle Ages: Studies in the History of Art* 15 (1985): 131–49, for a discussion of imagery on Persian ceramics.

4. T. W. Arnold, *Painting in Islam* (1928; reprint, Oxford, 1965), 1–40, is still the best overall discussion of this subject.

5. Contrast this with the conclusions of Hasan Javadi, "Women in Persian Literature: An Exploratory Study," in *Women and the Family in Iran*, ed. Asghar Fathi (Leiden, 1985), 37–59.

6. See Walther, *Women in Islam*, figs. 70, 57.

7. Wheeler M. Thackston, *A Century of Princes: Sources on Timurid History and Art* (Cambridge, Mass., 1989), 345.

8. The manuscript has been assigned to western Iran, Rayy, or Kashan by A. S. Melikian-Chirvani, "Varqe et Golshah," in *Arts Asiatiques* (1970), 71; to Baghdad, circa 1300 by M. S. Simpson, *The Illustration of an Epic: The Earliest Shah-Nameh Manuscripts* (New York, 1979); and to Baghdad, circa 1225 by Nora Titley, *Persian Miniature Painting* (London, 1984), 15.

9. Melikian-Chirvani, "Varqe," distichs 642, 647, 122–23.

10. Titley, *Painting*, 15.

11. According to the *Shah-Nameh Index*, the most frequently illustrated episodes include the stories of Zal and Rudabeh, the birth of Rustam, Rustam cleaves the witch, Tahmineh and Rustam, Siyavush and Sudabeh, Kay Khusraw crosses the Oxus with Farangis and Giv, Manizheh and Bizhan, Esfandyar slays the sorceress, Iskandar and Queen Qaydafeh, Bahram Gur and Azadeh, Gurdyeh and Shirin, and Khusraw Parviz.

12. Such as Malekeh and Sudabeh; see Javadi, "Women in Persian Literature," 38–39.

13. Oleg Grabar and Sheila Blair, *Epic Images and Contemporary History: The Great Mongol Shah-Nameh* (Chicago, 1980); Abolala Soudavar, "The Saga of Abu Sa'id

Bahadur Khan, the Abu Saʿid Name," in *The Court of the Il-Khans, 1290–1340*, ed. J. Raby and T. Fitzherbert (Oxford, 1996).

14. Grabar and Blair, *Epic Images*, 20.

15. Ibid., 49–50.

16. See A. K. S. Lambton, "Al-Marʾa, Women in Persia before 1900," in *Encyclopedia of Islam*, new ed., 6:481–85, for a discussion of women's position in Iran according to historical sources. M. Szuppe studies the relationship of women and power in sixteenth-century Iran in "La participation des femmes de la famille royale à l'exercice du pouvoir en Iran safavide au XVIᵉ siècle," pt. 1, *Studia Iranica* 23 (1994): 211–58; see also her chapter in this volume.

17. Marie Lukens Swietochowski and Stefano Carboni, *Illustrated Poetry and Epic Images: Persian Painting of the 1330s and 1340s* (New York, 1994), 21.

18. J. M. Rogers, Filiz Cagman, and Zeren Tanindi, *The Topkapi Saray Museum: The Albums and Illustrated Manuscripts* (Boston, 1986), 69, illus. 43, 44, bibliography therein.

19. For discussion of the role of Firdawsi's heroines, see Mahmoud Omidsalar's chapter in this volume.

20. See chapter 8 of this volume.

21. *Images of Paradise in Islamic Art*, ed. Sheila S. Blair and Jonathan M. Bloom (Austin, Tex., 1991), 17n.2, 22.

22. Ibid., 36.

23. J.-B. Tavernier, *Les six voyages de M. Jean-Baptiste Tavernier en Turquie, en Perse et aux Indes* (1713; reprint, Paris, 1930), 119.

24. Nimet Allam Hamdy, "The Development of Nude Female Drawing in Persian Islamic Painting," in *Akten des VII. Internationalen Kongresses für Iranische Kunst und Archaeologie, München, 1976* (Munich, 1979), 430–34.

25. Ibid., 435–37; and Massumeh Farhad, "Safavid Single-Page Painting" (Ph.D. diss., Harvard University, 1987), 227–31.

26. See A. A. Ivanov, O. F. Akimushkin, and T. V. Grek, *Albom Indiyskikh i Persidskikh Miniatyur* (Album of Indian and Persian miniatures) (Moscow, 1962), 50n.38, plate 83, for another version of this theme by the painter Muhammad Zaman. See Eleanor Sims, "The European Print Sources of Paintings by the Seventeenth-Century Persian Painter, Muhammad Zaman," in *Le stampe e la diffusione delle imagine e degli stili* (Bologna, 1983), 76, fig. 79, for an image of the engraving and an analysis of the formal relationship to Zaman's interpretation of the same subject.

27. Two artists of that name were active in this period: the first, the son of the preeminent Europeanizing painter of the seventeenth century, Muhammad Zaman ibn Haji Yusif-i Qumi; the second, the grandson of Ali Quli Jabbadar, another celebrated Europeanizing painter, active in the second half of the seventeenth century. This work is herein assigned to the former.

28. A fourth painting depicted the battle of Shah Ismail and the Uzbeks. See Sussan Babaie, "Safavid Palaces at Isfahan: Continuity and Change" (Ph.D. diss., New York University, Institute of Fine Arts, 1994), 177–212, for the most recent discussion of the decorative scheme of this palace.

29. Charles Texier, *Description de l'Arménie, la Perse et la Mésopotamie* (Paris, 1842), 127. See also Layla S. Diba with Maryam Ekhtiar, eds., *Royal Persian Paintings: The*

Qajar Epoch 1785–1925 (New York, 1998), catalog nos. 57–61, for images of female entertainers and consorts.

30. See Farhad, "Safavid Single-Page Painting," 243–44, for a description and a portrait of a courtesan and a shaykh by the painter Muhammad Yusuf, dated 1068/ 1658, cat. no. 52.

31. See Arnold, *Painting in Islam*, 5.

CONTRIBUTORS

Lois Beck is a professor of anthropology at Washington University in St. Louis. Her books include *Women in the Muslim World* (1978, edited with Nikki Keddie), *The Qashqa'i of Iran* (1986), *Nomad: A Year in the Life of a Qashqa'i Tribesman in Iran* (1991), *Nomads Move On: Qashqa'i Tribespeople in Post-Revolutionary Iran* (forthcoming), and *Women in Iran from 1800 to the Islamic Republic* (forthcoming, edited with Guity Nashat). She conducted anthropological research in Iran over a span of more than three decades, most recently in 2002, and she continues to pursue topics related to political, economic, and social change among nomadic and tribal people in Iran.

Richard W. Bulliet is a professor of Middle East history at Columbia University. He works primarily in social history with special interests in Iran. His scholarly books include *The Patricians of Nishapur* (1972), *The Camel and the Wheel* (1975), *Conversion to Islam in the Medieval Period* (1979), and *Islam: The View from the Edge* (1994). He coedited *The Encyclopedia of the Modern Middle East* (1996) and has published four novels on the modern Middle East.

Jamsheed K. Choksy is a professor of history, professor of Central Eurasian studies, and adjunct professor of religious studies at Indiana University. His books are *Purity and Pollution in Zoroastrianism: Triumph over Evil* (1989), *Conflict and Cooperation: Zoroastrian Subalterns and Muslim Elites in Medieval Iranian Society* (1997), and *Evil, Good, and Gender: Facets of the Feminine in Zoroastrian Religious History* (2002). His research covers the anthropology, archaeology, history, languages, linguistics, literatures, numismatics, and religions of the Near East, Central Asia, and South Asia. Most recently he codirected archaeological excavations in Baluchistan in Pakistan.

Layla S. Diba is an adjunct professor at the Bard Graduate Center for Studies in the Decorative Arts in New York City. She was the first woman museum director in Iran, a post she held from 1975 to 1979 at Tehran's Negarestan Museum of Eighteenth- and Nineteenth-Century Iranian Art. She edited and coauthored (with Maryam Ekhtiar) *Royal Persian Paintings: The Qajar Epoch, 1785–1925* (1998) to accompany an exhibition she organized in 1998–99 in New York, Los Angeles, and London. She writes on various aspects of Islamic art, specializes in the art of Iran in and after the seventeenth century, and is currently preparing for publication her research on the origins and development of Iranian lacquerwork.

Carole Hillenbrand is a professor of Islamic history at the University of Edinburgh. Her books include *Qajar Iran* (1983, edited with Edmund Bosworth), *The Waning of the Umayyad Caliphate* (1989), *A Muslim Principality in Crusader Times* (1990), and *The Crusades: Islamic Perspectives* (1999). She is currently preparing a translation and commentary on al-Ghazali's *Alchemy of Happiness.*

Fatemeh Keshavarz was born and raised in Iran. She is an associate professor of Persian and comparative literature at Washington University in St. Louis. Her book *Reading Mystical Lyric: The Case of Jalal al-Din Rumi* (1998) is a study of the literary contributions of this Persian mystic. She has completed a monograph on poetic expressions of spirituality in twentieth-century Iran.

Beatrice Forbes Manz is an associate professor of history at Tufts University. She is the author of *The Rise and Rule of Tamerlane* (1989) and the editor of *Central Asia in Historical Perspective* (1994). She is interested in the interaction of nomadic and sedentary societies in the medieval Middle East and Central Asia and is currently working on a monograph on government and society under the Timurid dynasty of the fifteenth century.

Julie Scott Meisami was a university lecturer in Persian at the University of Oxford from 1985 to 2002. In 2002–3 she held an Aga Khan fellowship in Islamic art and architecture at the Sackler Museum at Harvard University. Her books include *Medieval Persian Court Poetry* (1987), *Persian Historiography to the End of the Twelfth Century* (1999), *Structure and Meaning in Medieval Arabic and Persian* Poetry (2002), and several annotated translations from

Persian, including *The Sea of Precious Virtues (Bahr al-Fava'id): A Medieval Islamic Mirror for Princes* (1991) and Nizami's *Haft Paykar* (1995). She served as the editor of *Edebiyat: The Journal of Middle Eastern Literatures.*

Guity Nashat, a native of Iran, is an associate professor of history at the University of Illinois at Chicago. Her books include *The Beginnings of Modern Reform in Iran* (1983), *Women and Revolution in Iran* (1983, edited), *Women in the Middle East and North Africa* (1999, with Judith Tucker), and *Women in Iran from 1800 to the Islamic Republic* (forthcoming, edited with Lois Beck).

Mahmoud Omidsalar was born in Iran and currently works at California State University in Los Angeles. He is editing a critical edition of Ferdowsi's *Shahnama* with Jalal Khaleghi-Motlagh. His research concerns editorial theory, pre-Mongol Persian literature, Persian folklore, and ties between orality and textuality in classical Persian.

Maria Szuppe is a researcher at the Centre National de la Recherche Scientifique in Paris as part of the "Monde iranien" group. Her books include *Entre Safavides, Timourides et Uzbeks: Questions d'histoire politique et sociale de Hérat dans la première moitié du XVIᵉ siècle* (1992), *Inscriptions persanes de Char Bakr, nécropole familiale des khwaja Juybari près de Boukhara (Ouzbékistan)* (2002, coauthored with B. Babajanov), and several edited volumes on the late medieval and modern history of Iran and Central Asia, including *L'héritage timouride: Iran-Asie centrale-Inde, XVᵉ–XVIIIᵉ siècles* (1997), *Matériaux pour l'histoire économique du monde iranien* (1999, edited with R. Gyselen), and *Iran: Questions et connaissances,* vol. 2: *Périodes médiévale et moderne* (2002).

INDEX

Aba Bakr ibn Muhammad Juki (Timurid), 126

Abbasid rule, 38, 39, 113, 119n50

Abbas I (Safavid shah), 143, 146, 147, 148, 151, 160

Abbas II (Safavid shah), 220, 222

Abd al-Aziz (Timurid), 131

Abd al-Ghaffar, Abu Sa'id, 92, 93, 101n42; grandmother as wise woman, 92–93

Abd al-Latif (Timurid ruler), 126, 133, 134

Abd al-Malik ibn Marwan (caliph), 94

Abdi Beg Shamlu, 145

Abdullah Divana, 151

Abdullah Khan Ustajalu, 145, 155

abortion, 16, 36

Abu al-Abbas Ma'mun (Khwarazmshah), 87

Abu al-Fazl Bayhaqi. *See* Bayhaqi, Abu al-Fazl

Abu al-Hasan Ali (Khwarazmshah), 87

Abu al-Qasim Iraqi, 96

Abu-Hanifah, 41

Abu'l Hasan Ghaffari (painter), 230–31

Abu'l Qasim (painter), 225, 226

Abu'l Qasim Babur (Timurid), 133

Abu-Muslim, 39

Abu Sa'id (Ilkhanid sultan), 209

Abu Sa'id (Timurid ruler), 122, 123, 124, 132, 134, 136n5, 137n40

Achaemenian empire, 17–26; Greek accounts of, 19–21, 23; labor force participation by women in, 24–25; Mesopotamian influence on, 18; royal women of, 19–21, 24; women excluded from art of, 50

adab (secular) literature, 105, 113

adultery: Mesopotamian prohibition of, 12, 26; Qur'anic punishment for, 36, 41; shari'a punishment for, 41; "Stoning of an Adulteress," 231; Zoroastrian prohibition of, 31, 32

Afshar, I., 170

Afshar tribe, 153

agriculture: Achaemenian women in, 25–26; agrarian economy of Nile-to-Oxus region, 12–13; Indo-European women in, 16; Sasanian women in, 33–34

Ahmad (Timurid), 128

Ahmadabad-i Taft, 152–53, 166n54

Ahmad ibn Muhammad (Ghaznavid prince), 97

Ahmed, Leila, 63n12, 98n1

A'isha (wife of Muhammad, prophet of Islam), 43n34, 65n40, 94

A'isha (Jum'a) (wife of al-Bahiri), 73

Aka Biki, 125, 129, 130, 137n27

Ala al-Dawla ibn Baysunghur (Timurid), 123, 126, 132–35

Ala al-Din Qayqubad I (Seljuq sultan), 109

Alexander the Great, 22, 26, 106

Ali al-Rida (eighth Shi'i imam), 111, 112

Ali ibn Abi Talib (caliph), 60

Ali ibn Husayn (fourth Shi'i imam), 56

Murashu archive, 20, 24
al-Mustadi (caliph), 112
al-Mustansir (caliph), 113, 116
al-Musta'sim (caliph), 113
al-Mustazhir (caliph), 109, 111, 112
al-Mutawakkil (caliph), 59

Nahhunte-utu, 15, 42n15
Nasihat al-muluk (al-Ghazali), 106
al-Nasir (caliph), 109–10
Nasir al-Din Shah (Qajar shah), 230
Nihavand, 55
Nile-to-Oxus region: Achaemenians unite in, 17; Muslim conquest of, 40; pastoralism in, 5, 12–13; position of women in, 1–2, 6–7, 11. *See also* Iran; Iraq
Ni'matullahi, Vali Kirmani (sufi shaykh), 147
Ni'matullahi sufi order, 152, 164n24
Nippur, 24
Nisa'i (Nisati), 151
Nishapur, 68, 72–75, 79n5, 89, 96
Nizam al-Mulk, 82–83, 105–6, 114
Nizami of Ganjah, 186–87; misogyny in, 205n29; romantic epics of, 188, 203n9, 208; Shirin and wife Afaq, 189, 190, 199–201, 202, 204n16. *See also Khamseh; Khusrau u Shirin*
Nöldeke, T., 170
nomads, 6, 8, 13; in Arabia, 35, 38; Bakhtiyari, 42n7; depicted in painting, 227, 229, 230; in Iran, 227–28; Safavids and, 141, 161; Seljuqs and, 116; Turk and Mongol, 118n18; Turkish, 103, 107
no ruz (nav ruz) (New Year), 56, 159
Nura Khatun, 110
Nur al-Din (Timurid), 125, 126
Nur al-Din Kashi, 150
Nushtigin-i Khassa, 90

obedience, 32, 37
Olearius, Adam, 143
Olmstead, A. T., 23, 43n36
Omidsalar, Mahmoud, 9, 214
1001 Nights, 230–31
orientalism, 189, 204n15
Otanes, 20
Ottomans, 126, 127, 135n1, 154, 155, 164n26
Oxus river (Amu Darya), 49, 53, 141, 214

painting, Iranian, 206–36; angels and huris in, 216, 218; courtesans in, 230; dancers and entertainers in, 224–25; European influence in, 222–24; of ideal beauties, 214–22; literary heroines and consorts in, 208–14; nudes, 222, 224; Qajar portraiture, 225; repetition of compositions in, 208; under Safavids, 149, 164n27; urban women in, 230–32; women and society in, 226–32
painting, Islamic, 107–8
paradise: idealized feminine beauty in depictions of, 216, 218; Zoroastrian, 17
Pari-Khan Khanum I, 145, 149, 153, 168n80
Pari-Khan Khanum II, 156–58; daughter of Shah Tahmasp, 144; Khayr al-Nisa Begum opposes, 156–57, 160; loss of power by, 161, 162; mother Sultan-Aqa Khanum, 147; poem dedicated to, 165n35; remains unmarried, 144; Shahzada Sultanum as role model for, 156; vizier of, 154; wealth of, 152
Parsis, 50, 52
Parthian dynasty, 26, 51
Parysatis, 20, 21, 22, 24
pastoralism, 5, 12–13, 33–34, 118n18
Paykand (Baykand), 54
Perikhanian, Anahit, 63n12
Persepolis, 20, 24, 25, 44n44
Persian language, 39, 59, 86, 113, 150; literary works in, 187, 189, 201–3, 206, 233; New Persian, 48, 49; Pahlavi (Middle Persian), 26, 49, 50
Persians, 17–18, 19, 21, 23, 25, 39; clothes of, 143
Phaedyme, 20, 44n37
Pinikir (goddess), 14
Pir Muhammad ibn Jahangir (Timurid), 123, 130, 136n8
Plutarch, 21, 23
polygyny: in Achaemenian empire, 22, 23; in Ghaznavid dynasty, 82; in Qur'an, 35, 36; in Sasanian empire, 29–30; in Timurid dynasty, 128
pork, 60
Porukast (daughter of Zoroaster), 31
prayers, on Friday, 87–88, 104–5, 107
prostitutes: in Iranian painting, 230; in Seljuq period, 107; Zoroastrianism on, 16
Proto-Dravidians, 14
Purandukht (Borandukht), 28, 49

al-Qa'im (caliph), 108
Qajar dynasty, 224–26, 233
Qandahar, 156
Qarakhanids (Karakhanids), 88, 91–92,

of women in, 113; legal and literary views of women in, 104–6; marriage alliances in, 87, 108–10; Mas'ud I of Ghazna defeated by, 96–97; Mas'ud I proposes marriage alliances with, 100n35; medieval historical sources on women's roles in, 107–16; nomadic lifestyle in, 103; opposition to women in public affairs during, 82–83; painting of, 208, 212; political role of women in, 114–17; representation of women of, 207; Turkish women in, 107–8, 118n18; urban Persian women in, 107
Shad Malik (wife of Khalil Sultan, Timurid ruler), 131–32, 138nn59 and 60
Shafi'i (school of Islamic law), 41, 72, 73, 74, 79n5
Shahan (freedwoman of al-Mustansir, caliph), 113, 116
Shah-Beg(i) Khanum (Tajlu Khanum) (wife of Shah Isma'il, Safavi), 145, 149
Shah Begum, 149
Shahfarand (Shah i Afrid) (daughter of Sasanian prince, wife of Umayyad caliph), 56
al-Shahhami, Abu Nasr, 73
al-Shahhami, Zahir, 73
Shah Khatun, 88–89, 97, 100n30
Shahmalik (Timurid), 126–27
Shahnama (Ferdowsi), 170–85, 187–88, 208, 209, 211, 234n11; Afrasiyab, 176–77; Ardasher, 178–80; Ardavan, 178, 179, 180; Bahram-i Chubina, 182, 193, 197; Banugushasp, 177–78; Barmaya, 174, 175; Faranak, 174, 175; Farangis, 176, 214, 215; Fereydun, 174–76, 184n30; folk and oral versions of, 183n1, 184n13; Giv, 177, 214, 215; Golnar, 178–80, 181; illustrations of, 208, 211, 214, 215, 218, 233, 234n11; Jamshid, 173, 175; Kaykhosrow, 176–78, 214, 215; Piran, 177; Rustam, 182, 187–88; Shapur II, 180–82, 185n46; Siyavakhsh, 176; Ta'ir, 181; three parts of, 170; women in transitions of power in, 9, 171, 172–73, 178, 180, 181, 182–83; Zahhak, 173–75, 184n13
Shah Pasha Khatun, 145
Shahrbanu (daughter of Sasanian king, wife of Imam Husayn), 56
Shahr-Banu Khanum, 146
Shahriyar, 204n12

Shahrukh (Timurid ruler): Aka Biki and, 125; Aqa Biki and, 130; burial of, 129; Chinggisid wife of, 122; concubine mother of, 131; death of, 127, 133; displaces established dynastic line, 123; Tumen Agha and, 125; wife Gawharshad, 123, 124, 125, 126, 127, 131, 132–33, 142; wife Malikat Agha, 125, 128
Shahzada Khanum (Safiyah-Sultan Khanum), 147, 154
Shahzada Sultanum (Mahin Banu): as adviser to Tahmasp, 156, 157, 162; diplomacy of, 154; education of, 150; horse riding by, 151; remains unmarried, 144; as sister of Shah Tahmasp, 144; wealth of, 152; works dedicated to, 165n35
Sham'-i Jahan (Chaghadayid khan), 122
Shamkhal Sultan, 147, 157, 158
Shamlu tribe, 153, 166n59
Shapur (Sasanian king), 46n102
Shapur II, 180–82, 185n46
Sharaf-nama (Bidlisi), 148
Shari'a (daughter of Zumra), 73
shari'a, 37, 40, 41, 73, 83, 104; development of, 40–41; position of women in, 104
Shi'i Islam, 141, 150
Shilhak-Inshushinak, 15, 42n15
Shiraz, 107, 214
Shirin (Nizami's fictional character), 186–205; artistic rendering of, 214, 216, 217
Shirin (queen of Khusro II), 49
Shirvan, 145, 146
Shuhda al-Katiba, 113
Shutruk-Nahhunte, 15
Sima-yi du zan (Sirjani), 202
Simjuri, Abu al-Hasan, 96
Sirjani, Saidi, 202
Sitti Zarrin, 100n30
al-Siyaq li Ta'rikh Naisabur (al-Farisi): categories of women mentioned in, 72–75; number of women in, 68; women described in terms of male relatives in, 70; women excluded from, 75, 78
Siyar al-muluk (*Siyasatnama*) (Nizam al-Mulk), 83, 105–6, 114
slaves: Ibn Butlan on appraising, 107–8; among Safavids, 155; in Sasanian empire, 33, 51
Smerdis, 20
Soyurghatmish (Timurid), 128
Spain, 38

heroines from literary texts, 208–14; ideal beauty of, 214–26; in Sasanian art, 50; stock types, 208

women, seclusion of: in Achaemenian empire, 18, 21–22; encourages their depiction, 233; in Ghaznavid dynasty, 81; gradual emergence of, 3; introduction into Nile-to-Oxus region, 12; Islam and, 1, 11, 35; oppression associated with, 3; Qur'an on, 37, 41; as response to urbanization, 4–5; in Sasanian empire, 33; women's influence and, 12. *See also* harem

Xerxes I, 20, 25
Xerxes II, 18

Yadgar Muhammad (Timurid ruler), 134
Yanaltigin, 96
Ya'qub ibn Uzun Hasan (Aqqoyunlu sultan), 142, 154
Yazdagird III, 56
Yazdi, Sharaf al-Din Ali, 131
Yazid II (caliph), 56
Yazid III (caliph), 39
Yusuf, Amir (Ghaznavid prince), 90–92

Zahra Baji, 163n8
Zaman, Muhammad, 223–24, 235n27
Zand i Wahman Yasht, 61, 66n53
Zarifa (Zumra), 73
Zawzani, Abu Sahl, 93, 95
Zaynab Begum: adviser to Abbas I, 160; dignitaries in service of, 154; horse riding by, 151; letter writing by, 149; maintains her influence for years, 162; remains unmarried, 144; wealth of, 152–53, 166n55
Zaynab bint al-Shari, 113
Zoroaster, 15, 17, 31
Zoroastrianism: Achaemenians and, 18; on apostates, 58; creation myth of, 171–72; festivals of, 65n32; Islam replaces, 34, 55; next-of-kin marriage and, 16, 31–32, 44n62, 52; restrictive codes for women in, 7, 15–17, 52, 61; in Sasanian empire, 26, 27, 31–32; sharing wives permitted in, 31; veiling not practiced in, 50; women convert to Islam from, 55, 56, 57, 58; women's ritual role in, 52
Zumra (Zarifa), 73
Zumurrud Khatun, 111

The University of Illinois Press
is a founding member of the
Association of American University Presses.

Composed in 10.5/13 Minion
with Minion display
by Jim Proefrock
at the University of Illinois Press
Manufactured by Maple-Vail
Book Manufacturing Group

University of Illinois Press
1325 South Oak Street
Champaign, IL 61820-6903
www.press.uillinois.edu